POLIT
CO-OPEI
IN DIVIDED

A series of papers relevant to the conflict in Northern Ireland

Edited by Desmond Rea

GILL AND MACMILLAN

First published 1982 by
Gill and Macmillan Ltd
Goldenbridge
Dublin 8
with associated companies in
London, New York, Delhi, Hong Kong,
Johannesburg, Lagos, Melbourne,
Singapore, Tokyo

Reprinted in paperback 1983

7171 1323 X

Origination by Healyset, Dublin
Printed and bound in Great Britain by
Biddles Ltd.
Guildford and King's Lynn

Contents

EDITOR

Desmond Rea read economics and political science at Queen's University, Belfast and business administration at the University of California, Berkeley. Former Senior Lecturer in Business Administration at Queen's University, Belfast, he is Professor and Head of School of Applied Economics at the Ulster Polytechnic.

CONTRIBUTORS

Paul Arthur studied at Queen's University, Belfast. He is Senior Lecturer in Politics at the Ulster Polytechnic.

John Bristow studied at Manchester University. Formerly Lecturer in Economics at Queen's University, Belfast, he is now Fellow and Associate Professor of Economics, Trinity College, Dublin.

Bernard Crick studied at University College, London, the London School of Economics and Harvard University. He has taught and researched at the London School of Economics and Sheffield University and is currently Professor of Politics at Birkbeck College, University of London.

A.-P. Frognier was educated at the University of Louvain, Belgium, where he is now Professor of the Department of Political Science.

Norman Gibson studied at Queen's University, Belfast and at the University of Chicago. A former Harkness Fellow, he is Professor of Economics at the New University of Ulster. He is a member of the Royal Irish Academy.

John Hunter read psychology at Queen's University, Belfast. In 1977 he was awarded a United States Harkness Fellowship and from 1977 to 1979 he studied at Cornell University.

Patrick Keatinge studied at Trinity College, Dublin and the London School of Economics. He is Associate Professor of Political Science at Trinity College, Dublin.

Emil J. Kirchner studied at the University of Frankfurt and Western Reserve University. He is currently Director of Western European Politics, Department of Political Science, University of Essex.

Arend Lijphart studied at Principia College and Yale University. One-time Assistant and Associate Professor at the University of California, Berkeley, he was from 1968 to 1978 Professor of International Relations, University of Leiden. He is currently Professor of Political Science, University of California, San Diego.

John A. Oliver, one-time Permanent Secretary in the Northern Ireland Civil Service, held the following official positions in Northern Ireland: Officer in charge of the reshaping of Local Government (1966–69); Secretary to the Macrory Review Body (1970); and Chief Adviser to the Constitutional Convention (1975–77).

Bengt Sundelius studied at the University of Lund, Sweden and the University of Denver, Colorado. He is a Research Associate with the Institute of International Affairs, Stockholm and Associate Professor, Bradley University, Illinois.

Maurice J. C. Vile studied at the University of London. A Fellow of Nuffield College, Oxford, he is currently Pro-Vice-Chancellor and Professor of Political Science, University of Kent.

Preface

The continuing conflict in Northern Ireland is a reproach to British and Irish people everywhere, and a scandal in the Christian faith. It is nearer a 'solution' only in the sense that time moves on towards an unknown future day when some new factor, perhaps no more than a weariness of killing, will allow an interlude of peace. It is no nearer to the 'solution' which identifies the causes of conflict and takes effective steps to remove them.

The first necessity is to understand; but that is not easy either. The factual record of what has happened is exceedingly complex, and all of us, including the contributors to this volume, interpret it with little biases of selection and interpretation of which we are hardly conscious. Even if some grand representative committee could set down a totally neutral and reliable record of fact, this would only be a small advance; for what matters is not the fact but the myth, not the unemotional catalogue of events but the ways in which those events live in the minds of men today.

To be sensitive to ideas and feelings very different from one's own is hard indeed. It is simpler to give to the alien thought-process a false stereotype, an image created from a simplification and distortion of the past. But those now in conflict are men and women of the late twentieth century, influenced by their heritage but not determined by it. The Catholics who see Dr Paisley as just one of a line of Protestant bigots, and the Protestants who see the Provisional IRA as clones from the IRA stock of sixty years ago, are both preventing understanding because they accept the image as a substitute for the hard spiritual exercise of being sensitive to the reality.

The British administration, which rules the province as if it were a colony not ready for independence, can at least be given the credit for seeing that the situation has both a British dimension and an Irish dimension. Repeatedly, however, the Northern Ireland Office has been caught by the politicians' desire to get things moving, and has acted without an adequate sensitivity to the detail of the opposing myths. As Professor Krejci has pointed out in his remarkable book on *Ethnic and Political Nations in Europe* (Croom Helm, 1981), the English are conditioned by their long national history to think of 'nations' as defined by the occupation of territory, and find it difficult to understand an ethnic consciousness which is based on language or religion or culture rather than geographical area.

The danger of acting without an adequate sensitivity to the complex of ideas and myths is that one may make things worse. Bew and Patterson (*Journal of International Affairs*, vol. 36, no. 2) argue that the *unintentional* effects of British policy have been to exacerbate sectarian conflict. Another consequence of the urge to show progress is that constitutional ingenuity tends to be given an exaggerated importance. This book explores, most helpfully, a considerable variety of possible constitutional forms; but it must be recognised that, with goodwill, several different constitutional arrangements might be made to work, while without goodwill no arrangement, however cunningly balanced, stands any chance. The antagonists in the conflict will simply read and interpret the words of a constitution in differing ways, and myths about its real purpose will grow like mushrooms after rain.

It is right to expect British governments to keep on trying to mediate and to calm the situation, but their efforts are complicated by their difficulty in understanding how they themselves are seen. For the various myths about why the British are present, with English ministers and with military force, in a part of Ireland, and why they should want to stay or to leave, are pervasive and generally far wide of the mark. In consequence the statements of Ministers are not fully trusted, for where their assertions diverge from the myth, it is the myth which is believed. Or it is supposed that behind the Minister lurks a more powerful influence, perhaps from the Foreign Office or the Minister of Defence, which will in the end determine what is done.

Dr Oliver quotes Professor Rose's well-known words, 'the problem is that there is no solution'. But that is really a matter of the definition of words. There is no likelihood of a solution which restores normality at a stroke. But it is reasonable to seek a solution which converges towards peace, each round of trouble being a little less active than the last, and each showing some advance towards understanding. Since the nature of conflict is often to produce divergent situations, hate and suffering breeding more hate, even a slow convergence towards peace will not be easily obtained. And it is difficult to see how it can be obtained without reconciling leadership. There are historical examples of great reconcilers who began by belonging to one 'side' of a conflict; but it has to be said that men of the necessary quality and charisma are not so far to be seen in Northern Ireland, either among the committed leaders of communities or in the less committed centre. A Minister from across the water might perhaps start the process, but only if he was universally trusted to be sensitive, understanding and honest; and this is not a trust readily given to politicians.

While we wait for the man and their conjunction of events capable of beginning the convergence towards peace, the preparation can be made by resolutely and carefully increasing understanding of the issues, and by exploring alternative possibilities of progress. Professor Rea and his contributors have done Northern Ireland a notable service by the publication of this book. It throws light in dark places; and, though the light of reason will not of itself soothe a deeply emotional conflict, it can help to prevent errors which will make things worse, and prepare men's minds for a convergence towards peace.

Charles Carter

Charles Carter was educated at Rugby School and at St John's College, Cambridge. Formerly Stanley Jevons Professor of Political Economy and Corden Lecturer, the University of Manchester (1959-63), and Vice-Chancellor, University of Lancaster (1963-1979) he is currently Chairman, Research Committee, Policy Studies Institute. From 1959-63 he was Professor of Economics, Queen's University of Belfast and has been since 1977 Chairman, Northern Ireland Economic Council. In 1962 he wrote (with Denis Barritt) *The Northern Ireland Problem*.

Introduction

Since 1970 in Northern Ireland some 2,000 lives have been lost and more than 23,000 injuries have been sustained in what are euphemistically described as the 'troubles'. Countless hearts have been broken as a result. And today the two communities which make up Northern Ireland are almost entirely polarised. The conflict in Northern Ireland is one between different traditions, identities and allegiances. Cultural identity, religious belief, and loyalty to one's group are basic to all who live here. The result is that, as John Hunter points out below,

> put crudely, Northern Ireland's one million Protestants believe the maintenance of the Union with Great Britain is the only means of securing their future. On the other hand the half million Roman Catholics in Northern Ireland believe they can only secure their future within a United Ireland.

If the two communities are to live together in peace and harmony then appropriate political structures must be sought. Other divided societies have done so. Indeed experience elsewhere shows that there are a multiplicity of ways of democratically governing alienated communities and at the same time protecting minority rights. Should not the peoples of Northern Ireland, the Republic of Ireland and Great Britain examine other societies' solutions to conflict situations and thereby develop new insights that might lead to the solution of their own?

In the earnest belief that the people of the British Isles should indeed attempt to learn from the experiences of others the Glencree and Corrymeela Communities[1] nominated a

1

committee to plan a conference on the theme 'Northern Ireland, the Republic of Ireland and Great Britain: A Study Conference to Explore Models of Political Co-operation'. The Organising Committee,[2] having consulted a panel of experts,[3] decided upon the following objectives for the Conference:

(a) As background,
   (i) to attempt to understand more clearly the conflict in Northern Ireland and the evolution of constitutional policy;
   (ii) to examine the current political options, their economic implications and their advantages and disadvantages.
(b) By commissioning papers from experts, to make a thorough examination of different models of political co-operation attempted elsewhere.
(c) To consider the papers in detail at a conference as well as the possible application of the models from elsewhere, as elicited in the papers, to the particular situation in Northern Ireland.
(d) To disseminate the papers more widely.

The Organising Committee sought the advice of the panel of experts as to papers to be commissioned and from whom to commission them. The Conference took place at Queen's University, Belfast from 25 to 28 March 1981. It was subsidised by a grant from the Ford Foundation and an anonymous commercial benefactor. This volume is in fulfillment of the Conference's fourth objective. Its publication has been made possible by grants from the European Commission and the Ireland Fund respectively.[4]

The twelve papers fall into four parts. Parts I and II were commissioned to provide a backdrop to Parts III and IV. Part I contains two papers, one an analysis of the conflict in Northern Ireland and the other an examination of the evolution of constitutional policy in Northern Ireland. The three papers in Part II are concerned with what are widely seen as the current major political options facing the parties to the Northern Ireland conflict, their economic implications and their advantages and disadvantages. The six papers which make up Part III will enable the reader to examine different models of political co-operation attempted elsewhere in the world. The one paper in Part IV examines (with particular reference to the communiqués of the Republic of Ireland and United Kingdom governments of 21 May 1980 and 8 December 1980 respectively) 'political co-operation: the Anglo-Irish case'. The opinions expressed in these papers are of course the authors'.

DESMOND REA

REFERENCES

1. Glencree is a centre of reconciliation. Founded in 1974, its aim is, *inter alia*, to convince people in both parts of Ireland and elsewhere that violence is destructive of the very ends it seeks to achieve and to provide a programme of peace education. Address: Glencree Centre for Reconciliation, Enniskerry, Co. Wicklow. Telephone (01) 860962/3. The Corrymeela Community is a dispersed fellowship of Christians from different traditions in Ireland, who believe themselves to be called together as instruments of God's peace. Founded in 1966 the members are committed to work for a society whose priorities are, *inter alia*, mutual respect, and the participation of all. The Community runs a residential centre at Ballycastle, Co. Antrim devoted to the promotion of dialogue, study and understanding between all groups. Address: Corrymeela House, 8 Upper Crescent, Belfast BT7 1NT. Telephone: (0232) 25008.

2. The Organising Committee was Larry Bond, Louis Boyle, Geoffrey Corry, Rev. Shaun Curran, Judy Hayes, John Hunter, Rev. Dr John Morrow, Dr Edward Moxon-Brown, Professor Desmond Rea (Chairman), Dr David Stevens and Brigid Wilkinson.

3. Consultants to the Conference were Professor Ian Budge, University of Essex; Professor Bernard Crick, Birkbeck College, University of London; Rev. Dr R. R. Davey, Belfast; Professor René Jean Dupuy, University of Nice; Professor Norman Gibson, New University of Ulster; Professor Enda McDonagh, University of Notre Dame; Professor Cornelius O'Leary, Queen's University, Belfast; Dr John Whyte, Queen's University, Belfast; Dr Stanley Worrall, Belfast.

4. The Ireland Fund was organised in 1976 as a philanthropic, non-political, non-sectarian organisation. Its purpose is to generate funds in the United States and apply them to the furtherance of peace, culture and charity, primarily in Ireland. Over half of the Ireland Fund's grants have sought to promote peace and reconciliation in Ireland, and it is our belief that the publication of this book advances that goal. The Ireland Fund's registered office in the United States is at 300 Stadium Circle, Pittsburgh, Pennsylvania 15212, United States of America and its Executive Director is William J. McNally Esq.

PART I

BACKGROUND PAPERS

Part I contains two contributions which were commissioned as background papers.

1: AN ANALYSIS OF THE CONFLICT IN NORTHERN IRELAND
JOHN HUNTER

John Hunter starts from the (surely correct) assumption that 'any peaceful resolution of the conflict must involve drawing the two communities together within a framework which enables each to work for the common good' and he stresses that 'to understand fully the nature and origins of the conflict in Northern Ireland it is important to understand the views of the two communities and how their different perceptions of the conflict have evolved over the years'. It is his belief that '. . . the effect of (the divisive forces which continue to play on each community) could be mitigated by a conscientious attempt on the part of all parties to the conflict to understand the fears and aspirations which motivate their opponents'; and he concludes that 'in the absence of this understanding ignorance will continue to breed frustration and fear and retard the search for peace.' He uses various theories — categorised into the following four groups: political, religious, economic, and psychological — which have been advanced to explain the 'residue of basic and divisive issues', at the same time cautioning that 'none of these theories does justice to the complexity of the social worlds which exist in Northern Ireland and which underpin the present conflict.' He attempts to distinguish between those factors which are responsible for the genesis of the conflict and those which contribute to its intensity and longevity. He suggests that it

7

is the political factors which, because of their causal significance, are most important.

2: THE EVOLUTION OF CONSTITUTIONAL POLICY IN NORTHERN IRELAND OVER THE PAST FIFTEEN YEARS
JOHN A. OLIVER

John Oliver's terms of reference were to describe, explain and constructively analyse the evolution of constitutional policy in Northern Ireland since the period immediately prior to the current conflict, at the same time as drawing our attention to the relevant legislative and administrative changes. At each of the main 'turning points' he considers some of the alternative courses which were, he believes, open to the authorities but not taken: 'courses that were practical propositions within the reasonable bounds of political possibility at the time'. He concludes with a plea to the politicians for movement in the process of constructing the combined will to produce eventually a constitutional framework that is humane, just and capable of serving all the people.

1

An Analysis Of The Conflict In Northern Ireland

John Hunter

In 1970 a Belfast citizen was reported in *The Times* as saying, 'Anyone who isn't confused here doesn't really understand what is going on.' The sense of confusion grows as one examines the plethora of interpretations and theories which have been advanced in recent years to explain the nature and origins of the conflict in Northern Ireland. In an article in the *Economic and Social Review* Whyte[1] identifies eleven broad categories of analysis, one more than Lijphart[2] in his review article, while Darby draws on over 700 sources for his book *Conflict in Northern Ireland*.[3] Most of these sources were published in the five years which preceded the book's publication in 1976, and since then the deluge of books and articles has continued. Yet the search for a satisfactory synthesis continues.

However, the lack of agreement in academic circles is paralelled by that which exists outside university cloisters. Palley has remarked:

> It is a truism that no two Irishmen can agree on the history or interpretation of the problems of this island . . . Nor can anyone who has resided in this island for any length of time claim objectivity.[4]

Moreover the confusion many felt in 1969 and the early years of the 1970s, as their world collapsed in ruins around them, has all too often been transformed into the certainty which accompanies sectarian hatred and bitterness. Since 1970 over 2,000 lives have been lost and more than 20,000 injuries have been sustained and, despite many appeals for tolerance by various community and church leaders and the efforts of many voluntary organisations and statutory agencies to promote better community relations, the two communities in Northern Ireland have become almost entirely polarised.

9

Associated with this polarisation has been a heightened determination on the part of both communities not to compromise on even the most insignificant matter. Thus the journalist in search of local colour today would be more likely to find those he interviewed expressing trenchant and often bigoted views on the nature of the conflict. To understand fully the nature and origins of the conflict it is important to understand the views of each of the two communities and how their different perceptions of the conflict have evolved over the years. Clearly any peaceful resolution of the conflict must involve drawing the two communities together within a framework which enables each to work for the common good of society as a whole.

In exploring their fiercely held views it is necessary to remember that what may have actually happened in the past is of much less significance than what people believe happened. It is on the basis of the latter that the actions of people involved in the present conflict are determined. Thus what constitutes the reality of today's events is the product of yesterday's perceptions. In 1978, in his W. B. Rankin Memorial Lecture, Professor F. S. L. Lyons asked: '. . . have we in our entanglement with history locked ourselves into a hall of distorting mirrors so grotesque that we can no longer distinguish the realities of what has happened in this island from the myths we have chosen to weave about certain symbolic events?'[5]

Yet it is these myths which are often used to justify the barbaric acts of today's gunmen or to support what the outsider believes to be a most distorted interpretation of the nature of the conflict. But, when examined from the limited perspective available to the individual living in a closed community, which in ghetto areas of Belfast has been subject to stresses and strains of a well-nigh intolerable nature, such acts and views can appear to have a rational basis, however reprehensible they might seem to the outsider. This is particularly true where the perpetrators of terrorist crimes claim to be motivated by the same political aspirations as those of the community in which they live.

The phenomenon of the selective interpretation and unconscious distortion of events has been thoroughly explored by Burton. In his book, *The Politics of Legitimacy,*[6] he records his experiences over an eight-month period in 1972—73 when he lived in a tightly-knit Republican community in Belfast which he dubbed 'Anro'. His aim was to examine the social basis of IRA violence and to demonstrate that political violence can best be understood in terms of its social and political milieu.

He found the community character of Anro's social organisation, with its immensely strong ties of kin, class, religion and residence, forged a strong sense of social solidarity which proved well capable of soaking up the various attempts of the security forces to break Anro's own military activities. This strong sense of solidarity was built up over several generations, and, out of the accumulated experiences of its members during this time, there evolved what Burton describes as Anro's state of 'collective consciousness'. Within this state of collective consciousness he found there existed a 'level of mediated reality' which filtered and selectively interpreted views to produce and maintain a 'subjective social reality' which accorded with and confirmed the community's interpretation of the Northern Ireland problem and supported and strengthened the individual's partial and distorted perceptions of events. In such a fashion information was differentially received and selectively interpreted according to the experience and expectations of the receiving group.

Clearly this phenomenon is not unique to 'Anro': other Belfast communities on both sides of the sectarian divide evidence their own peculiar 'levels of mediated reality'. Nor is it likely that this phenomenon is limited to communities in troubled areas, or in Northern Ireland alone, for every group within society seems to possess the capacity to interpret events selectively to buttress its own limited perceptions of reality. Indeed without this coherence of view the group would probably not exist. In the Irish context evidence for the selective interpretation of events can be easily found in the differing interpretations of the same news items which appear in different newspapers. Moreover, each community in Northern Ireland largely operates in ignorance of the different political, social, religious and cultural traditions – the 'collective consciousness' — which govern the beliefs of the other and its response to the conflict.

It does seem likely, however, that the stresses and strains to which ghetto communities were subjected throughout the early 1970s produced within each a more consistent and intense interpretation of the nature of the conflict than would be true of communities living in less troubled areas. In the former the 'levels of mediated reality' would probably leave less scope for flexibility of interpretation or divergence of view, while evidence exists that those who did not fully endorse the traditional interpretation were branded as traitors and ostracised, or worse. In these circumstances the opportunities for reconciliation were reduced as communities became even further isolated from those across the sectarian divide. Meanwhile violence perpetrated by the self-styled defenders of each community was condoned and even legitimised through identifying the violence with the community's political aspirations. Thus during this period the only dynamic appeared to be that which drove the two communities further apart.

However, the diminution in violence over the last few years affords some hope that a return to near normality may reduce, although not eliminate, intercommunal tensions and loosen the forces which have bound each community into a cohesive and homogeneous body following a narrow sectarian path. With such a development, the 'level of mediated reality' and 'collective consciousness' of a community like 'Anro' may become more difficult to define and therefore to understand, although its basic principles are unlikely to be compromised or its political aims diluted. Recent years have also seen the establishment and growth of various groups pursuing different social and political goals in a non-violent manner. In 1978 Oliver estimated that the number 'of local neighbourhood community associations, tenants' associations, and action groups generally . . . must be something approaching 600'.[7] They are perhaps illustrative of a new life emerging from the violence and suggest that many groups are no longer content with the singleminded and inflexible pursuit of narrow traditional political goals.

Yet for the foreseeable future these unifying influences are likely to be of less significance than those divisive forces which continue to play on each community. The effect of the latter could be mitigated by a conscientious attempt on the part of all parties to the conflict to understand the fears and aspirations which motivate their opponents. In the absence of this understanding ignorance will continue to breed frustration and fear and retard the search for peace. It was Lyons who recently wrote that 'the recognition of difference especially by Irishmen themselves is a prerequisite for peaceful co-existence.'[8]

Working against any coming together of the two communities is the legacy of history. Unlike other societies in which the realities which concern their populations evolve and change over the years, the problem of defining Ireland's relationship with England has been an ever present concern of the Irish people over the last 400 years and more. Soon after the end of the First World War Churchill wrote:

> The whole map of Europe has been changed . . . The mode and thought of men, the whole outlook on affairs, the grouping of parties, all have encountered violent and tremendous changes in the deluge of the world, but as the deluge subsides and the waters fall we see the dreary steeples of Fermanagh and Tyrone emerging once again. The integrity of their quarrel is one of the few institutions that has been left unaltered in the cataclysm which has swept the world.[9]

Given the intensity of feeling this relationship has aroused over the years and the blood which has been spilt in attempts to resolve the quarrel, the task of bridge-building is formidable, particularly when it appears that the capacity of the various communities in Ireland for critical self-analysis and rational assessment has been long since lost, if it ever existed, in the mists of Irish history.

Moreover, it is facile to suggest that either an understanding of the 'collective consciousness' of opposing communities or the debunking of myths would in themselves resolve the problem and lead to the disappearance of the conflict. Both serve to reinforce the divisions between the communities in Northern Ireland but are not responsible for them. The elimination of myths will leave a residue of certain basic and divisive issues, sometimes of an irreconcilable nature. These issues are explored in this paper in the course of an analysis of the various theories which have been advanced to explain the nature of the conflict. None of these theories, however, does justice to the complexity of the social worlds which exist in Northern Ireland and which underpin the present conflict.

This analysis categorises the theories into four groups according to their primary emphasis — political, religious, economic and psychological. It is fair to say that no one group of theories affords a total explanation of the origins and nature of the conflict. The explanatory power of each is significantly enhanced by the incorporation of elements of the others. The analysis attempts to distinguish between those factors which are responsible for the genesis of the conflict and those which contribute to its intensity and longevity.

This framework is similar to that adopted by Palley who advocates examining the conflict by means of a multiplicity of conceptual frames:

> It is the lot of any writer on Northern Ireland to be driven into historical explanation. Indeed, most commentators succumb to an irresistible impulse to begin with an outline of the Stone Age in Ireland, and then proceed with generous interlardings of apposite quotations to an account of current dissatisfactions. Without such explanations the complexities of the problems afflicting Northern Ireland tend to be obscured by the most recent demands for particular political reforms or by the emotions conjured up by the last forceful excess — in current jargon 'the politics of the last atrocity'. But it is not sufficient merely to give historical explanations: the situation in Northern Ireland must be set in a multiplicity of conceptual frames.[10]

Analysis of the Northern Ireland problem by such means permits some synthesis of existing theories and facilitates an understanding of the complex interplay of the various political, social, economic, cultural, religious and psychological forces which together underlie it. Regretfully many of these reinforce each other, so strongly buttressing the divisions which exist between the two communities. Their congruence creates a problem of such intensity and intractability that to focus on one aspect to the exclusion of another is to be guilty of a dangerous oversimplification — dangerous in that it underestimates, indeed ignores, the difficulties involved in the search for a peaceful resolution of the conflict.

Theories of the Conflict
(1) Political Theories

At the core of the Northern Ireland problem is a quarrel over political power and who should exercise it, which Palley describes as a problem of 'political nationalism'.[11] Put crudely, Northern Ireland's one million Protestants believe the maintenance of the Northern Ireland state is the only means of securing their future. On the other hand the half-million Catholics in Northern Ireland believe they can only secure their future within a united Ireland. Jackson has therefore defined the problem as that of a 'Double Minority':

> Within their own enclave the Protestants of Ulster, one million strong, outnumber their Catholic brethren by two to one. But in the wider context of Ireland they themselves are easily outnumbered three to one.[12]

Traditional Republicanism glosses over the problem of the double minority and in its simplest form defines all the people of Ireland as one homogeneous nation which has been artificially divided by the machinations of British imperialism. Meanwhile Unionism justifies the continued partition of Ireland by virtue of the existence of two nations or races with different cultures, loyalties and religious beliefs, conveniently and necessarily separated by a land frontier.

To determine the validity of these and other political interpretations of the nature of the present conflict, it is necessary to return to the early seventeenth century and briefly trace the main political developments in Ireland since then. The reader will be spared the return to the Stone Age referred to by Palley! This analysis will also provide the backcloth against which various religious, economic and psychological interpretations of the conflict will be later examined, and will hopefully debunk many of the myths which underlie and at times underpin the differing political viewpoints of the various parties to the conflict.

The starting point for an examination of Ulster's history over the last four hundred years is its geography. Based on the work of the geographer Professor Estyn Evans, Lyons notes that the main reason why Ulster was the last stronghold of the old Gaelic civilisation was the 'natural barrier of small hills, forests, bogs, lakes and water courses'[13] which separated it from the rest of Ireland. 'Behind this barrier there developed a region differentiated from others by its climate, its geology and its human geography.'[14] This natural partition meant there was more trade and communication with Scotland than with the southern part of the island, and resulted in the presence of a comparatively significant number of Scots in the present counties of Down and Antrim, well before the Flight of the Earls in 1607. The Earls of Tyrone and Tyrconnell were the last of the Gaelic chiefs to hold out in their Ulster strongholds against English rule and after their flight to Europe by boat from Lough Swilly their vast estates were confiscated. The crown's plan was to displace the native Irish from these lands and replace them by loyal English and Scottish settlers who through the imposition of English law and administration would effectively crush the old Gaelic culture and usher in an age of peace and stability. In practice it did not work out as planned. Soon it became apparent that the resources of the state were inadequate to organise the plantation of Ulster on a piecemeal basis, so the City of London and its wealthy Livery Companies were invited to assist.

Articles of agreement drawn up in 1610 granted the County of Londonderry and parts of Donegal, Tyrone and Antrim to the City of London which established the Irish Society to organise their management and development. In turn the Society parcelled out large tracts of land to individual companies but again resources proved inadequate and although the native Irish were often forced back onto poorer land on high ground they were generally not totally dispersed and often lived cheek by jowl with the new settlers for whom they worked as labourers and tenant farmers. It is therefore not surprising to learn that grantees of lands were required to build 'bawns' or fortified walled cottages to which settlers could retire in times of difficulty. The precarious frontier existence of the settlers was demonstrated by the rebellion of the native Irish in 1641. The massacre of planters and their families in isolated settlements confirmed the treachery and savagery of the native Irish and provided the excuse for swift and bloody retribution. However the main significance of the rebellion lay in its reinforcement of the feeling of insecurity on the part of the settlers and the development of what has since been described as a siege mentality. Moreover, this insecurity was often expressed in religious terms, for unlike the native Irish and the earlier Anglo-Norman invaders of the twelfth century (who were both Roman Catholics), the newcomers espoused an uncompromising Calvinism with an emphasis on Puritan values. It was this religious dimension which effectively prevented the assimilation of the newcomers, with their different culture and traditions, by the native Irish, and sowed the seeds of the present conflict and divisions.

However, it was the defeat of the Catholic King James II fifty years later by the forces of William of Orange which was to seal the division between Planter and Gael. The victories of William's forces at Londonderry, Aughrim and the Boyne confirmed and strengthened the former's authority and power and provided in later years convenient and emotive symbols to recall the deliverance, imagined or otherwise, of Ulster's Protestants from the fearsome prospect of Roman bondage.

The years which followed saw the enactment of the harsh Penal Laws which prohibited both Catholic and Presbyterian from holding government office or from sitting in parliament. Catholics were further prohibited from purchasing land. The saying of Mass and the training of priests were also outlawed. However, Stewart records that except for those laws which buttressed the political power of the Protestant Ascendancy the Penal Laws were generally 'much more stringent in the letter than in the enforcement.'[15] Since the Presbyterians had been attracted to Ulster by the promise of religious toleration such laws constituted a grave infringement of their liberty and Barritt[16] records that by the end of the eighteenth century a quarter of a million Presbyterians had emigrated to America. There they rapidly made their mark. During the American War of Independence George Washington is reported to have said that 'if he were defeated everywhere else he would make his last stand among the Scotch-Irish of his native Virginia.'[17]

The revolt of the American colonies, together with the French Revolution, was to have a significant impact on some of the more liberal Presbyterians who remained. As a consequence of the political frustrations they felt, they formed the radical society of United Irishmen in Belfast in 1791. According to Stewart, 'the United Irishmen held the view that no reform or political progress was possible in Ireland until Dissenter and Catholic united to isolate the Irish executive and overthrow the power of the Anglican Protestant Ascendancy.'[18] The movement sought to repeal the Penal Laws, to reform parliament and to establish an independent Ireland, although some of those who joined it, including its leader, Wolfe Tone, who was born an Anglican, were less concerned with the Penal Laws than with breaking the connection with England, 'that never failing source of all our political evils'.[19]

The Society drew its initial support predominantly from middle-class Presbyterians in certain clearly defined urban areas. But it had no following among Protestant farmers or more significantly among Protestants living in areas where the memories of the 1641 massacre were still fresh, despite the passage of 150 years. Catholic support came later as the organisation sought to expand its membership, and paradoxically it came from the ranks of the Catholic secret agrarian society, the 'Defenders', whose members were a good deal less idealistic than their Presbyterian fellows. Indeed in 1795, the year which saw the foundation of the Protestant Orange Order, there were open sectarian battles between the 'Defenders' and the Protestant 'Peep O' Day Boys'.

The insurrection of 1798 degenerated into sectarian massacres on a scale reminiscent of those of the seventeenth century and reinforced yet again the basic mistrust and fear each community had of the other. While the rising proved abortive — it was easily defeated and its leaders were executed or banished to France – its significance to later generations of Republicans lived on. To them it represented the uniting of Catholics and Protestants in the pursuit of an Ireland free from English rule. However this linkage was very limited in both scope and duration, for the Presbyterian founders of the United Irishmen were a radical minority and not representative of Presbyterians in general. Moreover, events were later to conspire to link Catholicism with Irish nationalism in an unbreakable bond. This conjunction was viewed with foreboding by those remaining radical Presbyterians who could not but perceive that any representative Irish parliament would inevitably be dominated by Catholic members and their values and led them, by the late nineteenth century, to make common cause with the adherents of the established church – an alliance their more conservative colleagues had long before accepted. This trend was enhanced by the dependence of the relatively more prosperous Ulster economy on trading links with England and Scotland. Thus over the years there occurred the fusion of the religious and political divides which is still recognisable today.

The 1798 rebellion provided the government in London with an excuse to abolish the short-lived Irish parliament, which had been established in Dublin in 1782 at the instigation of the Anglo-Irish ascendancy who controlled its affairs. The Act of Union of 1801 bound Ireland to Britain in legislative union and was to be accompanied by Catholic emancipation. However it took nearly thirty years for Catholic emancipation to materialise following the election to Westminster of Daniel O'Connell – a Catholic – at the Clare by-election in 1828. Attention then focused on the repeal of the Act of Union and the establishment of an independent legislature for Ireland: 'We have our viceroy and our Irish peers; we only want a House of Commons which you could place upon the same basis as your Reformed Parliament.'[20] O'Connell's espousal of constitutional nationalism had little success and soon the repeal movement was overshadowed by a tragic event of great significance – the potato famine of 1845–47.

The effect of the famine was traumatic and devastating. Within the space of five years the total population of Ireland declined by about a quarter from its peak of around eight million. Nearly one million died and the remainder emigrated. Over the remaining years of the century many followed the example of those who had left Ireland's shores, so that by the year 1900 the population had decreased to around four million.

The disastrous impact of the famine was compounded by the laissez-faire policies of the government in Westminster, at whose door the responsibility for the million deaths which had occurred was unequivocally laid. It is hardly surprising that the famine left a legacy of hatred towards England which was then carried overseas by those who emigrated, particularly those who went to the United States.

Although there had been a brief violent reaction to English indifference to Ireland's sufferings in the unsuccessful Young Ireland rising of 1848 it was not until ten years later that the secret society, the Irish Republican Brotherhood, better known as the Fenians, was formed. It became the first in a long line of revolutionary groups dedicated to the establishment of an Irish republic, and although its rising in 1867 was, like its predecessors, abortive, the emigration of many of its leaders stiffened the resolve of those overseas to see Ireland freed from oppressive English rule.

Meanwhile at Westminster the Repeal Movement in favour of a federal relationship with England had given way to the Home Rule movement in favour of self-government. Under Parnell's leadership the Home Rule party fastened on the land question as a vehicle to mobilise broad support for Home Rule, and in 1879 Parnell assumed the presidency of the Land League which had been founded by Davitt. Ever since the plantation, the ownership of land had been an inflammatory issue. Throughout the eighteenth and early nineteenth centuries the pressure for land had grown ever more intense as the population rose, despite the precarious livelihood it provided. The famine was accompanied by widespread evictions as tenants were dispossessed of their land for their failure to pay their rents. Then in the 1870s cheap food imports caused a slump in the market for agricultural produce and profit margins declined, once again creating insecurity for the tenant. As a consequence of the disruptive tactics used by Parnell at Westminster to highlight the land issue, Gladstone's Liberal government passed the Land Act of 1881, which gave security of tenure to the tenant and also provided for Land Courts to assess 'fair' rents. With the land question out of the way the Irish Parliamentary Party, reinforced by its election victories in 1886, could once again concentrate on Home Rule.

By 1885 Gladstone was convinced of the merits of Home Rule but his first Home Rule Bill in 1886 was defeated in the Commons. A similar fate befell his second Home Rule Bill in 1893 which was defeated in the Lords. By then Parnell had died, discredited as a result of his amorous liaison with Mrs O'Shea. With his death the Irish impetus for a constitutional settlement lost momentum, while the scandal which surrounded his marriage to Mrs O'Shea in the year before his death caused a split in the Irish Parliamentary Party from which it never recovered.

Meanwhile in Ireland 1893 saw the formation of the Gaelic League by Douglas Hyde and others. Its formation represented a reaction against the dominance of English culture throughout Ireland. Its aim was to revive the Irish language and create a distinctively Irish culture; although non-sectarian and non-political many of its followers were so inspired by it that later they became inextricably linked with militant republican nationalism.

Gladstone's Home Rule Bills in 1886 and 1893 had not gone unopposed in Ireland. Ulster had traditionally returned a number of Unionist MPs to Westminster who sided with the Tories in their opposition to both bills. The Unionist MPs and their supporters believed independence would have dire consequences for Ulster. Firstly, they considered it would imperil Ulster's prosperity, for Belfast relied heavily for her raw materials and exports on the English market. Secondly, they believed an independent Ireland would pose a threat to civil and religious liberties, for they feared the new state would be dominated by the Roman Catholic Church. Lastly, they believed an independent Ireland would dissolve the strong cultural ties between Ulster and England.

Nevertheless despite Unionist and Tory opposition Asquith's Liberal government forced the third Home Rule Bill through parliament in 1912. Opposition to the measure grew rapidly in Ulster and in 1912 half-a-million Ulster Protestants, under the leadership of Sir Edward Carson, signed a 'Solemn League and Covenant' which pledged the signatories

. . . to stand by one another in defending for ourselves and our children our cherished position of equal citizenship in the United Kingdom and in using all means which may be found necessary to defeat the present conspiracy to set up a Home Rule Parliament in Ireland. And in the event of such a Parliament being forced upon us we further solemnly and mutually pledge ourselves to refuse to recognise its authority.[21]

The following year a provisional government was set up to assume power illegally in Ulster should Home Rule come to pass. It quickly became clear this was no idle threat for gun-running, carried out under the noses of the authorities, provided the necessary weapons to equip the Ulster Volunteer Force (UVF) to fight, if necessary, the forces of the crown. Stewart records that the UVF, with nearly 100,000 members, was very well organised. It had its own cavalry, motor car corps, ambulance and nursing services, signallers, despatch riders and a special strike force and 'lacked only artillery and aircraft.'[22] Furthermore the UVF's preparations for armed resistance enjoyed the support of the Tory party at Westminster, whose leader, Andrew Bonar Law, said in 1912: 'I can imagine no length of resistance to which Ulster can go in which I should not be prepared to support them, and in which, in my belief, they would not be supported by the overwhelming majority of the British people.'[23] Meanwhile in the rest of Ireland a rival force was established — the Irish Volunteers.

The threat of civil war loomed large until, in 1914, the advent of the First World War caused the Home Rule Act to be put into cold storage for its duration. The UVF pledged support for the crown and fought in France, but the Irish Volunteers split on the issue. A large majority, now calling themselves the National Volunteers, supported the war but the radical anti-war minority retained the old name of Irish Volunteers. When the war was over the Home Rule Act was replaced by the Government of Ireland Act of 1920, which provided for the partition of Ireland. This change in policy was due to a number of factors, not least of which was the significant opposition to the Home Rule Bill in Ulster before the war. Moreover, Ulster regiments formed from the UVF had distinguished themselves by their gallantry during the war and in particular had suffered heavy loss of life at the Battle of the Somme in July 1916. Within the space of two days the 36th Ulster Division lost 5,500 officers and men killed, wounded and missing and won four Victoria Crosses. Although Southern Irish losses in France were also heavy the loyalty and bravery of the Ulstermen was perceived to be in marked contrast to those who, a few months before the Battle of the Somme in 1916, had taken Dublin by surprise and proclaimed a republic from the steps of the GPO. They too sealed their covenant in blood, for the rising was crushed and its leaders executed — a punishment perhaps understandable in the context of the bloody war in Europe, but which nonetheless converted thousands overnight to the cause of Irish nationalism. Significantly out of the ashes of the 1916 rising grew the Irish Republican Army whose membership was drawn in the main from the most extreme republican element in the Irish Volunteers.

When the possibility of partition had first been mooted, during passage of the Home Rule Bill, Redmond, the leader of the Irish Parliamentary Party in the Commons, had said: 'Ireland is a unit . . . this two-nation theory is to us an abomination and a blasphemy.'[24] However in 1919 Lloyd George expressed himself unwilling to coerce Ulster Unionists into an independent undivided Ireland because he believed they were

. . . as alien in blood, in religious faith, in traditions, in outlook — as alien from the rest of Ireland in this respect as the inhabitants of Fife or Aberdeen . . . To place them under national rule against their will would be as glaring an outrage on the principle of liberty and self-government as the denial of self-government would be for the rest of Ireland.[25]

This belief ignored, of course, the presence and political aspirations of a sizeable Republican minority in the six counties which were to become Northern Ireland. Notwithstanding Lloyd George's views, those who framed the Act clearly did not intend the partition which resulted to be permanent, for the Act provided for the establishment of a Council of Ireland: 'with a view to the eventual establishment of a parliament for the whole of Ireland and to bring about harmonious action between the parliaments and governments of Southern Ireland and Northern Ireland.'[26]

While this Act resulted in the establishment of a separate parliament for Northern Ireland, its provisions were not accepted in the South and an insurrection followed the exclusion of six of Ulster's nine counties from the jurisdiction of an all-Ireland parliament. The Anglo-Irish Treaty of 1921 which the British government eventually reached with the Sinn Fein party which had decimated the Irish Parliamentary Party in the 1918 elections, resulted in the creation of the Irish Free State with dominion status, i.e., a self-governing territory of the then British Empire. The Treaty was finally implemented only after the conclusion of a brief but bloody civil war.

Since then there is evidence that the two parts of Ireland have grown further apart. From the beginning Northern Ireland felt under threat as the IRA launched a campaign of murder and violence designed to undermine the authority of the new government and prevent it from functioning effectively. At various times over the next fifty years they returned to the offensive in an effort to dislodge the local administration, claimed by its leaders to be a Protestant parliament for a Protestant people. Representatives of the Catholic minority were consigned to the role of permanent opposition with no prospects of exercising political power. It is hardly surprising that Nationalist members initially refused to take their seats while other members of the minority refused to participate in the 'public' life of the state. Rose records that in the twelve Stormont elections between 1921 and 1969 the Unionists never won fewer than forty of the fifty-two seats while the only real issue for the Unionist party throughout most of that time was the preservation of the border with the Catholic republic. The extent of the Unionists' political power was so complete that on only one occasion during the entire life of the Northern Ireland parliament did a 'Nationalist' bill obtain government support and become law. The Wild Bird Act 1931 was a measure Darby suggests 'even the most ingenious argument could not make controversial'.[27]

The record of the Northern Ireland government before the Second World War has been analysed by Buckland in his book, *The Factory of Grievances*. He concludes:

> The new government inherited a divided and disadvantaged society. It did little to relieve the disadvantages, but helped to confirm and deepen the divisions thus establishing a pattern of government and politics which ended in violence.[28]

The depth of those divisions was such that even the political reforms introduced since 1969 seem to have had little healing impact — equal voting rights for all local and Westminster elections, the reorganisation of the police, the replacement of the B Specials, the transfer of responsibility for housing from local councils to a central authority, the introduction of procedures for dealing with complaints against statutory bodies and the establishment of a Fair Employment Agency.

Meanwhile policies of successive governments in the South of Ireland over the past half century have served to confirm and justify Unionist intransigence, despite frequent public pronouncements in favour of the peaceful reunification of Ireland. The fears of Ulster Unionists that Home Rule in 1914 would lead inevitably to Rome Rule and threaten their civil and religious liberties were validated by the enshrining of the Catholic social code within the Constitution of the Republic in 1937, creating what has been described as a 'theocratic' state. Thus Unionists believed their objections to Home Rule were retrospectively justified and their actions at that time legitimised. Article 44 of the Constitution recognised the special position of the Catholic Church within the state: 'The State recognises the special position of the Holy Catholic Apostolic and Roman Church as the guardian of the faith professed by the great majority of its citizens.'[29]

Even though this article was repealed thirty-five years later, nonetheless it remains the belief of Ulster Protestants that the Catholic Church continues to be all-powerful in matters affecting what it chooses to define as moral issues. It came as little comfort to Ulster Protestants in 1980 to hear that Dr Noel Browne could not find one member of Dail Eireann to support his bill to change the laws of the state to permit divorce. The open sale of contraceptives is also prohibited by the state while laws regarding the censorship of books and films were only reformed in 1967.

However, the article which most incensed Unionist opinion in 1937 and continues to do so to this day is Article 2: 'the national territory consists of the whole island of Ireland.'[30] In the view of Ulster Unionists this article serves to encourage the various IRA factions in the latter's attempts to reunite Ireland by violent means. Indeed distorted minds could even cite this article to legitimise and justify their actions. The Unionists' view is confirmed by the Republic's apparent determination not to permit the extradition to Northern Ireland of those wanted for questioning in respect of terrorist crimes.

According to a recent survey carried out by the Economic and Social Research Institute,[31] while 90 per cent of Protestants and 64 per cent of Catholics in Northern Ireland favour extradition, the population of the Republic is evenly divided. In the same survey 71 per cent of the Republic's population expressed opposition to the removal from the Constitution of the territorial claim. In addition the population of the Republic was evenly divided on the value of legislation to permit divorce as a 'step to bring about a solution'. Furthermore the same survey found 74 per cent of the population of the Republic were anti-Northern Protestant. It is no wonder Lyons believes that ' . . . few people in the Irish Free State seem much interested in either the structure or ideology of Ulster Unionism'[32] while Beckett has remarked, 'The real partition of Ireland is not on the map but in the minds of men.'[33]

However, it is simplistic to believe that Irish unity will be brought about by the promise of divorce legislation and other constitutional changes. Lyons has drawn attention to the fallacy of the belief that the Northern Ireland Protestant is 'possessed of an insatiable lust for looser marriage bonds and unlimited contraceptives'.[34] Indeed one aspect of the common ground which exists between Unionist and Nationalist is a rigid conservatism in respect of moral values. One of the few occasions on which unanimous all-party votes have been recorded in various District Councils in Northern Ireland was to condemn the proposals of the then Labour government to bring the law on homosexuality in Northern Ireland into line with that in England and Wales.

Thus in respect of these constitutional matters the policies of successive governments in the Republic have served to strengthen and buttress Unionist opposition to a united Ireland and to confirm and validate its worst fears. According to the ESRI survey 89 per cent of Northern Protestants wish to remain within the United Kingdom as do 50 per cent of Northern Catholics. The authors of the survey conclude: 'These figures cast considerable doubt on the traditional assumption of a common viewpoint and purpose in a nationalist community defined as including Northern Ireland Catholics.'[35] Meanwhile in terms of the whole population of the island the ESRI study estimates only between 48 per cent and 52 per cent are in favour of a united Ireland. However, it is only fair to record that the ESRI survey has been the subject of academic criticism for alleged methodological weaknesses.[36] Despite this state of affairs no government in the Republic has even formulated and adopted a specific programme designed to win the hearts and minds of Ulster Unionists and encourage them, with suitable social, religious and financial guarantees, to accept a united Ireland. It is therefore hardly surprising that the Ulster Unionist believes that successive governments in the Republic have wished to coerce him into a theocratic state, within which he believes his freedom will be constrained through state interference in his private life. To quote Stewart:

> In the long run the decisive factor in partition . . . is the simple determination of Protestants in north-east Ulster not to become a minority in a Catholic Ireland. It is towards weakening this determination that all the efforts of Irish nationalism ought in theory to have been aimed. Instead these have been largely directed to strengthening it in every possible way.[37]

The historical analysis so far has treated Ulster Unionists as a single homogeneous group, yet the last decade has seen their fragmentation into a number of different political parties, each claiming to represent traditional mainstream unionism. Even in 1968, before the outbreak of the present troubles, Professor Rose[38] collected data which cast doubt on the traditional belief of Unionists that they constituted a single homogeneous group. Only 39 per cent of the Northern Ireland Protestants he interviewed claimed to be British. Thirty-two per cent claimed to be Ulstermen while 20 per cent claimed to be Irish. In marked contrast 76 per cent of Northern Ireland Catholics claimed to be Irish, 15 per cent British and only 5 per cent Ulstermen. Lijphart believes these figures show that the problem of nationality is not the key to the conflict and that Northern Ireland could best be described as a plural society in which the subgroups exercise differential political rights. Such a theory appears to Lijphart to fit the facts well for he goes on to say: '. . . government by consensus is impossible in plural societies and . . . either coercion or political instability must ensue.'[39] However, perhaps he overestimates from Rose's data the extent of the fragmentation on the Unionist side, for both those groups which consider themselves British or Ulster, constituting 71 per cent of the total, would be vehemently opposed to a united Ireland. Moreover, it seems likely that the figure of 20 per cent of Protestants who in 1968 would have considered themselves Irish would now be much reduced as a consequence of the polarisation which has taken place over the last decade. Thus the groups Rose identifies are probably sub-groups of a more basic division.

Another interesting explanation for Rose's data and for the fragmentation of the previously monolithic Unionist Party is recorded by Whyte.[40] He quotes Miller's 'no nation' or 'contractarian' theory to explain the Ulster Protestant's position. The latter still operates on a pre-nationalist basis, never having fully experienced the nationalist phase of European development. According to Whyte the essence of the theory is that subjects owe conditional allegiance to a ruler, and are entitled to look after their own interests if their ruler fails to do so. Whyte points out that this theory

> . . . helps to explain how Unionists serenely avoid the crisis

of national identity which Nationalists so often predict for them. It fits in with much of the rhetoric of present day unionism.[41]

Notwithstanding the fragmentation of the old Unionist Party one would still imagine that the gap between Unionist and Nationalist or Protestant and Catholic remains very wide. Rose's data suggest otherwise for he found, admittedly during a time of relative peace and tranquillity, that both Protestants and Catholics in Northern Ireland believed they had more in common with each other than with either Southern Irishmen or Englishmen. Moreover, Whyte's analysis of Rose's data leads him to conclude:

> It was only on strictly political issues and on a cluster of questions relating to ecumenism that Protestant and Catholic attitudes differed widely . . . The picture which emerges is not of a province divided into communities: it is rather that of a single community divided on particular issues.[42]

This thesis conflicts somewhat with that elaborated by Lyons in his book *Culture and Anarchy in Ireland: 1890– 1939.* He claims that at the very heart of the Irish conflict lies a 'collision of a variety of cultures' whose 'diversity has been a force which has worked against the evolution of a homogeneous society and in doing so has been an agent of anarchy rather than of unity.'[43] Among the four cultures he identified in the W. B. Rankin memorial lecture at Queen's[44] were the 'Gaelic' and the 'Presbyterian' cultures. The Gaelic revival at the end of the last century was stimulated by the stifling influence of the dominant English or Anglo-American culture, which Yeats described as that 'filthy modern tide', and emphasised its rural and Catholic identity while espousing a nationalist ideology. It was this culture that Sinn Fein ('ourselves') symbolised at the elections in 1918 when it displaced the older Irish Parliamentary Party, to the annoyance of George Russell (AE) who wrote:

> The cultural implications of the words Sinn Fein are evil. We are not enough for ourselves. No race is. All learn from each other. All give to each other. We must not be afraid

of world thought or world science. They will give vitality to our nationality.[45]

In contrast Lyons described the Presbyterian culture as 'the product conjointly of colonisation, of Calvinism and of industrialism'[46] which emphasises the Protestant work-ethic, combined with Puritan values.

It is interesting that no trace of these two cultures can be found in Rose's data Perhaps the 'filthy modern tide' has already submerged both the 'Gaelic' and 'Presbyterian' cultures or Rose's questionnaire was too insensitive to pick up cultural variations. Alternatively, it may well be that each of these cultures separately coexists with the Anglo-American. The former may operate at an ideological level and the latter on an everyday practical plane. Indeed unless one is a recluse it would appear difficult to avoid being part of the Anglo-American culture.

This might help explain the longevity and intensity of the present conflict if its origins lie in the collision between these two irreconcilable and idealistic cultures, whose relevance to life in modern Ireland is questionable. Moreover, as Lyons himself has pointed out, these cultures are incapable of living apart, for each is the product of the other and unable to live independently from it. Thus each provides the reinforcement necessary for the continued existence and vitality of the other.

One purpose of this brief analysis of the historical origins of the present conflict has been to demonstrate how complex these origins are and how, over the centuries, events have reinforced each other and driven ever deeper the wedge between the communities in Northern Ireland. The central question throughout this long period has been who should exercise political power in Ireland.

However, those who analyse today's conflict in Northern Ireland have a number of additional dimensions of more recent origin to consider. One important dimension not already touched upon is Britain's reduced role in world affairs. It is therefore difficult to believe that Britain has any longer any strategic or economic interest in any part of Ireland which requires the maintenance of a military presence.

The reverse is more likely to be true given the parlous state of the United Kingdom economy and the huge financial subventions required by the Northern Ireland exchequer, currently running at around £1,000 million annually. There seems therefore no reason to doubt the sincerity of the British government's oft-repeated assurance first made at Sunningdale in 1973: 'if in the future the majority of the people of Northern Ireland should indicate a wish to become part of a united Ireland, the British government would support that wish.'[47]

A further dimension of more recent origin is the significant divisions which exist within the two communities in Northern Ireland as well as between them. While these intra-community divisions add significantly to the complexity of the problem and reduce the already dim prospects for any speedy and peaceful resolution to the conflict they nonetheless confuse and obscure the basic division between the two communities over the central question of the constitutional future of Northern Ireland.

While the elucidation of this central question is primarily a function of historical analysis there are other dimensions to the conflict which require examination. The next to be considered is the religious dimension.

(2) Religious Theories

While the issue of political nationalism lies at the root of the Ulster problem more often than not the problem is defined in religious terms and starkly presented as a conflict between Protestants and Catholics. Although Jackson uses these labels to define the conflict as the problem of a double minority, he is careful to say that the conflict is not doctrinal in nature. In this he has the support of Stewart and de Paor. The former believes that '. . . the quarrel is not about theology as such and remains in its modern form stubbornly a constitutional problem, though religion is the shibboleth of the contending parties.'[48] De Paor's view is similar. He believes religious bigotry is 'not the root of the matter' and that the two religious parties to the conflict do not quarrel with one another 'because of matters of theology or faith'[49]

On the other hand the Dutchman Heslinga[50] believes the

Irish border is in the last resort a religious frontier while O'Brien asserts that if religion is a 'red herring' then it is a 'red herring about the size of a whale'[51] These views are supported by the research undertaken by Harris during 1952 and 1953 in Ballybeg into the importance of religion and its impact on social relationships in a small rural community. She found that, although members of the two religious groups evidenced tremendous good will and tolerance towards each other, nonetheless 'all social relationships are pervaded by a consciousness of the religious dichotomy.'[52]

The key to understanding the importance of the religious dimension lies in the symbiotic relationship which exists between political and religious institutions. Thus Fitzgerald's statement that 'the Irish problem is quite simply the fruit of Northern Protestant reluctance to become part of what they regard as an authoritarian Southern Catholic State'[53] can be understood as a political statement as much as a religious one. Moreover Jackson's interpretation of the problem as that of a double minority and his use of the labels Protestant and Catholic can be understood in the same way.

The existence of this symbiotic relationship and its development can be clearly seen in the context of the history of Ireland. By the time of the emergence of the Home Rule movements in the mid nineteenth century the political divide between those who favoured an independent Ireland and those who opposed any constitutional change was also a religious divide. Catholicism had become identified with nationalism and the Gaelic culture, while Protestantism with its Puritan values espoused the unionist cause. Thus religious labels became, and remain, a shorthand way of identifying the different parties to the conflict and the religious descriptions 'Catholic' and 'Protestant' are in large measure synonyms for 'nationalist/republican' and 'unionist' respectively.

Yet it is facile to believe that there is no doctrinal element to the conflict for, although the issue is at heart a constitutional one, the traditional values of the two protagonists largely flow from their different religious faiths. Thus not only do different religious principles to a large extent define the social and cultural values of the two communities, they also serve to differentiate and consolidate them. Nowhere is this more clearly recognised than in working-class areas of Belfast, where unfortunately the perceptions each community has of the other's religious faith are grossly distorted and based on myth rather than reality.

Roman Catholics are generally believed by Protestants in Ulster to be dominated by a monolithic and authoritarian church which seeks to impose its beliefs not only on its own people but in the context of the Republic on the whole population, whether Protestant, Catholic or Jew. The Catholic Church's opposition to divorce, contraception and abortion is enshrined in the Republic's legislation and Constitution, so limiting the human rights of the Republic's citizens, and interfering in their private lives. Moreover, in the opinion of Ulster's Protestants the Catholic Church still has sufficient influence in the Republic to ensure the defeat of any proposed legislative changes it perceives to be contrary to its teaching and beliefs. The Ulster Protestant also identifies the Catholic Church with nationalist politics and Gaelic culture, each of which constitutes a threat to his continued existence in Ireland. The more extremist Protestants would even link the Catholic Church with the IRA on the basis of graveside ceremonies of an unmistakeably military nature for IRA men killed in action. Such displays appear to them to indicate that the Catholic Church either condones IRA violence or is actively implicated in it. Finally the Ulster Protestant believes that with a united Ireland the effect of the Catholic Church policy on mixed marriage, and the obligation to bring up the children of such marriages as Catholics, would lead in time to the extinction of the Protestant race in Ireland.

This latter fear has some validity, for Walsh[54] has documented the decline in the number of Protestants in the Republic since 1921, when, according to the first census held after the introduction of partition there were 221,000 Protestants. Their numbers have since declined by approximately 10 per cent each decade, until now they form around 5 per cent of the population. Among the reasons Walsh adduces for this decline is the impact of mixed marriages in which the children are brought up Catholic. The decline has been such that in 1978 Fitzgerald stated, 'This continued and rapid erosion of this section of our population is one of the most potent weapons of extremists'.[55]

Protestant fears have been succinctly stated by Gibson:

> The very heart of Protestant fears is the historic Catholic claim to be the one true universal church and the ultimate arbiter of religious truth ... This feeling of Protestants and the sense of insecurity and vulnerability which goes with it ... is strengthened by their widespread conviction that the Church would wish to impose an exclusive Catholic ethos throughout the state, and through the power of the state impose its moral and social teaching on all members of society.[56]

While Protestants tend to fear Catholics for their religion, Catholics on the other hand tend to fear Protestants for their political and social control. The Roman Catholic in Ulster sees Protestant clergymen occupying positions of some power and influence in various political parties. It would appear therefore that Protestant Churches have no need to influence clandestinely various political parties, for the representatives of each are one and the same. The Roman Catholic cannot but conclude that politics and religion, as practised by his Protestant fellow-countrymen, are inextricably interwoven. This view is confirmed by the power which the Roman Catholic perceives is exercised by the Orange Order. Throughout the century the Orange Order has been the cement in the Protestant political power-structure and until recently the ladder to political success. Although it is closely identified with the Protestant churches, to the Roman Catholic observer the Orange Order derives its strength not so much from basic Christian principles as from a fanatical hatred of the Church of Rome and its antichrist Pope. Yet the Order itself formally requires its members 'to abstain from all uncharitable words, actions or sentiments towards Roman Catholics,'[57] an aim which Barritt and Booth believe many think 'more honoured in the breach than the observance'.[58] Furthermore, the Roman Catholic perceives the Protestant churches as possessing their own inflexible beliefs based on a stern and uncompromising Calvinism with its emphasis on the Protestant work ethic and Puritan values.

Both these limited perspectives confirm the truth of Swift's opinion of many years ago: 'We have just enough religion to make us hate, but not enough to make us love.'[59] They illustrate the level of ignorance and misunderstanding which exists between Roman Catholics and Protestants. Yet although neither perspective is totally false there appear to have been few concerted attempts on the part of the major religious denominations in Ireland to promote and preach in concrete terms the message of Christ the peacemaker and reconciler in the context of Ulster's divided and violent community. Rarely have the churches dissociated themselves from the activities of divisive organisations or actively tried to reduce the sectarian hatreds which exist within their congregations, for which they must bear their share of responsibility. Even within the churches it can be difficult to determine whether the message being preached is a political or a religious one, such is the extent of the overlap between these spheres. Thus O'Brien has drawn attention to 'the role of the churches [in] encouraging, exalting and extending the kind of tribal self-righteousness which forms a culture in which violence so easily multiplies.'[60]

On the other hand there were several corporate activities which the major denominations engaged in during the 1970s. These included the annual conference at the Ballymascanlon Hotel attended by the leaders of the major churches, the latter's peace campaign in December 1974 and the reports prepared on a variety of topics by a number of Joint Study Groups comprising representatives of the Irish Council of Churches and the Roman Catholic Church, of which the best-known is entitled 'Violence in Ireland'.[61] However, it is arguable that these activities have had little impact on the man in the pew.

Throughout this century there has been a strong link between violence and religious fervour. The deeply religious poet, Patrick Pearse, three years before his execution in 1916 for his part in the Easter rising, emphasised the redemptive nature of a blood sacrifice:

We may make mistakes in the beginning and shoot the wrong people; but bloodshed is a cleansing and a satisfying thing and the nation which regards it as the final horror has lost its manhood. There are many things more horrible than bloodshed, and slavery is one of them . . . without the shedding of blood there is no redemption . . . as the blood of the martyrs was the seed of saints, so the blood of the patriot will be the sacred seed from which alone can spring new forces and fresh life into a nation that is drifting into the putrescence of decay.[62]

This statement, made in an age when attitudes to violence were perhaps different to our own, should be set against the view expressed by Pope John Paul on his recent visit to Ireland:

> I proclaim with the conviction of my faith in Christ . . . that violence is evil, that violence is unacceptable as a solution to problems, that violence is unworthy of man. Violence is a lie for it goes against the truth of our faith and the truth of our humanity.[63]

Russell has investigated the attitudes of today's children in Northern Ireland towards violence. He found a strong connection between the strength of religious feeling of school children and the violence of their attitudes. Strongly religious Protestant children appeared to be 20 per cent more likely to endorse the use of violence for political purposes than their less religious fellows, while among Roman Catholic children the comparable figure was 30 per cent.[64]

The churches must also bear a heavy responsibility for the divisive effects of segregated education. Children grow up without the opportunity to meet with and learn from their peers across the sectarian divide. In these circumstances it is hardly surprising that myths and prejudices flourish and the miasma of superstition and mistrust grows, unchecked by any knowledge of or contact with the other community. Indeed Darby believes 'children see their own segregation as confirmation and approval of Northern Ireland's community division'[65] while Fraser suggests that 'the practical end-result of Ulster's education policy is this: sectarian abuse is the only verbal exchange socially sanctioned and rioting the only joint activity possible.'[66]

Fraser, like others, advocates primary school integration —

'the one initiative that would contribute more than any other single factor to the prospect of peace in Ulster'.[67] However, there are those who adopt a less sanguine view and, while agreeing that integrated education or at least the existence of joint extra-curricular activities, would do much to dispel many myths, prejudices and rumours, believe Fraser's view shows a touching but unrealistic faith in the value of formal education as a means of achieving a permanent change in attitudes and outlook, particularly when those attitudes have become engrained through many generations and reinforced in various ways throughout the short life of the child. Thus Russell claims that surveys he conducted among 4,000 Protestant and Catholic schoolboys on intercommunal group friendships in Northern Ireland showed that in general 'friendship between religions — when it was found — modified extreme social and political attitudes among schoolboys in the North without specifically weakening religious beliefs and practices.'[68]

In their book, *A Society Under Stress,*[69] the Harbisons outline a more optimistic view. Joan Harbison believes that, based on a study by McKernan, 'a consensus of values and ideals . . . may exist among the young'[70] regardless of religious affiliation, and feels this constitutes a sound basis on which to build inter-communal friendship, particularly since research findings suggest the skills of ethnic discrimination in Ulster are not acquired before the ripe old age of eleven, compared with five in the United States, where the colour of one's skin immediately identifies the individual's ethnic origins. Joan Harbison also refers to research which demonstrated that the views of Protestant and Catholic children about each other became gradually less stereotyped when the children were placed in a situation of enforced contact in an assessment centre for a five-week period. Moreover, this change in attitude appeared to be retained, at least over the short term, when their attitudes were retested five weeks after leaving the centre, during which time they had had no contact with the other side.

Although many of the studies to which the Harbisons refer are based on small samples, they nonetheless provide some support for the view that integrated education could lead in time to at least a reduction in the level of hostility between the two communities.

(3) Economic Theories

Another conceptual frame within which the Northern Ireland conflict must be examined is the economic one.

The history of Ireland provides ample evidence to support those who believe in an economic basis to the conflict, although whether the evidence is sufficient to establish a causal relationship between economic factors and the current violence is questionable.

The Plantation of Ulster effectively displaced the native Irish from the better land, where they were replaced by loyal settlers from England and Scotland, for whom they then worked, with a burning sense of injustice, as labourers. Thus from the early seventeenth century there was some disparity between the standards of living of Planter and Gael and this has continued to the present time, although Rose would argue the disparity is not as great as might be imagined. He admits his data, gathered in 1968, show there is a tendency for Catholics to be less well off than Protestants but he points out that '. . . given their larger numbers in the population . . . there are more poor Protestants than poor Catholics in Northern Ireland.'[71]

The later years of the seventeenth century and the decades which followed saw the imposition of various laws designed to protect the English market from the import of various Irish products including woollen goods, glass, cattle and cotton. This legislation coupled with a cheap food policy conspired to maintain the Irish economy as a whole in a depressed state. Only in Ulster, with the development of its textile and shipbuilding industries in the late nineteenth century, did a limited degree of prosperity develop. These industries were heavily dependent on the British market both for their raw materials and for their exports and it is therefore hardly surprising that among the most determined antagonists of Home Rule in the early twentieth century were many Belfast industrialists fearful that Home Rule would limit their access to the English market. The validity of their fears was confirmed by the trade war which took place between Britain and the Irish Free State in the 1930s.

Indeed the industrialisation of Belfast is, Lyons[72] believes, one of the main keys to an understanding of the genesis of the present conflict. The creation of the textile and ship-building industries around the estuary of the river Lagan produced a tremendous demand for labour and Belfast became a magnet for farm workers seeking to escape from grinding rural poverty and the insecurity of agricultural life in the years that followed the famine. Its population expanded from around 19,000 at the start of the nineteenth century to nearly 400,000 by its close. However, all too often the state of rural poverty was only to be replaced by one of urban poverty, as the newcomers found themselves living in slum conditions in well-defined tribal areas, where their own safety and convenience of worship could be assured. The tensions of life in these tribal areas of Belfast during the last century were such that between 1813 and 1913 fourteen major riots occurred. The same tribal areas exist today.

Sectarian hatreds were exacerbated by the competition for jobs and houses, while unscrupulous employers and politicians sought to undermine the labour movement by banging the sectarian drum and by practising religious dis-crimination in the recruitment of labour. In 1907 James Larkin came to Belfast as an organiser for the National Union of Dock Labourers. His organisation of cross-channel dockers in the port of Belfast soon led to a strike in support of higher wages and better working conditions which spread rapidly to carters, coalmen and the police. However, this unprecedented unity between Catholic and Protestant was to be short lived, for the employers, ably assisted by newspaper proprietors and the Orange Order, described the strikes as a Fenian plot and Larkin as a papist agitator bent on achieving the destruc-tion of the Northern economy. The strikes petered out and eventually the workers returned on much the same terms as before. Ironically six years later, during the Dublin strikes and lockout, Larkin was portrayed by the Dublin employers as a tool of British imperialism.

This skilful exploitation of sectarian hatreds has led some writers to favour a Marxist interpretation of the conflict. According to this interpretation, the capitalist bourgeoisie has artificially fomented the conflict by splitting the working class on sectarian lines, so diverting what is at heart a class struggle between the proletariat and the bourgeoisie into a religious struggle between Protestant and Catholic. This class struggle can only be settled, they believe, when Ireland has been reunited. Thus tongue in cheek Engels wrote: 'Ireland still remained the Holy Isle whose aspirations must on no account be mixed up with the profane class struggles of the rest of the sinful world.'[73]

In practice the loyalty of the proletariat has been cemented by differential discrimination whereby those in positions of authority, generally but not always Protestants, have afforded to their co-religionists positions of privilege particularly in terms of employment and housing. The reforms introduced over the last ten years have largely outlawed such practices but their legacy remains, for example in terms of higher unemployment rates among Catholic workers, as evidenced by the findings of the recent Belfast Welfare Rights Project.[74]

However, while Whyte believes the evidence of discrimination recorded by the Cameron Commission and by Darby in fields such as employment, the allocation of houses, and the determination of electoral boundaries cannot be seriously questioned, he suggests that 'the real question for examination is not whether discrimination has taken place, but how much.'[75] He quotes Rose who found that in 1968:

> Whatever may have been true in particular areas, there was no great aggregate discrimination against Catholics in the provision of either public housing or public employment ... Only about 10 per cent of Catholics mentioned religious discrimination as an obstacle to their getting a job.[76]

Whyte also points out that although the evidence from census data would indicate that there is a cumulative disadvantage associated with being a Catholic this may not be totally due to discrimination. Thus the higher unemployment levels among Catholics referred to earlier could at least in part be explained by the absence of employment opportunities in certain towns, geographically remote from Belfast and therefore unattractive to employers, where Catholics are in a majority, for example Strabane, Londonderry and Newry.

Birrell is another supporter of the theory that there is an economic basis to the conflict. He has pointed out that during the early 1970s rioting was most severe in towns which ranked highest on a number of indicators of social need:

> Relative deprivation provides a persistent underlying cause of civil disturbance in Northern Ireland. The only effective solution seems to be to remove its causes.[77]

The association between high levels of social deprivation and violence in Belfast has been documented by Boal and others.[78] They have shown that those areas suffering from a concatenation of adverse social and environmental circumstances, including high unemployment, poor housing, low pay, large families, and high levels of infant mortality, are all those which have been most affected by violence. Such conditions clearly aggravate community tensions and provide a fertile environment for the growth of violence which in turn exacerbates the social malaise and generates yet more unemployment and poverty. To give but one example of the high level of social deprivation in Northern Ireland, the Housing Conditions Survey of 1974 found 19.6 per cent of housing stock or approximately 90,000 dwellings, was unfit.[79]

However, the absolute level of social and economic deprivation is believed by sociologists to be not as important as how the level compares with neighbouring areas. Gurr suggests that it is the discrepancy between legitimate expectations and the actuality of life which gives rise to frustration, which in turn finds an outlet in aggression. The level of aggression is then proportionate to the discrepancy and to the likely benefit to be derived from it. According to Gurr the process can be reversed '. . . if discontented people have or get constructive means to attain their social and motivational goals, few will resort to violence.'[80] However the link between adverse economic circumstances and violence, in Irish history, is tenuous. Budge and O'Leary have pointed out that in nineteenth-century Belfast the cycle of sectarian rivalry coincided not with economic factors but with political events.[81]

In a variant of the Marxist interpretation Boserup[82] argues that it is not the British bourgeoisie which is responsible for the conflict in Northern Ireland but differences within the capitalist class, between two forms of capital. The older form of capitalism is locally based, depending on declining industries and relies on discrimination to keep its workforce loyal. The newer is based on international capitalism, is non-discriminatory and is described by Boserup as the 'welfare state of managerial capitalism'. The latter represents moderate Unionism and the former extreme Unionism.

Although this interpretation helps to explain divisions within the Unionist camp it is facile to account for the present troubles without reference to the differing political aspirations of the Catholic and Protestant communities. Moreover, although the international capitalism identified by Boserup is likely to be conservative in political outlook, economic expediency seems more likely to determine its activities than either political ideology or reformist zeal. The attractiveness of Northern Ireland's comparatively cheap labour to multinational companies is emphasised by Jackson and Smyth[83] who believe that one source of the conflict lies in Northern Ireland's role as a supplier of cheap labour to the European market. The 'periphery' suffers economic deprivation when compared with the 'centre'.

The British and Irish Communist Organisation argues that differential economic development has been responsible for the evolution of two nations in Ireland. That organisation lays the blame for the present conflict at the door of the Southern Irish bourgeoisie.

> . . . to claim that the Protestant bourgeoisie is dividing the working class is the reverse of the truth. It is the Catholic nationalist of the south who play this role by stirring up the Catholic minority in the North against acceptance of the state in which they live, thus preventing the development of working-class unity in Northern Ireland.[84]

This theory, like Boserup's, ignores the cumulative political history of the island and also overlooks the problem of the lack of national identity among the Protestants of Northern Ireland which Rose uncovered, and which was discussed in an earlier section. It may also require revision in the light of the rapidly closing gap between the Southern and Northern economies. The latter's traditional superiority is gradually disappearing. The North's traditional industries – shipbuilding, engineering and textiles – are in decline and new ones have been difficult to attract in the violent atmosphere of the last decade, while there has been a tremendous growth in the economic development of the Republic, although signs of strain have appeared recently. The Fine Gael pamphlet, 'Ireland – Our Future Together', published in 1979 lists the financial and economic benefits which would accrue to Northern Ireland in the event of an agreed federal solution to Ireland's political division. It is therefore conceivable that in the not too distant future the Republic of Ireland may be able to offer the prospect of a higher standard of living within a united Ireland to the population of the North than it currently enjoys within the United Kingdom. However, it seems doubtful that economic benefits would alone persuade the one million Protestants of Northern Ireland to set aside their fears and throw in their lot with the three million Catholics of the Republic. Moreover, this analysis ignores the huge subvention which Northern Ireland currently obtains from the British exchequer, of around £1,000 million per annum.[85] It is unrealistic to suppose, as do some Republicans, that such a subsidy would continue indefinitely were a united Ireland to be established tomorrow.

Data collated by Rose[86] also throw light on the extent to which 'class' is perceived to be important by Northern Ireland's population. He found that in 1968 it was the weakest of four variables he identified as reflecting strong social identifications and commitments. While 42 per cent of his sample considered 'religion' and 38 per cent 'nationality' to be important only 23 per cent referred to 'political party' and 12 per cent to 'class'. Moreover, Rose found a low correlation between political party and class, which was hardly surprising given the emphasis of the two major political parties of that time – the Unionists and the Nationalists – on the border and its maintenance. It was and still remains the only major issue in Northern politics. Rose therefore concluded that the conflict in Northern Ireland is intractable precisely because it is not about economic issues but about non-bargainable issues of religion and nationality: 'There is then little scope for politicians to lead people along class lines.'[87]

If the Marxist interpretation of the Northern Ireland conflict is to be successful in explaining the genesis of the conflict it must establish a causal link between class differences and the present violence. This it fails to do. Rose's data would indicate class is a relatively insignificant facet of life in Northern Ireland while the cumulative political history of Ireland would suggest that even if employers have in the past sought to control their employees by practising religious discrimination in jobs and by banging the sectarian drum, the division between Catholic and Protestant has some objective basis in reality and cannot be described as artificially created by the machinations of these same employers. It cannot be denied that employers have taken advantage of intercommunal divisions between Catholic and Protestants, as indeed have politicians, but responsibility for the divide itself cannot be ascribed to them. Indeed O'Brien believes the Northern Ireland problem is 'distorted or analysed out of existence by the Marxist interpretation.'[88]

Finally, even though economic factors may not be responsible for the conflict in Northern Ireland they doubtless play their part in its exacerbation. The amelioration of economic adversity and social deprivation could do much to reduce community tension. Gibson has written: 'I remain convinced that sustained full employment, a reasonably rapid rate of economic growth and a dramatic improvement in housing availability and conditions would do an enormous amount to lessen political tension and make peaceful evolution possible.'[89]

(4) Psychological Theories

There is no question that the violence in Northern Ireland over the past decade has had a psychological impact on its population, particularly in Belfast. One has only to remember the searing sense of shock felt by the whole community on hearing of the carnage resulting from the bomb explosion in the crowded Abercorn restaurant during the early days of the troubles to realise how inured people have become to the continued violence. The population's emotions have been blunted and the prolonged violence has desensitised many to the sufferings of those directly affected.

While this legacy of the troubles is serious enough in itself, the early 1970s produced some evidence to suggest the violence was having a seriously deleterious effect on children. Fraser, a psychiatrist who worked in Belfast, has described the trauma experienced by children who had been exposed, usually inadvertently, to violent situations, in some cases a riot, in others a bomb, explosion or a gun battle.[90] However, such instances, while nonetheless serious in themselves, are perhaps exceptional, for Harbison, writing in 1980, believes that

... the evidence suggests that the children of Northern Ireland are somehow learning to cope. Their behavioural problems are certainly no more severe than other urban children.[91]

She quotes the results of studies which suggest children in inner London are more likely to be behaviourally disturbed than those in Belfast. In these studies 14.2 per cent of London children were deemed anti-social and 7.7 per cent neurotic, compared with 12.9 per cent and 3.3 per cent respectively for Belfast children.[92]

The apparent absence of severe and widespread behavioural disturbance among children exposed to violence illustrates the resilience of human nature and its capacity to cope with stressful events. Nonetheless, in the case of adults there is some evidence to suggest that the 1970s have seen a significant increase in the use of prescribed drugs by people living in ghetto areas of Belfast.[93] One reason that has been advanced for the troubles' lack of significant psychological impact is that wars seem normally to be accompanied by a decline in psychiatric admissions. This phenomenon is probably due to a strengthening of community ties and a lowering of social barriers in the face of a common enemy. However in Belfast the enemy is generally not easily identifiable, except in so far as uniformed members of the security forces are identified as the enemy.

Fraser believes that it has been in those fringe areas bordering on the scenes of the greatest violence that there has been the most significant increase in tension and anxiety and suggests that 'anxiety not experience [of violence], is the outstanding stressor.'[94] Indeed he feels there may conceivably be a therapeutic benefit associated with the stimulus of involvement in a riot. Although an acute short-term emotional reaction may follow exposure to danger, Fraser believes chronic anxiety states of a long-term nature requiring hospitalisation tended during the early 1970s to occur in those fringe areas close to the greater violence. Around this same time Lyons found that there had been a significant decline in depressive illnesses affecting both sexes and all ages in social groups IV and V living in riot areas. Meanwhile rural Co. Down evidenced an increase in the number of male depressives over the same period.[95]

Uncertainty as to the psychological impact of the troubles on the population of Northern Ireland has not prevented some observers from advancing psychological theories as explanations for the troubles. In considering such theories it is once again important to ensure that factors which undoubtedly contribute to and intensify the violence are not also given causal significance. Moreover, it is important to strip away the jargon associated with such interpretations, which often appear to suggest a scientific validity for the analysis which may be spurious. Thus Stewart has written that 'one has always to remember that facts well enough known to every Belfast street urchin have to be translated into learned jargon for university professors abroad.'[96]

The simplest psychological explanation for the troubles suggests that each society, particularly at a time of change, requires an 'outgroup' or 'scapegoat' onto which it can project its frustrations at its own inability to satisfactorily resolve the problems it faces. In this way society suppresses the reality of its own inadequacies and deficiencies and attributes its failings to the scapegoat who is accused of being responsible for the creation and escalation of the problems the society faces. The resulting image of the scapegoat, to whom is often attributed various unsavoury and false characteristics including racial defects, provides a rationale for the expression of prejudice to the extent that it legitimises acts of discrimination and even violence. Since according to this theory the characteristics of this pariah group are in reality illusory and fictitious, it should be possible, given an understanding of the psychological processes at work, to unscramble the distortions and restore peace and understanding. In the Northern Ireland context each community views the other as the scapegoat which is responsible for its political and economic difficulties, to the extent that Jackson describes Northern Ireland thus: 'A society suffering a deep psychosis in which rational thought and action are invariably overtaken by emotional spasms the moment it comes under stress.'[97]

This theory is enhanced by those such as Ardrey and Lorenz who believe man has an innate intuitive propensity to engage in violence – a propensity described by Ardrey as 'the mark of Cain'.[98] According to Ardrey, this is linked to a strong sense of the importance of territoriality and the need to defend it at all costs – a concept not unrelated to the Irish situation in which the cry 'not an inch' has been frequently heard.

However, both Montague[99] and Gurr[100] reject this thesis. Both believe the real causes of behaviour are learned; hence while men have the capacity for violence they neither have a need for it nor is there within man a river of destructive energy seeking an outlet. Violence, according to Gurr, is the outcome of frustration; and he accepts Freud's concept of the frustration – aggression mechanism in which the aggression is often displaced onto a scapegoat or outgroup particularly where such a group is easily identifiable and is near at hand. Significantly this theory does not absolve mankind of responsibility for its own actions.

A great deal of work has been done in the United States on the phenomenon of scapegoating and the development of prejudice in the context of relationships between black and white. Berkowitz has identified four factors which influence the choice of a scapegoat in the United States – visibility, strangeness, prior dislike and proximity.[101] All are present to varying degrees in Northern Ireland, particularly proximity.

The phenomenon of scapegoating is a specific and extreme example of the way in which stereotypes of a more general nature evolve. Vinacke has defined stereotyping as 'the tendency to attribute generalised and simplified characteristics to groups of people in the form of labels and to act towards members of those groups in terms of these labels.'[102] Thus although prejudice and discrimination may begin with the definition of an outgroup in terms of its stereotype it is the content of that stereotype and its truth or falsity, which proves the existence of prejudice. Therefore the analysis of stereotypes held by a particular community both of itself and others, demonstrates the community's own values and how far short of those values other groups fall.

Research into the phenomenon of stereotyping in Northern Ireland has been carried out by O'Donnell.[103] His research led him to the surprising conclusion that the 'real' stereotype Protestant and Roman Catholic have of each other is remarkably consistent with the 'supposed' stereotype each imagine the other would have, regardless of age, socioeconomic class, sex and geographical location. Thus:

> In sum the 'real' stereotype that Protestants have of Roman Catholics is that they are ordinary enough people but Irish — nationalist — Republican. They are seen as brainwashed by priests, having too many children, and as being superstitious and bitter.[104]

On the other hand Roman Catholics supposed

> they would be banded as disloyal Republicans, determined to overthrow the powerholders through murderous IRA/Sinn Fein tactics. They also thought they would be described as priest-ridden bigots, too lazy to work and yet expecting the state to support their irresponsibly large families.[105]

Meanwhile Roman Catholics perceive themselves

> as fine, ordinary decent Irish people. However, they think they are deprived of power, so it is reasonable that they see themselves as long-suffering, unfortunate and insecure.[106]

A similar consistency exists in respect of the real and supposed stereotypes Roman Catholics have of Protestants:

> Roman Catholics . . . think Protestants are in control of

the country and are determined to remain in control, even at the cost of bitter murder. This is because they are seen to be loyal Orangemen, ordinary British people.[107]

On the other hand Protestants supposed:

they would be called loyal, British, Orange, power-holders, that they would be seen as bitter, narrow-minded bigots, and as murderous enemies determined not to give an inch.[108]

Meanwhile Protestants perceive themselves as

fine, ordinary, decent, British people . . . loyal Orangemen, determined to remain in power and maintain their hard-working, conservative ethic.[109]

The significance of O'Donnell's work, completed in the mid 1970s, lies not just in the consistency between the real and supposed stereotype but in their relationship to the perception each group has of itself. The above descriptions would suggest each of the two communities in Northern Ireland has a remarkably perceptive understanding of the real characteristics of the other and that the stereotype each holds of the other contains much that is accurate and valid for the group as a whole. These stereotypes are therefore far from imaginary creations based on the prejudices of each community.

While O'Donnell's research was confined to Northern Ireland MacGreil investigated 'intergroup attitudes' in Dublin.[110] These attitudes are the building blocks from which stereotyping grows, and from which the existence of social prejudice can be inferred. MacGreil defines attitudes as 'positive or negative dispositions which dispose a person to behave favourably or unfavourably towards particular foci'[111] and he believes the attitudes people form are the product of their culture, social environment and their personalities. According to MacGreil the most important psychological factors which are conducive to the development of social prejudice are frustration, aggression, anxiety and insecurity. Meanwhile prejudice itself enables the individual to simplify and rationalise the world around him at the same time as it affords him or her security and prestige from membership of the in-group to which he or she is affiliated. Like other researchers before him he also identified the authoritarian and demagogic personality types as being particularly prone to prejudice, the extent of which was 'explained in part by age, sex, education, occupation and religious attitudes.'[112]

In the context of the present study MacGreil's book is particularly interesting for the light it sheds on the attitudes of Dubliners to the problem of Northern Ireland. He found 85 per cent of his sample held that Protestants in the Republic had more in common with Roman Catholics in the Republic than they had with their fellow Protestants in Northern Ireland and 59 per cent felt Roman Catholics in Northern Ireland had more in common with Northern Protestants than they had with their fellow Roman Catholics in the Republic. Moreover 'Unionists' were held in such low regard by Dubliners that they lumped them together with such other out-groups as itinerants, communists, alcoholics, criminals, atheists and militant Republican groups! MacGreil concluded that 'Dublin respondents perceive an ethnic sub-division of Ireland into a Northern (6 counties) and a Southern (26 counties) community.'[113]

The findings of both MacGreil and O'Donnell must be interpreted cautiously. Both made extensive use of questionnaires to derive their raw data and, as MacGreil himself admits, not every attitude identified in a questionnaire reaches behavioural expression. Questionnaires solicit spontaneous responses which on reflection might be considered erroneous or inappropriate in real life, and there may be ordering effects from the sequence of questions. Moreover, the attitudes one holds could conceivably be inconsistent and this fact only recognised when the time comes to express them in behaviour.

The behavioural expression of one's attitudes may also be limited by legal constraints. For these reasons many researchers supplement the use of questionnaires, or replace them, with direct observation of the individual's behaviour. Clearly in many circumstances this is impractical, particularly where the observer's presence is likely to interfere with the subject's behaviour. In any event such research is more time-consuming and expensive.

The various factors involved in psychological interpretations of the conflict clearly throw some light on the dynamics of the interaction between the two communities. Based on an understanding of the psychological phenomena discussed in this section of the paper, various attempts have been made to facilitate communication and create trust and understanding between members and leaders of opposing factions in what have been described as psycho-dynamic workshops. The results of such workshops have been disappointing and the concept has been largely discredited, despite its theoretical value as a way of dispelling myths and illusions. However, as Burton has pointed out, myths and illusions often constitute reality for individuals involved in the conflict and even if they can be dispelled there remain to be resolved various divisive political issues, often of an irreconcilable nature. Moreover, with the best will in the world a workshop in an academic setting still constitutes an artificial environment, within which it is impossible to effectively encompass and control the myriad of complex and often intractable problems which constitute the Northern Ireland conflict.

Such a workshop conducted at Stirling University in Scotland in 1972 by two American psychologists, Doob and Foltz, has been severely criticised by Boehringer.[114] He draws attention to the danger participants attending such workshops run. Not only can they suffer psychological damage from the destruction of their cherished ideals in a highly-charged, intensely emotional setting, but they can experience serious 're-entry' problems, including physical danger on returning to their own communities whose members are still locked in sectarian conflict and who have not had the benefit of the workshop's revelations. Inevitably therefore these workshops largely ignore the realities of everyday life in a ghetto community where the pressure to conform for the safety of the group as a whole may be well-nigh irresistible.

From theories of social prejudices such as that advanced by MacGreil it is tempting to suggest that psychological factors lie at the root of the present conflict. This interpretation conveniently absolves society from blame, for the problem becomes one of 'treating' those whose prejudiced behaviour provides evidence of mental illness or psychological disturbance. However, such behaviour may well reflect the realities of life when viewed from the limited perspective of an individual living in a violent ghetto community. Thus, rather than being an aberrant response to the world around him such behaviour may be totally rational and derive its justification from his group's own values. For these reasons Fairleigh suggests that 'far from being a symptom of individual disorder the behaviour called prejudice may be acquired through the normal mechanisms of attitude formation and may be a predictable and interlocking response to other realities of the social environment.'[115]

O'Donnell's work shows that the stereotypes each community holds of the other in Northern Ireland have some basis in reality and are far from being the illusions that some social scientists suggest. His work and that of MacGreil throw light on some of the psychological processes which define the relationships between the two communities within Northern Ireland and between Northern Ireland and the Republic. An understanding of these processes does much to explain the intensity of the present conflict and its intractability and throws valuable light on the dynamics of inter-personal and inter-group relationships in the context of the present violence.

Nonetheless, in the unlikely event that these psychological processes could be fully understood and controlled, there would still remain various divisive questions to be resolved. Recognition of these psychological factors as contributory to the conflict might well aid the search for a satisfactory resolution to the problem at the root of the conflict — the future constitutional position of Northern Ireland.

Conclusion

This paper has briefly outlined and analysed a number of the major theories that have been advanced to explain the nature and origins of the Northern Ireland conflict. None of these theories can be dismissed, for each contributes to and enriches that explanation. Thus the conflict flows from and is intensified by a complex interplay of various political, social, cultural, religious, economic and psychological forces which generally operate in a single direction to drive the two communities in Northern Ireland further apart.

While this interplay of congruent forces is of crucial importance in explaining the intensity and intractability of the present conflict, the paper suggests that certain forces — principally political ones — are of greater importance than others because of their causal significance. Thus the question of Northern Ireland's constitutional future is believed to lie at the heart of the present conflict.

This does not mean that the political dimension should be the sole focus of attention. On the contrary the reverse is true, since at the present time and for the foreseeable future, the problem of Northern Ireland's constitutional future does not appear amenable to peaceful resolution, given the irreconcilable nature of the demands made by opposing political parties. Moreover, present intercommunal tensions are such that any attempt at compromise on their part would almost certainly result in political suicide.

The more practical alternative is to concentrate on the amelioration of those other forces which drive the two communities apart in the hope that an atmosphere of trust and goodwill can gradually be built up, based on an appreciation of the other's traditions and aspirations, which in time will dispel the fears and hatreds of today and lead to changes in attitudes and perhaps a willingness to consider alternative models of political co-operation.

REFERENCES

1. J. H. Whyte, 'Interpretations of the Northern Ireland Problem: an Appraisal' *Economic and Social Review*, Vol. 9, No. 4, 1978.
2. A. Lijphart, 'Review Article: the Northern Ireland Problem: Cases, Theories, and Solutions', *The British Journal of Political Science*, Vol. 5, No. 1, June 1975.
3. J. Darby, *Conflict in Northern Ireland: The Development of a Polarised Community*, Gill and Macmillan, Dublin 1976.
4. C. Palley, *The Evolution, Disintegration and Possible Reconstruction of the Northern Ireland Constitution*, reprinted from Anglo-American Law Review 1972, Barry Rose Publishers in conjunction with The Institute of Irish Studies 1972.
5. F. S. L. Lyons, *The Burden of Our History*, the W. B. Rankin Memorial Lecture, The Queen's University of Belfast, 1978, p. 8.
6. F. Burton, *The Politics of Legitimacy*, Routledge and Kegan Paul, London 1978.

7. J. Oliver, 'Ulster Today and Tomorrow', *Political and Economic Planning*, Vol. XLIV, Broadsheet No. 574, p. 61.

8. F. S. L. Lyons, *Culture and Anarchy in Ireland 1890–1939*, Clarendon Press, Oxford 1979, p. 13.

9. W. S. Churchill, in A. T. Q. Stewart, *The Narrow Ground: Aspects of Ulster, 1609–1969*, Faber and Faber, London 1977, p. 179.

10. C. Palley, op. cit., p. 368.

11. ibid., p. 370.

12. H. Jackson, *The Two Irelands – The Problem of the Double Minority: A Dual Study of Inter-Group Tensions*, Minority Rights Group Report No. 2, Rev. Ed. 1972, p. 4.

13. F. S. L. Lyons, op. cit., pp. 115–16.

14. ibid.

15. A. T. Q. Stewart, *The Narrow Ground: Aspects of Ulster 1609–1969*, Faber and Faber, London 1977, p. 103.

16. D. P. Barritt and C. Carter, *The Northern Ireland Problem*, Oxford University Press, Oxford 1962.

17. A. T. Q. Stewart, op. cit., p. 105.

18. A. T. Q. Stewart, op. cit., p. 101.

19. F. S. L. Lyons, *Ireland Since the Famine*, Collins/Fontana, London 1973, p. 3.

20. D. O'Connell in A. C. Hepburn (ed.), *The Conflict of Nationality in Modern Ireland*, Edward Arnold Ltd, London 1980, p. 14.

21. 'Solemn League and Covenant' in A. C. Hepburn, op. cit., p. 76.

22. A. T. Q. Stewart, *The Ulster Crisis, Resistance to Home Rule 1912–14*, Faber and Faber, London 1967, p. 168.

23. A. B. Law in *The Conflict of Nationality in Modern Ireland*, p. 75.

24. J. Redmond in *The Conflict of Nationality in Modern Ireland*, p.78.

25. D. Lloyd George, in C. Palley, op. cit., p. 372.

26. Government of Ireland Act, 1920. S. 2(1).

27. J. Darby, op. cit., p. 112.

28. P. Buckland, *The Factory of Grievances: Devolved Government in Northern Ireland, 1921–39*, Gill and Macmillan, Dublin 1979.

29. The Constitution of Eire, 1937, Article 44.

30. The Constitution of Eire, 1937, Article 2.

31. E. E. Davis and R. Sinnott, 'Attitudes in the Republic of Ireland Relevant to the Northern Ireland Problem', Vol. 1, *Economic and Social Review Institute Paper No. 97*, Dublin 1979.

32. F. S. L. Lyons, *Culture and Anarchy*, p. 173.

33. J. C. Beckett, quoted in G. Ecclestone and E. Elliott, *The Irish Problem and Ourselves*, Church Information Office Publishing, London 1977, p. 5.

34. F. S. L. Lyons, *The Burden of Our History*, p. 21.

35. E. E. Davis and R. Sinnott, op. cit., p. 143.

36. K. Heskin, 'How Valid are the ESRI's Findings?' *Irish Times*, 29 and 30 October 1979.

37. A. T. Q. Stewart, *The Narrow Ground*, p. 162.

38. R. Rose, *Governing Without Consensus*, Faber and Faber, London 1971.

39. A. Lijphart, op. cit., p. 88.
40. J. H. Whyte, 'A Political Scientist's View' in J. Darby (ed.), *A Critique of 'Governing Without Consensus'*, Northern Ireland Community Relations Commission, Belfast 1972.
41. J. H. Whyte, 'Interpretations of the Northern Ireland Problem', p. 270.
42. J. H. Whyte, 'A Political Scientist's View', p. 2.
43. F. S. L. Lyons, *Culture and Anarchy*, p. 2.
44. F. S. L. Lyons, *The Burden of Our History*.
45. G. W. Russell, quoted in F. S. L. Lyons, *Culture and Anarchy*, p. 167.
46. F. S. L. Lyons, *The Burden of Our History*, pp. 18, 19.
47. Sunningdale Agreement, see *Times* leader 21 May 1980.
48. A. T. Q. Stewart, *The Narrow Ground*, p. 180.
49. L. de Paor, *Divided Ulster*, Penguin, Harmondsworth 1970, p. 13.
50. W. M. Heslinga, see G. Ecclestone and E. Elliott, *The Irish Problem and Ourselves*, Church Information Office Publishing, London 1977, p. 4.
51. C. C. O'Brien, *States of Ireland*, Hutchinson, London 1972, p. 148.
52. R. Harris, *Prejudice and Tolerance in Ulster*, Manchester University Press, Manchester 1972, p. xi.
53. G. Fitzgerald, *Towards a New Ireland*, Knight, London 1972, p. 64.
54. B. Walsh, *Religion and Demographic Behaviour in Ireland*, Economic and Social Research Institute, Dublin 1970.
55. G. Fitzgerald reported in *Belfast Telegraph* in 'Mixed Marriage: The Official Attitude that may change and the Promise that Won't', 22 February 1980.
56. N. Gibson, quoted in R. Davey, *Old Fears and New Hopes for Ireland*, Audenshaw Papers, No. 74, Yorkshire 1980.
57. Text of oath of membership of Orange Order, quoted by K. Heskin, *Northern Ireland: a Psychological Analysis*, Gill and Macmillan, Dublin 1980.
58. D. P. Barritt and A. Booth, *Orange and Green, A Quaker study of Community Relations in Northern Ireland*, Northern Friends Peace Board, Belfast 1972.
59. J. Swift, quoted in *The Irish Conflict and the Christian Conscience*, Pro Mundi Vita, Belgium 1973.
60. C. C. O'Brien, op. cit., p. 290.
61. *Violence in Ireland: A Report to the Churches*, Christian Journals Ltd., Belfast 1976.
62. P. Pearse, quoted in Lyons, *Culture and Anarchy*, p. 90.
63. Pope John Paul II quoted in R. Davey, *Old Fears and New Hopes for Ireland*, Audenshaw Papers, No. 74, Yorkshire 1980.
64. J. Russell, reported in J. Darby, *Segregated Schooling – Does it contribute to Sectarianism?*, p. 63.
65. J. Darby, *Segregated Schooling – Does it contribute to Sectarianism?*, p. 65.
66. M. Fraser, *Children in Conflict*, Penguin, Harmondsworth 1974, p. 163.

67. ibid., p. 164.
68. J. Russell, reported in *Irish Times*, 'No Solution in North', based on paper delivered to 5th Annual Conference of Educational Studies Association of Ireland, 14 April 1980.
69. J. Harbison and J. Harbison, *A Society Under Stress*, Open Books, London 1980.
70. J. Harbison, 'The Children of Northern Ireland', *New Society*, 17 April 1980, p. 101.
71. R. Rose, op. cit., p. 289.
72. Lyons, *Culture and Anarchy*, p. 138.
73. F. Engels, quoted in R. Rose, op. cit., p. 275.
74. E. Evason, *Ends That Won't Meet: A Study of Poverty in Belfast*, Child Poverty Action Group, London 1980.
75. J. H. Whyte, 'Interpretations', p. 260.
76. ibid.
77. D. Birrell, 'Relative Deprivation as a Factor in Conflict in Northern Ireland', *The Sociological Review*, Vol. 20, No. 3, 1972, p. 338.
78. F. W. Boal, P. Doherty and D. Pringle, *The Spatial Distribution of Some Social Problems in the Belfast Urban Area*, Northern Ireland Community Relations Commission, Belfast 1974.
79. Housing Conditions Survey, Northern Ireland Housing Executive, Belfast 1974.
80. T. R. Gurr, *Why Men Rebel*, Princeton University Press, Princeton, New Jersey 1970, p. 69.
81. I. Budge and C. O'Leary, *Belfast: Approach to Crisis, A Study of Belfast Politics, 1613–1970*, Macmillan, London, 1973, pp. 91–5.
82. A. Boserup, *Who is the Principal Enemy? Contradictions and Struggles in Northern Ireland*, Independent Labour Party, London 1972.
83. J. A. Jackson and J. M. Smith, 'Sociological Aspects', in J. Darby (ed.), *A Critique of 'Governing Without Consensus'*, pp. 5–7.
84. J. H. Whyte, 'Interpretations', p. 262.
85. R. W. Hutchinson and J. Sheehan, *A Review of Selected Indicators of Economic Performance in Northern Ireland and the Republic of Ireland during the 1970s*, Co-operation North, Dublin 1980.
86. R. Rose, op. cit.
87. ibid., p. 388.
88. C. C. O'Brien, op. cit., p. 15.
89. N. Gibson, 'Economics and Consensus', in J. Darby (ed.), *A Critique of 'Governing Without Consensus'*, p. 13.
90. M. Fraser, op cit.
91. J. Harbison, op. cit., p. 100.
92. ibid., p. 101.
93. D. J. King, C. McMeekin and P. C. Elmes, 'Are We as Depressed as We Think We Are?', *Ulster Medical Journal*, Vol. 46, 1977.
94. M. Fraser, op cit., p. 79.
95. H. A. Lyons, 'Depressive Illness and Aggression in Belfast', *British Medical Journal*, 1972, 1.

96. A. T. Q. Stewart, *The Narrow Ground*, p. 141.
97. H. Jackson, op. cit., p. 4.
98. R. Ardrey, *African Genesis*, Atheneum, New York 1961.
99. M. F. A. Montague, *Man and Aggression*, Oxford University Press, Oxford 1968.
100. T. R. Gurr, op. cit.
101. L. Berkowitz, *Aggression: A Social Psychological Analysis*, McGraw Hill, New York 1962.
102. Vinacke, quoted in E. E. O'Donnell, *Northern Irish Stereotypes*, College of Industrial Relations, Dublin 1977.
103. E. E. O'Donnell, *Northern Irish Stereotypes*, College of Industrial Relations, Dublin 1977.
104. ibid., p. 96.
105. ibid., p. 105.
106. ibid., p. 103.
107. ibid., p. 101.
108. ibid., p. 105.
109. ibid., p. 103.
110. M. MacGreil, *Prejudice and Tolerance in Ireland*, College of Industrial Relations, Dublin 1977.
111. ibid., p. 11
112. ibid., p. 530.
113. ibid., p. 525.
114. G. H. Boehringer, H. Bayley, V. Zeruolis and K. Boehringer, 'The Destructive Application of Group Techniques to a Conflict', *Journal of Conflict Resolution*, Vol. 18, No. 2, June 1974.
115. J. Fairleigh in *Sectarianism – Roads to Reconciliation*, Papers read at 22nd Annual Summer School of the Social Study Conference, August 1974, Three Candles Limited, Dublin 1974, p. 8.

BIBLIOGRAPHY

Ardrey, R., *African Genesis*, Atheneum, New York 1961
Barritt, D. P. and Booth, A., *Orange and Green: A Quaker Study of Community Relations in Northern Ireland*, Northern Friends Peace Board, Belfast 1972
Barritt, D. P. and Carter, C., *The Northern Ireland Problem*, Oxford University Press, Oxford 1972
Berkowitz, L., *Aggression: A Social Psychological Analysis*, McGraw Hill, New York 1962
Birrell, D. 'Relative Deprivation as a Factor in Conflict in Northern Ireland', *The Sociological Review*, Vol. 20, No. 3, 1972
Boal, F. W., Doherty, P. and Pringle D., *The Spatial Distribution of Some Social Problems in the Belfast Urban Area*, Northern Ireland Community Relations Commission, Belfast 1974
Boehringer, G. H., Bayley, H., Zeruolis, V. and Boehringer, K., 'The Destructive Application of Group Techniques to a Conflict', *Journal of Conflict Resolution*, Vol. 18, No. 2, June 1974

Boserup, A., *Who is the Principal Enemy? Contraditions and Struggles in Northern Ireland*, Independent Labour Party, London 1972

Buckland, P., *The Factory of Grievances: Devolved Government in Northern Ireland, 1921–1939*, Gill and Macmillan, Dublin 1979

Budge, I. and O'Leary, C., *Belfast: Approach to Crisis, A Study of Belfast Politics, 1613–1970*, Macmillan, London 1973

Burton, F., *The Politics of Legitimacy*, Routledge and Kegan Paul, London 1978

Darby, J. *Conflict in Northern Ireland: The Development of a Polarised Community*, Gill and Macmillan, Dublin 1976

Darby, J. (ed.), *Critique of 'Governing Without Consensus'*, Northern Ireland Community Relations Commission, Belfast 1972

Davey, R. *Old Fears and New Hopes for Ireland*, Audenshaw Papers No. 74, Yorkshire 1980

Davis, E. E. and Sinnott, R., *Attitudes in the Republic of Ireland Relevant to the Northern Ireland Problem*, Vol. I, Economic and Social Research Institute, Paper No. 97, Dublin 1979

de Paor, L., *Divided Ulster*, Penguin, Harmondsworth 1970

Ecclestone, G. and Elliott, E., *The Irish Problem and Ourselves*, Church Information Office Publishing, London 1977

Evason, E., *Ends That Won't Meet: A Study of Poverty in Belfast*, Child Poverty Action Group, London 1980.

Fitzgerald, G., *Towards a New Ireland*, Knight, London 1972

Fraser, M., *Children in Conflict*, Penguin, Harmondsworth 1974

Gurr, T. R., *Why Men Rebel*, Princeton University Press, Princeton, New Jersey 1970

Harbison, J., and Harbison, J., *A Society Under Stress*, Open Books, London 1980

Harbison, J., 'The Children of Northern Ireland', *New Society*, April 1980

Harris, R., *Prejudice and Tolerance in Ulster*, Manchester University Press, Manchester 1972

Hepburn, A. C. (ed.), *The Conflict of Nationality in Modern Ireland*, Edward Arnold, London 1980

Heskin, K., *Northern Ireland: A Psychological Analysis*, Gill and Macmillan, Dublin 1980

'Housing Conditions Survey', Northern Ireland Housing Executive, Belfast 1974

Hutchinson, R. W. and Sheehan, J., *A Review of Selected Indicators of Economic Performance in Northern Ireland and the Republic of Ireland During the 1970s*, Co-operation North, Dublin 1980

Jackson, H., 'The Two Irelands — The Problem of the Double Minority: A Dual Study of Inter-Group Tensions', Minority Rights Group Report, No. 2, Rev. Ed. 1972

King, D. J., McMeekin, C. and Elmes, P. C., 'Are We as Depressed as We Think We Are?', *Ulster Medical Journal*, Vol. 46, 1977

Lijphart, A., 'Review Article: The Northern Ireland Problem: Cases, Theories and Solutions', *The British Journal of Political Science*, Vol. 5, No. 1, June 1975

Lyons, F. S. L., *The Burden of Our History*, W. B. Rankin Memorial Lecture, Queen's University of Belfast 1978
Lyons, F. S. L., *Culture and Anarchy in Ireland 1890—1939*, Clarendon Press, Oxford 1979
Lyons, F. S. L., *Ireland Since the Famine*, Collins/Fontana, London 1973
Lyons, H. A. 'Depressive Illness and Aggression in Belfast', *British Medical Journal*, London 1972
MacGreil, M., *Prejudice and Tolerance in Ireland*, College of Industrial Relations, Dublin 1977
Montague, M. F. A., *Man and Aggression*, Oxford University Press, Oxford 1968
O'Brien, C. C., *States of Ireland*, Hutchinson, London 1972
O'Donnell, E. E., *Northern Irish Stereotypes*, College of Industrial Relations, Dublin 1977
Oliver, J., 'Ulster Today and Tomorrow', *Political and Economic Planning*, Vol. XLIV, Broadsheet No. 574, London 1978
Palley, C., *The Evolution, Disintegration and Possible Reconstruction of the Northern Ireland Constitution*, Barry Rose Publishers, London 1972
Rose R., *Governing Without Consensus*, Faber and Faber, London 1971
Sectarianism — Roads to Reconciliation, Social Studies Conference, Three Candles Ltd., Dublin 1974
Stewart, A. T. Q., *The Narrow Ground: Aspects of Ulster, 1609—1969*, Faber and Faber, London 1977
Stewart, A. T. Q., *The Ulster Crisis: Resistance to Home Rule, 1912—1914*, Faber and Faber, London 1967
The Irish Conflict and the Christian Conscience, Pro Mundi Vita, Belgium 1973
Violence in Ireland: A Report to the Churches, Christian Journals Ltd., Belfast 1976
Walsh, B., *Religion and Demographic Behaviour in Ireland*, Economic and Social Research Institute, Dublin 1970
Whyte, J. H., 'Interpretations of the Northern Ireland Problem: An Appraisal', *Economic and Social Review*, Vol. 9, No. 4, 1978

2

The Evolution of Constitutional Policy in Northern Ireland over the past Fifteen Years

John A. Oliver

The 1960s

The period of fifteen years laid down in the terms of reference points back to the mid 1960s, possibly the high point in the life and work of the Northern Ireland parliament. Although essentially a devolved institution under the Government of Ireland Act, 1920, the local parliament had achieved something of the character of a federal relationship with parliament and government in London on account of London's self-imposed restraint from interference in local or transferred matters. Under Section 75 of the 1920 Act Westminster retained supreme authority over all persons, matters and things but had in practice refrained from intervening.

The scene in the mid-Sixties was a promising one. Parliament at Stormont had developed into an efficient legislative machine. The Roman Catholic Nationalist Party had been persuaded to accept the role of official opposition. The province was enjoying one of its longest periods of relative stability and tranquillity. The economy was expanding and the industrial base was broadening under a stylish programme of industrial promotion backed by a thorough-going support programme in roads, housing, water, effluent and industrial training. An ambitious Regional Plan for physical development was in force, embracing (amongst much else) the bold concept of a stop-line on the growth of Belfast and the even bolder concept of a new regional city in Co. Armagh. The second university was being planned as well as the new Ulster Polytechnic College. Infant mortality had been brought down to the level of 23 in every one thousand live births from close on 100 in the early Twenties; unemployment had been brought down from around 20 per cent in the Thirties to 6 per cent though with wide local variations. Two new pioneering administrative departments had been formed in 1964, one to deal with all the main social services and the other with all the main physical development services. Professional, trade and local government bodies from Great Britain, as well as American news organisations, were more and more coming to hold conferences in Ulster and to study aspects of the local scene.[1]

To appreciate the degree of satisfaction that reasonable people could feel in the state of affairs reached by 1966 under devolution it is necessary to go back and recall the situation in which parliament and government had been founded in 1921.

The Origins of the State

Violence was raging throughout Ireland. The new parliament was being created out of the torn fragments of a written constitution intended for a situation different in many ways from that which in fact developed. The population was small and the taxable and rateable capacity extremely limited. There were no natural resources apart from the land and the people. And most important of all, the new parliament started without the attendance of the Roman Catholic and nationalist representatives, as the whole settlement of 1920 had failed to win their confidence or support.[2] Nevertheless the legislative and administrative system which was built up brought great benefits to the people. Agriculture was most vigorously promoted, with constant improvement in scientific advice, methods, machinery, marketing and subsidies. Forests and Forest Parks were developed to a high standard. Electricity was provided ahead of need and taken to the people. Water supplies and sewerage were steadily extended. The educational system was transformed and improved with enormous benefits to successive generations of children; and was administered so as to cope acceptably with that most sensitive of problems, government grant-aid and supervision of an otherwise independent Roman Catholic and Church-managed system of primary and secondary schools and training colleges. Cash benefits under the various social schemes were assessed and paid to all with clockwork efficiency and the greatest impartiality. Housing advanced in many notable forms — in municipal form under many but not all of the local councils, in the much valued Private Enterprise Subsidy Schemes and in the Housing on Farms Scheme. No fewer than 150,000 houses had been built between 1945 and 1966, to approved modern standards accommodating over one-third of the whole population. Road-building was promoted on a scale and to a standard of design and beauty that became the envy of road builders and road users visiting the province. Hospitals were modernised and a comprehensive national health service introduced. In the contentious matter of local government reform a programme started in March 1966 had reached a useful stage of progress by 1967 and a further more positive stage by 1969, urging a simplified one-tier system of modern local government with the fullest range of important responsibilities.³

Stormont Legislation
   It is not true to say, as is often alleged, that all this legislation was a mere carbon-copy of British legislation. That allegation was effectively dealt with by the United Kingdom Royal Commission on the Constitution (Kilbrandon) in 1973 which specially examined a selection of the statutes and concluded that while some were closely modelled on British statutes — such as the national insurance codes, for good and obvious reasons — about a half (in so far as one can make a count in such matters) were in whole or in part peculiar to Northern Ireland.⁴ The rest were of a technical nature. The mention of just a few developments in the legislative and administrative history of the province will evoke popular memories of special arrangements legislated for in several very different aspects of public life: the abolition of spirit-grocers; the closing of public roads on specified days to allow international car and motor-cycle racing; the R licence for newly qualified car-drivers; the Tuberculosis Authority that did itself out of a job in ten years; the unique arrangement (under which so many Ulster farmers and their sons benefited) whereby the Ministry of Agriculture was closely interlinked at all points with the Faculty of Agriculture at the Queen's University; and the incomparable Housing Trust that

reached a standard of design and management that caused ordinary passers-by to comment, 'That's a brave nice estate; it must be the Housing Trust.'

The practice of framing legislation partly on a British model and partly on local adaptations of it, far from being merely some unworthy compromise, turned out in fact to be a most useful device. It enabled the subordinate parliament to take the legislative results of British experience and expertise, wait for a time to see how they worked, to benefit from their mistakes (as the saying went) and then to add fitting adaptations to meet local conditions. Indeed Nicholas Mansergh (one of the early authorities on the constitution of Northern Ireland) goes so far as to describe this particular process as 'the greatest contribution ... to the ordinary citizens of Northern Ireland'.

By any standards the achievements of the parliament and government of Northern Ireland were considerable; given the pervading conditions of violence and political instability they were very considerable indeed. These conclusions are borne out in different terms and with much greater detachment by the Kilbrandon Royal Commission in its unanimous report.[5]

The Civil Service

It is an open secret that much of the initiative, drive and energy behind these administrative achievements (and, be it said, behind much of the legislation, too) came from the Northern Ireland Civil Service. But that says little. The maintenance of such a service, its pay and conditions, its freedom to operate and to initiate have all to be ascribed to the good sense of successive ministers who saw the value of a positive administration at work on non-political matters. Senior officials enjoyed close contact with ministers, as well as direct working relations with opposition members and with local authorities, including — perhaps (in some ways) especially — with the eleven local councils that had permanent Catholic and Nationalist majorities. Above all they could see quick and direct results for their labours and derived much personal satisfaction in that way. Whatever the political arguments for or against devolution, the existence of a responsive civil service showing a lot of initiative, deriving much job satisfaction and earning respect from the public is without a shadow of doubt one of the great benefits.

It may help to place on record two aspects of civil service work under devolution that are seldom mentioned in public.

There were close, unreported working relations with opposite numbers in Dublin, between officials who knew what had to be done and what had to be avoided. How else would all those matters of cross-border concern have been managed under a devolved regional parliament having no statutory power to embark on foreign relations with an independent country, least of all with one that not only refused to recognise the Northern regime but maintained a claim over the Northern territory in Article 2 of its 1937 Constitution: railways, road passenger and freight traffic, roads, drainage, infectious diseases, animal health, fisheries, electricity?

Next there was the high degree of personal attention given to the individual citizen in his dealings with the administration. The unchallengeable witness here was Sir Edmund Compton who had the literally unique experience of acting as Ombudsman simultaneously for the United Kingdom and for Northern Ireland:

> The quality of administrative performance compares well; indeed the individual citizen frequently gets a better service from a Northern Ireland Ministry than he would get from a United Kingdom Department; an individual here received noticeably higher consideration than those in any other part of the United Kingdom.[6]

All in all, it is not surprising therefore that W. N. Osborough could sum up the whole position as follows: 'Were it not for the inherent instability in the order of things and the violence and civil strife that took over in the years after 1968, the achievements of the Northern Ireland Civil Service might well have been written in letters of gold.'[7] Though most officials — past even more than present — would modestly disclaim that golden tribute in the light of their personal shortcomings and the inner knowledge of their failure to do all that they might have done, it is relevant to this paper that amidst the welter of harsh words spoken over Ulster those tributes are on record.

Without for one moment suggesting that every initiative taken by the Northern Ireland government under the Matthew and Wilson regional plans, the Lockwood report and many other programmes in the Sixties was as well thought out or as well presented as it might have been, it is right to say that across their whole range the initiatives made up a sizeable volume of social, economic and physical change. Each step produced, as it would have in any society, a certain measure of criticism; in this divided community it produced an even larger measure of suspicion and hostility from the Roman Catholic population. This very fact lay at the root of much of the unrest and violence that were to follow. If, for example, the government had not promoted the concept of a second university, endorsing the Lockwood committee's recommendation of Coleraine as the site, and if the government had instead simply allowed the Queen's University to expand quietly, then the outburst of anger over the choice of Coleraine in preference to Londonderry would not have taken place. In the same way, if the Belfast built-up area had simply been allowed to go on expanding and nothing so eye-catching as a new regional city in Co. Armagh had been driven forward, the bitter anti-Unionist suspicion attaching to that particular development could never have arisen. In similar but less distinctive ways the siting of each new factory or institution in Coleraine, Antrim, Larne, Ballymena, Carrickfergus, Bangor and so on evoked deep suspicions of bias and sectarianism in the minds of Roman Catholic and Nationalist leaders in Londonderry, Strabane and Newry which the siting of other factories in those areas and the huge amount of public investment there did nothing to assuage.

Clearly these suspicions, genuinely held and ably articulated, reflected a new aspect of the old traditional distrust felt by Roman Catholic and Nationalist people, namely the protest of a rising generation of young people educated under the tripartite educational system of secondary education open to all under the 1947 Act. Not content with the old-style oratory of the Nationalist Party leaders this new generation of educated young people in their twenties and thirties wanted to express their dissatisfaction in more direct and relevant language. In this they were fortuitously aided by the rapid extension of television news coverage and they were encouraged also by the examples of student protest in America, France and Germany in those very years. In a historical perspective there was, after all, little to be surprised at in this outburst of discontent at a time when so much positive work was being undertaken by the state. As the nineteenth-century French historian de Tocqueville put it: that which is tolerable where no change can be foreseen becomes intolerable once change is seen to be possible. Revolt, after all, has come in many societies not at the time of greatest deprivation but at a time of rising expectations.

Alternative Courses

In this paper the opportunity will be taken at each of the main turning points to consider some of the alternative courses which were open to the authorities but not taken, courses that were practical propositions within the reasonable bounds of political possibility at the time. There is no intention of animadverting on any of the political parties or their leaders. Rather than stir up old controversies and apportion credit or blame, the method is to bring forward real issues and real choices out of real experience, still relevant for consideration today, since the essence of the Ulster political situation changes little.

As renewed violence broke out in 1968 and 1969, requiring the intervention of British troops and British Ministers, and as the Northern Ireland government embarked on a belated programme of political change, it is helpful to consider what they might reasonably have done before that stage was reached in the long though troubled years of their unbroken power.

It would have been possible to stamp out discrimination in the siting and allocation of houses in those local authorities in which it occurred. Many had a good record and the Housing Trust (the biggest housing authority by far) had an unimpeachable record; but with political will and administrative skill evil practices could and should have been stopped.

Something could have been done to reduce discrimination in employment. It would be wrong to suggest that legislation can eliminate such practices, for their roots go deep in society and the practices are subject to many pressures of history, tradition and geography. But an independent Staff Commission for Local Government and a Fair Employment Agency could well have been included in the industrial relations legislation passed in 1963 and 1965 and could have helped create a different climate, as the Ulster trade union movement was known to be anti-sectarian in its philosophy.

The opportunity was missed in the post-war reconstruction years of 1945–50 (when the National Health Service, the new Welfare service, and the National Insurance Schemes were being created, the Poor Law Authorities abolished and the local administration transformed) to carry through a total re-casting of the local government system. Even if all of that could not have been managed politically, the electoral wards that were becoming more and more out of date with the shifting of populations – producing anomalies that both favoured and disfavoured the Protestant and Unionist position – could have been regularised, as they eventually were under the 1971 scheme with total acceptance.[8]

With greater courage the anomaly of the ratepayer's franchise in elections to local councils – in itself a perfectly reasonable restriction that applied both to Protestant and Roman Catholic voters but which had become a bone of contention and a totem-pole of complaint – could have been abolished in the Electoral Law of 1962 and the law for local council elections simply brought into line with the law for elections to the Stormont parliament.

Let no one imagine that the problems of policing in Ireland started in 1921. The recruiting, equipping and training of the regular forces and the special constabularies had been a source of complaint and counter-complaint for generations past:

> The formula of tinkering with the police was tried after each successive outbreak (in the nineteenth century) and always without the slightest effect ... Lord Hunt in 1969 was, whether he knew it or not, following a well-established precedent.[9]

While the building up of the Royal Ulster Constabulary into a competent professional force can be counted an achievement in all the difficult circumstances, the 'B' Special Constabulary clearly outlived their hour. Evoking support only from the Protestant population, they remained too long the unregenerate heirs of an out-of-date tradition. Conversion into a fresh new Police Reserve actively seeking recruits from the whole population was clearly the necessary step to take (for experience has shown the enormous value of a corps of part-time constables who know their own neighbourhood intimately). The time to take that step was without question around 1962 when to the relief of the whole population (Protestant and Roman Catholic) the police had quietly and unaided subdued an IRA military campaign that had harassed the Border areas for six years.

Roman Catholic Participation

At a deeper level greater efforts could have been made to associate the Roman Catholic population with the government and administration of the Province; and the governing political party with all their power and influence were clearly the people to initiate the moves and to provide many more openings for Roman Catholic leadership in public affairs. It would have required from the Minority some marked response, a degree of trust and a large measure of open commitment. In a word, participation. In another word, power-sharing.

Some informal talks did take place on this very matter in the Sixties but the pity was that the two sides persisted in seeing the impasse over and over again from two quite different points of view. The Roman Catholic political leaders saw it as continuing evidence of Protestant ascendancy and discrimination against their faith. The Protestant political leaders (little concerned about the religious faith of their opponents, if they but knew it) saw them as self-declared enemies of the state and by definition unsuitable to hold high office in and for the state. As that divergence of view lay so close to the heart of the Ulster problem it is a pity that the talks were not pursued and the issue resolved, eased or at any rate clarified in those conditions of relative peace and stability.

Rapid Changes

Be all that as it may, the hard fact is that 1968 and 1969,

with protest, violence and an atmosphere of rebellion, precipitated the Province into the state of instability and turmoil from which it still suffers. The development which is most relevant to this paper is the spate of legislative and administrative changes which flowed thick and fast from 1969 till 1972: the civilisation and disarming of the Royal Ulster Constabulary; the abolition of the Ulster Special Constabulary; the creation of the Police Authority; the transfer of powers of prosecution from the police to a Director of Public Prosecutions; the creation of a Police Reserve; the establishment of the Ulster Defence Regiment within the British Army; the appointment of a Parliamentary Ombudsman and of a Commissioner for Complaints, the abolition of the ratepayer's franchise in local elections; votes at eighteen in all elections; the re-drawing of all local government boundaries and wards; the creation of a new Ministry of Community Relations and also of a Community Relations Commission; declarations of equality of employment opportunity; codes of employment procedure; training facilities for the whole public service; a points system for the allocation of public authority housing; the ending of the Housing Trust and the creation of the Housing Executive as the sole public housing authority in the Province; the enactment of an Incitement to Hatred Act; and, perhaps most far-reaching of all in a historical sense, the total transformation of the local government system under the perceptive and clear-headed Macrory recommendations.

This large, intricate and immensely contentious programme was conveniently summarised and explained by the Northern Ireland government in its noteworthy document, *A Record of Constructive Change,* in August 1971. It is interesting to recall the tone of exasperation with which this Parliamentary Paper opened: 'In face of unsubstantiated allegations that it has failed to honour its obligations under the Downing Street Declaration (of 1969) the Government of Northern Ireland has decided to place the facts clearly and succinctly on record'.[10] It certainly did, in ten terse pages.

In one sense it was humiliating for the Northern Ireland government to have to promote such a hurried programme of legislative and administrative change under the combined pressure of the British government on the one hand and of protest, violence and insurrection on the other. The very fact of being hustled into such a list of quickly devised arrangements caused the local political leaders to lose face with their own supporters. Many of them were simply outraged at any aspersion being cast upon the police forces. Many others had more reasoned objections, for example to the destruction of one of the public bodies with which they considered Ulster had set an example to the British Isles, namely the Housing Trust; to the consequent position of considerable danger in which fully half the population could become tenants of one municipal landlord; to the obvious duplication of an Ombudsman and a Commissioner for Complaints; to unnecessary complications being added to the already sizeable machinery of government in a very small province, for example, a Ministry of Community Relations and subordinate to it, eyeball to eyeball, an appointed Commission as well.

There was, of course, a realistic viewpoint taken by some of the Unionist leaders who saw in this bizarre situation the heaven-sent opportunity of being able to carry out a number of reforms which they would for years past have wished to make but could not achieve politically. They saw the active interest of the British government as a valuable and rare reinforcement to them in governing a most difficult community.

Those were, however, much finer feelings than the feelings of the Protestant and Unionist population towards the Roman Catholic representatives as each of these concessions was granted. With surprising naivety they expected them to express gratitude, only to find them (in the best radical traditions) in no mood to express thanks, looking on each concession as a right and treating each announcement (and they came thick and fast) merely as the occasion for making some further demand.

Looking back, what alternatives were open? The Unionist leaders could well have said to the British government: 'If you want these things done, do them yourselves by using your over-riding powers in Section 75 of the Act of 1920. After all, the matters in question are essentially civil rights — or are being demanded as such. Is it not reasonable that civil rights should be guaranteed by the central authorities in London for all parts of the United Kingdom?'

Another course would have been to use all available political and diplomatic skill to work out a concordat with the Roman Catholic leaders (and invoking the active support of the British government who all this time were maintaining a presence inside Stormont Castle). The concordat would have said:

> We shall promote the changes you are demanding on condition that you then agree to support the system; we shall proceed stage by stage, and before we advance to stage 2 and 3 and so on we shall have to get from you an undertaking to accept nomination to public boards, take part in elections, to share the responsibility for unpopular consequences, to stick at and not withdraw and above all to speak up and defend the system both inside and outside Ulster. After all, your campaign is clearly directed towards improving the system; it is up to you, surely then, to help make it work and not to abstain every time you dislike something.

The sad fact was that violence was increasing, the pressure on police and army rising and the general atmosphere deteriorating with the result that neither of those alternatives could in practice be adopted. The heat was on.

Parliamentary Accord

The one exception, the one matter over which Nationalist and Unionist politicians came close to some sort of accord, was the speech by the Northern Ireland Prime Minister on the opening of a new session of parliament on 22 June 1971 (the fiftieth anniversary, incidentally, of the opening of the parliament by King George V). He outlined a set of proposals (home-brewed this time and not in response to specific pressure or demand) that foresaw an enlargement in the size of the Commons, a change in the composition and role of the Senate and the setting up of subject Committees in the Commons with substantial powers and with some chairmen drawn from the opposition.[11]

Abstention

The initiative drew a welcoming response, even a fulsome one, from Roman Catholic opposition spokesmen. The debate bears re-reading for it was sustained at a high level.[12] It seemed that a high-water mark had been reached and that there was hope for parliamentary co-operation again. Unfortunately that hope was dashed a few weeks later when the Catholic opposition decided — for what was to them a genuine, serious reason connected with the shooting of Seamus Cusack and Desmond Beattie by the British army in Londonderry — to go into abstention again. To be clear, this took place in mid-July 1971, before the introduction of internment, not after it, as is widely said. The drastic but by no means unprecedented step of internment of IRA suspects without trial came in August 1971 and led to unparalleled violence, disruption and withdrawal from public life. The arguments and the consequences are too well known to need rehearsing here.

But two administrative aspects do bear summarising with an eye to the present and the future. As part of the protest against internment some Roman Catholic leaders called for a rent and rates strike. It was not only that it caused untold difficulty for the administration. When the leaders painted the slogan 'Rent Spent' on the footpaths of Newry, encouraging the tenants to stop setting aside for rent and rates and leading them to believe that one day some feeble government would grant an amnesty and wipe out the debts, they laid the basis for accumulating debts over the years and compulsory deductions from cash benefits from which many individual citizens have not yet recovered and which still add to their poverty and misery.

The second consequence affecting public administration was the refusal of four elected local councils to continue to discharge their functions. This was meant to express in dramatic form their particular sense of outrage against internment and their contribution to the wrecking of the political system that introduced the hated measure. When creditors, from business firms to unskilled workmen, started clamouring for their money, when builders could not complete their contracts to build houses and when citizens were unable to

get the everyday permits and licences to which they were
entitled, government felt forced to intervene. All four councils
had to be abolished, their functions placed in commission
and the responsibility for running their affairs entrusted to
the Stormont Ministry, to one senior official for all four,
as it happened. The alternative course of action would have
been the purist approach of leaving the local ratepayers to
suffer and to see for themselves the full consequences of the
action of those whom they had elected.

End of Stormont Parliament
   All this, together with the events on the streets of Londonderry on Sunday 30 January 1972, led the British government
to the view that they must intervene more closely. The
proposition was put to the Northern Ireland government that
they should surrender to London all powers of law and order
(widely defined), placing the local leaders in an acute dilemma. Clearly they had no illusions about the joys and satis-
factions of conducting law and order functions; they had had
after all fifty years of direct experience on top of centuries
of historical experience; and they knew only too well how
extremely difficult the task would prove for any British
government. In a pragmatic sense they could see advantages
in handing over those functions while remaining in office.
As a matter of principle, however, they took the view that
law and order (in the widest interpretation) were essential
to any government; that they could not call themselves a
government without those powers; and so, on that matter of
basic principle, they declined the proposition and resigned,
knowing that this would mean the end of their parliament,
government and their whole system.[13] And so the parliament
of Northern Ireland ended as it began, in conditions of
violence and abstention.
   The alternative open to the local leaders was clear. It was
to have carried on, preserved their parliament and system of
government, promoted their Green Paper on the improvement of the parliament and, with responsibility for law and
order then in impartial British hands, to have sought a fresh
understanding with the Catholic and nationalist leaders in
the favourable spirit of June 1971. Internment would, of

course, have been a huge stumbling block for the nationalists but the British government would presumably have phased it out (as they eventually did in other circumstances). The abstention of the Nationalist members would obviously have been a stumbling block in the eyes of the Unionists but then the cause this time — dissatisfaction over shootings in Londonderry in July 1971 — would have become a matter for the British and not the Northern Ireland authorities. The popular distress of the Protestant population over the loss of the parliament and government, with the particularly sordid violence that followed, would have been avoided. At a deeper level the vacuum in local leadership which then quickly developed would have been avoided. It is ironic that twenty months later many of the same Unionist leaders in the new power-sharing Northern Ireland Executive should be gladly taking office on a brand-new constitution which rigorously excluded law and order functions![14]

The Dungiven Parliament

Meantime an odd development in constitutional policy had taken place in the form of the 'Dungiven Parliament', mounted by the abstaining Roman Catholic MPs and Senators. In order to demonstrate in a vivid way their total rejection of the parliament of Northern Ireland they summoned in the autumn of 1971 an alternative assembly. It met in the Castle Ballroom, Dungiven, Co. Londonderry on 26 October, assuming the pretentious and misleading title, 'The Assembly of the Northern Irish People.' Although useful as a propaganda exercise the Dungiven Parliament met only twice and then came to an end.[15]

Direct Rule and the Darlington Conference

Reverting to the mainstream of constitutional developments in March 1972, it is important to note that (as so often in human affairs) the least thought and preparation went into the very system of government that was to change the whole course of local history and to dominate the scene for Ulster, Eire and Britain for the following decade: direct rule. Brian Faulkner's version of British government thinking and presentation in February and March 1972 gives a spirited account of constitution-making in harsh reality.[16] Direct rule came into force quickly and smoothly, from the passing of the Northern Ireland (Temporary Provisions) Act through Westminster in a couple of days to the arrival of Mr Whitelaw and his Ministers and their settling in, along with their advisers, at Stormont Castle.

Let it be said that the burden on these British Ministers was immense. Having to operate on six bases — their homes in England, their constituencies there, the office in Whitehall, the Westminster Commons or Lords, Stormont Castle and the various Departments in Belfast, Netherleigh and Bangor — entailed a huge amount of travelling, work, strain and physical danger in an atmosphere lacking any local political support. It still imposes those burdens today, ten years later.

The British government's next step — the Darlington Conference of September 1972 — was useful in showing that the main Unionist Party, the Alliance Party and the Northern Ireland Labour Party were co-operative and constructive parties and not just bitter losers in the direct rule revolution. But the full value of Darlington was lessened by the refusal of the SDLP to take part and to a lesser extent by the absence also of Dr Ian Paisley and Mr Bill Craig, all for clearly stated reasons.

The Local Councils

The melancholy sequence of events which led — bit by bit and without deliberate intent on the part of anyone — to the destruction of the local council system needs to be threaded in to the narrative here if the complete constitutional story is to be kept in mind.

The Stormont White Papers of 1967 and 1969 on the Re-Shaping of Local Government were succeeding in building up some public opinion in favour of a fully developed modern system of about seventeen single-tier local councils with the widest range of powers. The violent events of 1969 (and in particular the sweeping decision of October 1969 to abolish the Housing Trust and take the housing function away from local councils) made necessary a new wholesale review by Sir Patrick Macrory and others in 1970. In essence their report (Cmd. 546) said four things: in such a small province with only slender rateable capacity it is sensible to concentrate the bigger and more expensive services at the centre, either in appointed boards or in the existing Ministries; the Stormont parliament is there to supervise them day-by-day and as a provincial body would benefit from having that job to do; but to discharge that duty properly it would need to be enlarged and to adjust its procedures (on lines eventually promulgated in the 1971 Green Paper on parliament);[17] when all that has been settled, then feel free to create as many local councils within reason (based on each traditional market town and its supporting area around) as local opinion wants, giving them merely the remaining small functions to discharge. The act embodying these sweeping changes was passed by the Stormont parliament in March 1972. It was, ironically, the last act to be passed. A few days later the parliament itself was swept away, the very key-stone on which the whole edifice depended. The outcome in practice then was a set of twenty-six local councils and nine area boards for education, health and social services (alongside many other appointed boards with highly important duties) all operating without the supervision, checking, criticism, publicity and local political leadership which the system so obviously needed. Probably the most unhappy of outcomes.

The alternative course, once the parliament was abolished and direct rule came in, would have been to repeal the Local Government Act and allow the traditional system of county and district councils to carry on, with any necessary tidying up; with the introduction of Proportional Representation in 1973 there could well have evolved a revived local government system. Another option would have been to let the 1972 act be carried into effect (as in fact happened) and to substitute for the dismantled parliament one new, elected, province-wide body with the sole duty of administering all the local services commonly regarded as 'local government' and relieving direct rule ministers of the greater part of that unwelcome burden.

Border Poll

When H. M. Government later in 1972 presented to parliament their legislation for the holding of a referendum in

Ulster so that Ulster people could declare under secret ballot their wishes on the crucial question of remaining in the United Kingdom, it must have seemed to Members of Parliament a most sensible, reasonable, fair thing to do. In effect the Border Poll held on 8 March 1973 was boycotted by all the Roman Catholic and nationalist parties and only 600,000 voters out of a possible million took part. The fact that 98.9 per cent of those who voted supported the union with Britain revealed nothing that was not known before. Under the subsequent act of 1973 parliament nevertheless went on to provide for the holding of a similar poll not earlier than 9 March 1983. So the concept of the Border Poll is still alive statutorily as part of the constitutional process.[18]

Was this elaborate but abortive Border Poll the best that could be arranged? The questions put: 'Do you want Northern Ireland to remain part of the United Kingdom' and 'Do you want Northern Ireland to be joined with the Republic outside the United Kingdom?' were possibly too stark.[19] The terms of remaining or leaving might have been included. Better still perhaps would have been a series of options graded from full integration into the United Kingdom right through federalism, devolution, independence to various forms of association with the Irish Republic, with voters invited to number them in the order of their preference. This might have encouraged the nationalist parties to take part and, if so, would then have revealed a great deal more about people's attitudes. It is not enough to contend that such a complex referendum would have been too difficult for the voters, for they were (and are) sophisticated electors, as they proved three and four months later (in May and June of that year) when they operated with consummate ease the complex and wholly unfamiliar system of Proportional Representation (Single Transferable Vote).[20]

The 1973 Constitution

In the Northern Ireland Constitution Act of 1973 the British government and parliament took a large step towards laying down in firm terms the position, powers and duties of a devolved assembly as well as the limitations upon it. Although the elected body and the related executive body were to collapse and disappear within less than a year the act still remains on the statute book and embodies in principle such constitutional provisions as exist to-day. It was a remarkable piece of draftsmanship, embodying all essential powers and duties in a neat and understandable form along with a schedule of statutory repeals affecting hundreds of existing Westminster statutes ranging from the Wild Creatures Act of 1971 to the Aden, Perim and Kuria Muria Islands Act of 1967!

The core of the matter, however, turned out to be the composition of the Executive or cabinet. Section 2 (1) (b) laid down the principle that it had to be 'widely accepted throughout the community'. Then the Secretary of State (after a series of confidential soundings) constructed in November 1973 an Executive intended to satisfy that principle – a coalition of Mr Faulkner's Unionist Party, the SDLP and the Alliance Party followed by the many-sided conference at Sunningdale in December at which the British government, the government of the Irish Republic and the three participating parties from Ulster took part. The new power-sharing Executive took office on 1 January 1974 but was driven out of office on 29 May 1974.

This is not the place to examine all the many complex political issues which haunted and eventually killed the Executive – and with it, of course, the Assembly and the whole structure – but some comment on the broad constitutional provisions in the scheme is relevant.

The tone of the 1973 Act, as contrasted with the tone of the 1920 Act, was work-a-day and practical with arrangements slimlined and tailored to the position of a subordinate legislature in a devolved system in a small province. Acts of Parliament were to be merely measures, Ministers to be merely Heads of Departments and so on. Although this was regarded by many of the Protestant and unionist people as belittling and indeed as even vindictive on the part of London, these particular aspects of modernisation were probably justified, though they could have been better prepared and more sympathetically presented. In the same way the abolition of the office of Governor was a crude step, read as a regrettable measure, even if a logical one. But one of the biggest changes of all received little criticism at the time and has barely been mentioned since. This was the big change from a two-chamber system — Commons and Senate — to a unicameral system of a directly elected Assembly alone. The reader may wish to reflect on this matter. It is all very well cutting an Ulster legislature down to size in the sense of removing some of the frills and paraphernalia of parliament but a thought should be spared for the realities of the political, electoral and social scene. If ever any country needed a second chamber, surely it is Ulster. With, for the forseeable future, an electorate divided on the fundamental question of national allegiance and any directly elected assembly certain to reflect and embody that division; with a permanent minority facing a permanent majority; and with the citizens (whatever their individual social, economic or cultural problems and opinions) feeling obliged by fear at each crucial stage to support their political leaders on the basic issues of nationality and the constitution: then surely the need in 1973 was to create a second chamber (with powers however small) to represent and speak and act for the Catholic population as such on their human problems; for Jews and Quakers never likely to win any elections; for young people; for culture and the arts, for conservation, for wildlife and for all the things for which a highly-charged and strongly political elected chamber can seldom find time or inclination. It was already clear by 1973 that there were new developments in the community based on disillusion with the established parties, and taking the form of street politics, defence committees, neighbourhood associations, tenants' groups and so on and so on. While no such senate or second chamber could have stayed the onrush of political events in 1974 it could at least have given public, ordered and recorded expression to new feelings that were seething underneath and that have gradually intensified ever since. One of the strongest threads running through the world-famous Peace Movement, for example, has been utter rejection of the political parties and of the normal political processes. While that Movement has lost much of its impetus (for other reasons) those feelings of distrust still remain and are not being catered for or assuaged in any way.

Another Initiative

Resuming the broad narrative in 1974, the next development after the overthrow of the power-sharing Executive was the speedy production by Britain of yet another set of proposals for constitutional advance. Their White Paper of July 1974 proposed an elected Constitutional Convention for 'the time has come to give representatives of all the people of Northern Ireland the opportunity to meet together to discuss the future': and asked not only for power-sharing as one of the requirements but actually went so far as to lay down: 'There must be some form of power-sharing'.[21] Subsequent discussion papers issued by H. M. Government pointed firmly in the same direction, leading candidates for election to the Convention (as well as the general public) to take it as settled British policy that political power-sharing would be one of the inescapable parameters (to use the jargon of the time). The best example was probably Discussion Paper 2 of November 1974 which said in the plainest language: 'There must be some form of power-sharing and partnership.'[22]

To most unionists it came as a relief and to most nationalists as a bitter blow when Westminster handed down the relevant Act of Parliament providing in considerable detail for the procedure of the Convention but without even mentioning the issues of partnership or power-sharing. The only basic requirement was the insipid one of considering what provision for the government of Northern Ireland is likely to 'command the most widespread acceptance throughout the community there.'[23] Even this tame request proved equivocal as the meaning of the key-phrase 'the most widespread acceptance' lent itself quite obviously to two conflicting interpretations in the sense of: *either* extremely wide acceptance *or* an acceptance wider than that likely to be gained by other provisions (e.g. 35% as against 30% and 25% and 10% for other proposed arrangements).

From the very outset there were two separate approaches, each perfectly legitimate and sustainable: the SDLP relying on the British White Paper and other clear government statements while the Unionist group relied on the very different but equally firm ground of the law itself. This is plain from the documents in the Convention Report. The Convention never recovered from being cast in this disastrous scenario.[24] There were many other reasons of a totally different nature and it may be helpful to the reader to take some note of them in case at some stage in future another Convention be proposed.

The Convention at Work

The Constitutional Convention was a wholly elected body, returned after an electoral campaign conducted on the lines of a parliamentary election, complete with manifesto, canvassing, speeches of intention and commitment and so on. The meeting-place accorded to the Convention by the British government was the Commons Chamber of the former Stormont parliament, along with all its accommodation and services, including Hansard, library, vote office, whips' offices and, perhaps most significant of all, the services of the clerk of the former parliament with his expert and dedicated parliamentary staff.

The outcome was forseeable. The members comported themselves as if they were members of a parliament, with party discipline, whips, order papers and all the rest. More important, they took the line, the old-fashioned but very honourable line it seemed, of feeling obliged to stick by their manifestos and refuse to bend, bow or budge. More serious still, the Unionist members dedicated themselves to the principle of 'open agreements openly arrived at', obviously in reaction against the methods of secret negotiation used at Sunningdale in December 1973.

Given such an atmosphere the Convention could proceed only along the well-known parliamentary lines of set speeches made with an eye to the Press Gallery and to Hansard, confrontation, party manoeuvre and frequent recourse to the division lobby. One possible opening came with the challenging speech of Mr John Hume on 19 June 1975 when in a philosophical passage he laid bare the realities of the two conflicting traditions, courageously calling on the Unionists to re-examine theirs and calling with even greater courage on his own supporters to give up many of the romantic myths that they cherished. The chances for any real meeting of minds or for any quiet negotiation, bargaining, or give and take were extremely poor. Apart from one move towards the concept of 'voluntary coalition' (as distinct from enforced or contrived power-sharing) which arose in August—September 1975 and quickly disappeared again, there was no promise of a deal, an informal grouping, a late-night huddle, or any cabal. The more extreme members did not even meet in the parliamentary bar, since one group were of a convivial nature while their opposite numbers were the sternest of teetotallers. As one wit on the staff put it: 'It seems around here that every smoke-filled room carries a serious health warning!' A 'deal' would have helped because, as Professor Richard Rose has put it, the choice is between a deal and a document. The Constitutional Convention chose 'the document' with a vengeance and in the end voted through on firm majority lines a competent and in itself entirely proper case for a straightforward British-style, orthodox, majority-vote parliament in a federal relationship to Westminster but unrelated to the current hopes for a form of partnership.[25]

In such informal and off-the-record meetings as were organised by the Chairman of the Convention (and there were many) the discussion amongst the elected members quickly became immensely complex, more complex than seemed necessary. The already complicated cat's cradle of relationships between all the many parties in Northern Ireland, between them and the Irish Republic and between them and Britain, was made more complicated and harder to unravel by two things: the intense attitudes of most of the members and the over-subtle interpretation they placed on each and every word or action of the British government. To less subtle minds the simple truth seemed to be that all the evidence since Darlington in 1972 showed that the British wanted to hand back devolved power the very moment some locally agreed scheme was settled. The essence of the constitutional geometry seemed to be: the greater the local agreement the greater the amount of devolution.

What could — within the bounds of practical politics — have been done to help the Convention serve Ulster better? The act could have embodied the guide-rules so clearly sketched in non-statutory documents. The Convention could have been a nominated one, nominated after consultation with the political parties; or could have had at least one nominated bench; or could have been in two parts: a small nominated delegation to negotiate in confidence and behind closed doors, reporting back to an open and elected body. This body could meanwhile have been kept usefully and happily occupied on the practical day-to-day concerns of the constituents — jobs, housing, benefits, schools, roads, water, sewerage and so on — for the Convention was the only elected, Province-wide assembly then existing and many constituents persisted, not surprisingly, in sending their queries to the Members only to find that these carefully elected representatives were not authorised or encouraged to deal with such mundane matters.

Another course which the Constitutional Convention itself could well have taken was to have invited evidence from the public. It would possibly have been helpful to them and certainly a healthy thing in itself to have drawn the views in particular of the astonishing number of informal street and neighbourhood groups that were then forming, struggling to find expression for new thinking and constantly throwing up new leaders. The dust sheets could have been taken off the Senate Chamber and a succession of vehement, voluble but neglected groups given the opportunity for once of a hearing by the very body that was to consider the future of 'all the people'.

So much emotion had been spent on the concept and practice of 'power-sharing' in the unhappy experience of 1974 that power-sharing had become in many quarters a dirty word. Yet the many practical and perfectly honourable forms that partnership government can take in a modern state have been widely studied and favourably viewed as workable models of political co-operation.[26] Some were reflected in the British government's White Paper, 'A Working Paper for a Conference' published in November 1979 in preparation for the Atkins constitutional talks.

The Political Parties

This may be a useful point at which to take stock of the development of the political parties. Fragmentation is the word that best describes the scene. Whereas for fifty years and more the stage had been occupied by the two main parties, the Unionist Party and the Nationalist Party (with interesting but transient departures from time to time), that pattern was shattered by the stormy events of the late Sixties and Seventies. Where there had been one Unionist party, at least three developed: the mainstream Official Unionist Party, the Democratic Unionist Party and the Vanguard Unionist Party; by 1974 there had been added the Unionist Party of Northern Ireland in support of that section of the unionists who took part in the power-sharing experiment of that year. Since then a new small party has emerged: the Popular Unionist Party. Likewise on the nationalist side the Nationalist Party gave way to new emerging groups of which the biggest and most stable by far has been the Social Democratic and Labour Party formed in August 1970, as the voice for anti-unionism and for the unification of Ireland by peaceful means and by consent. Of the other parties representing shades of nationalist and republican feeling the most consistent on the political stage has been the Republican Clubs/Workers' Party on a programme related severely to housing, jobs and the standard of living of working people within a philosophy that leads logically to the class struggle. The Irish Republican Socialist Party and the Irish Independence Party also operate today.

The other significant development was the creation in 1970 (out of the non-political New Ulster Movement) of the Alliance Party embracing both Protestants and Roman Catholics on a political programme that is wholly and unequivocally in favour of partnership between Roman Catholics and Protestants in government. Lacking sufficient support across the Province to influence national events in any major way its greatest impact lies today in the very fact of maintaining a non-confessional stance and in presenting a centre position within local councils. Throughout all these developments the Northern Ireland Labour Party has continued to function on policies closely akin to those of the British Labour Party.

One relevant conclusion from this short survey of the parties is surely that, under any new constitutional arrangement, no one party is likely to be able to muster an overall majority as the Unionist Party did for so long. Put another way, any future government or executive formed on party political lines would have to be a coalition of parties, for so long as can be forseseen.

Direct Rule Possibilities

When the Convention came to an end in March 1976 the British government were, understandably, determined to let things settle and to take time before making any new move on the constitutional issues.

What was less understandable was the manner in which they continued to operate direct rule, then running for over four years. It was clear to all that they would have to keep direct rule going for some considerable time. With the IRA campaign of violence still in force and evoking sporadic and vicious retaliation from loyalist extremists and with signs appearing of a decline in the economy, there would have been an opportunity for introducing some new elements, for engaging local participation and for broadening the administration. The utter steadfastness with which the British parliament and government have shouldered all the burdens of direct rule is characteristic; but so also is the conservatism with which they have adhered to the pattern laid down so hastily in March 1972.

When urging power-sharing or coalition on politicians in the extremely difficult circumstances of Ulster, rent by deep and grievous constitutional disagreement, it would surely be becoming to display something of the same attitude in the immeasurably easier circumstances of Westminster. In other words, what better example of power-sharing than for H. M. Government of the day to have appointed (in consultation with the Leader of H. M. Opposition) someone from the opposing party to be one of the Junior Ministers under direct rule?

Again, if history, geography and tradition count in the government of Ulster (as is widely argued) then surely the close contact and sympathy with Scotland over so long (longer probably than with England) must count for something and could have been usefully recognised by the inclusion of an experienced Scottish politician in the direct rule team in 1976.

One life peer from Ulster was recently created, specifically to strengthen Ulster representation in the House of Lords. And he has done so with great acceptance. If that is so, why not create further life peers from Ulster and ask them to serve within the direct rule administration and answer for their actions in the Lords? Indeed why not give duties and minor office to a couple of Ulster members in the Commons and convert their role in that House into a more positive one?

It is not just in the United Kingdom context that such practical changes in the colour and texture and acceptability of direct rule would have been useful and possible. From January 1973 onward the European dimension was looming larger and larger: entry into the EEC in 1973, the referendum in 1975, the parliamentary elections in 1979. Ulster was affected in many ways, through the export of her manufactured goods, the Common Agricultural Policy (CAP), regional aid, fisheries and much else. To have involved local people increasingly in all those aspects of British relations with Europe might have been more fruitful than treating direct rule purely as a normal branch of London administration (however unreal this seems to most of the British public and however unappealing to most Members of Parliament). Readers will doubtless think of other ways of 'Ulsterising' direct rule.

Membership of the EEC has meant for Ulster some closer working relations with the Republic of Ireland, a member for the same length of time and a beneficiary, too, under the regional aid and the CAP. Experience so far has not given evidence of any prospect of easing the Ulster question in that wider and more promising context as was hoped at one time. Professor Richard Rose has written:

> Many talk about a solution to Ulster's political problem but few are prepared to say what the problem is. The reason is simple. The problem is that there is no solution.[27]

Without going all the way along a road of pessimism and despair it is possible to argue that if the 'narrow ground' of the problem makes it insoluble within Ulster then perhaps the wider scope of the EEC might make it more amenable. This is not happening. The talks in Dublin in December 1980 between the United Kingdom and Ireland as neighbouring members of EEC have not so far done anything to allay the chronic fear and the feeling of insecurity felt by Ulster Protestants. It would be wise to take stock realistically of the main sequence of recent events in the relations between the two parts of this island as seen from the North: the O'Neill overtures, his reception of Sean Lemass at Stormont in 1965, his visit to Dublin, his total overthrow; the Darlington talks; the Border Poll; the Sunningdale Conference and its rejection; the Council of Ireland and its total and utter rejection; the Constitutional Convention Report; the activities of the IRA; the strong distaste for unification with the Republic still revealed by opinion pools, in particular that of the Economic and Social Research Institute, Dublin, 1979.

The Atkins Talks

From the point of view of H. M. Government the official position is clear. Although the Atkins talks of 1979–80 did not lead to any agreed conclusion they were sufficient to enable the government to focus the issue on to the possibility of a devolved assembly with wide powers but with firm statutory arrangements for partnership either within the Assembly or within the Executive. That is the choice offered.

It may be helpful to the reader to have before him a short summary of the proposals of H. M. Government that were placed on the table in July 1980: (a) a province-wide legislalature or Assembly based on one single body of about eighty members elected on PR(STV); (b) a wide range of local functions similar to those exercised by the power-sharing Executive of 1974; (c) an advisory council to consult with the Secretary of State on his reserved powers; (d) departmental committees; and (e) safeguards against discrimination.[28]

So far as the crucial question of the formation of the government or cabinet or executive is concerned, two options were offered. One ensures that any party with substantial representation in the Assembly would have a seat or seats in that executive, a sort of guaranteed and automatic coalition. The other option seeks to achieve balance by creating a Council of the Assembly (on which minority representatives would have a prominent place) with power to block, delay or refer back the proposals of the executive. In a word the choice is offered between balance and partnership within the executive itself or balance and partnership within the wider assembly.

What is more, the government pledges itself in the relevant White Paper of July 1980 'to embark on the fullest possible programme of consultation and discussion'.[29] This surely is the chance for constructive minds in all those aspects of life in which Ulster is so strong — business, farming, trade unions, education, administration and the professions — to step forward and put the clamant needs of the people before political doctrines and differences which could well be placed on ice for a decade or two.

Independence

While events move slowly on, the possibility must be taken seriously of some sudden breakaway movement towards independence for Ulster. Although none of the main political parties has so far campaigned for such a step, there is one well-informed and potentially strong body which does advocate independence, namely the New Ulster Political Research Group. When one recalls the latent anti-English feelings apparent in all sections of the Protestant population within the broader tradition of loyal support for Britain and the Commonwealth; the continuation of openly declared IRA violence; the rapid decline in the economy; the complex problems of high costs, low pay, poverty and persistent debt; the slump in foreign investment; the apparent neglect of Ulster by the English establishment, it is not difficult to see the possibility of a strong campaign being mounted. Add to this the seductive argument that only an independent Ulster could encompass the two conflicting allegiances and substitute for the provocative union jack and the provocative tricolour some new unifying emblem such as the Giant's Causeway or the fuchsia bush.

A Combined Will

I would plead for more and more people in all walks of life to speak up, to voice the feelings of 1981 (whatever they are) rather than of 1971 or 1921, to look to the future rather than the past, to substitute positive ideas for negative slogans, to keep in mind the actual real men, women and children of the Province and to ask the politicians of all parties, small as well as big, for quicker movement in the long process of constructing the combined will to produce eventually a constitutional framework that is humane, just and capable of serving all the people. A deal before a document.

REFERENCES

1. See successive editions of the Ulster Year Book HMSO, Belfast, for various facts and figures.
2. See *Royal Commission on the Constitution*, Cmd 5460, HMSO, London 1973, pp. 49–56.
3. See *The Reshaping of Local Government*, Cmd 517, HMSO, Belfast 1967 and *The Reshaping of Local Government*, Cmd 530, HMSO, Belfast 1969.
4. See *Royal Commission on the Constitution*, Cmd 5460, HMSO, London 1973, pp. 3, 379.
5. ibid., pp. 377, 378.
6. Report of Ombudsman, 26 January 1971, for Northern Ireland, Sir Edmund Compton 2076; also *Belfast Telegraph*, 27 January 1971 (Press Conference).
7. W. N. Osborough in the *Irish Jurist*, Vol. XII, 1977, pp. 389–92.
8. See Local Government Boundaries Act (Northern Ireland) 1971 and subsequent scheme by Sir Frank Harrison.
9. A. T. Q. Stewart, *The Narrow Ground*, Faber and Faber, London 1977.
10 Northern Ireland Government, *A Record of Constructive Change*, Cmd 558, HMSO, Belfast 1971.
11. These proposals were elaborated in a Green Paper entitled *The Future Development of the Parliament and Government of Northern Ireland*, Cmd 560, HMSO, Belfast 1971.
12. See House of Commons (Northern Ireland) Report, Belfast, Column 269.
13. This short account of an historic event is confirmed tersely by the *Royal Commission on the Constitution*, Cmd 5460, HMSO, London 1973, p. 55, para. 177.
14. See Northern Ireland Constitution Act 1973, Schedule.
15. Ian McAllister, *The Northern Ireland Social Democratic and Labour Party*, Macmillan, London 1977.
16. See Brian Faulkner, *Memoirs of a Statesman*, Weidenfeld and Nicolson, London 1978, ch. 12.
17. See Green Paper on *Parliament, Northern Ireland*, Cmd 560, HMSO, Belfast 1971.

18. See Northern Ireland Constitution Act 1973, Section 1, Schedule 1.
19. Northern Ireland (Border Poll) Act 1972, Schedule.
20. For a lengthy list of possible options, see J. Oliver, 'Ulster today and tomorrow', *Political and Economic Planning*, Vol. XLIV, Broadsheet 574, London 1978.
21. White Paper on the Proposed Constitutional Convention, Cmd 5675, HMSO, Belfast 1974, p. 16, para. 45(a).
22. Northern Ireland Office, *Constitutional Convention: Procedure*, HMSO, Belfast 1974, p. 3, sub-para. (a).
23. Northern Ireland Act 1974, Section 2(1).
24. See 'Proposals in Principle' tabled by the SDLP on 23 September 1975, p. 54, para. 1; also 'Official Report of the Convention', p. 11, para. 17. Both are in the main *Report of the Convention*, HMSO, Belfast 1976.
25. For a detailed account of the mechanics of the Convention, see *Blackwood's Magazine*, Edinburgh 1976.
26. For a discussion of these forms, see J. Oliver, op. cit.
27. Richard Rose, *Northern Ireland – A Time of Choice*, Macmillan, Washington and London 1976, p. 139.
28. Northern Ireland Office, *Proposals for Further Discussion for the Government of Northern Ireland*, Cmd 7950, HMSO, Belfast 1980.
29. ibid., p. 17, para. 64.

BIBLIOGRAPHY

Blackwood's Magazine, Edinburgh, August 1976

Faulkner, Brian, *Memoirs of a Statesman*, Weidenfeld and Nicholson, London 1978

Green Paper on Parliament, Cmd 560, HMSO, Belfast 1971

House of Commons (Northern Ireland), Official Reports

Local Government Boundaries Act (Northern Ireland) 1971

McAllister, Ian, *The Northern Ireland Social Democratic and Labour Party*, Macmillan, London 1977

Northern Ireland Act 1974

Northern Ireland (Border Poll) Act, 1972, Schedule

Northern Ireland Constitution Act 1973

Northern Ireland Government, *A Record of Constructive Change*, Cmd 558, HMSO, Belfast 1971

Northern Ireland Office, *Constitutional Convention: Procedure*, HMSO, Belfast 1974

Northern Ireland Office, *Proposals for Further Discussion for the Government of Northern Ireland*, Cmd 7950, HMSO, Belfast 1980

Oliver, J. A., 'Ulster Today and Tomorrow', *Political and Economic Planning*, Volume XLIV, Broadsheet 574, London 1978

Oliver, J. A., *Working at Stormont*, Institute of Public Administration, Dublin 1978

Osborough, W. N., review of Oliver, J. A., 'Working at Stormont', the *Irish Jurist*, Vol. XII, 1977, pp. 389—92

Quekett, A. S., *The Constitution of Northern Ireland*, HMSO, Belfast 1946

Report of the Northern Ireland Convention, HMSO, Belfast 1975

Rose, Richard, *Northern Ireland — A Time of Choice*, Macmillan, Washington and London 1976

Stewart, A. T. Q., *The Narrow Ground: Aspects of Ulster, 1609—1969*, Faber and Faber, London, 1977

The Re-Shaping of Local Government, Cmd 517, HMSO, Belfast 1967

The Re-Shaping of Local Government, Cmd 530, HMSO, Belfast 1969

Ulster Year Book, Various Editions, HMSO, Belfast

PART II

THE POLITICAL SYSTEMS AND ECONOMICS
OF THE CURRENT OPTIONS

As has been stated, the papers in Part I were commissioned as background papers. The following three papers, which make up Part II, complete the back-drop; they are concerned with what are widely seen as the current major political options facing the parties to the Northern Ireland conflict, their economic implications and their advantages and disadvantages.

3: POLITICAL AND ECONOMIC INTEGRATION
NORMAN GIBSON

Norman Gibson begins by considering some aspects of political integration, and points out that successive United Kingdom governments have made it clear that they desire direct rule to be temporary, to be a means towards more permanent institutional arrangements. Next he examines some significant features of economic integration as it affects first the whole of Ireland and subsequently Northern Ireland; with respect to the latter he questions the overall benefits of the economic integration of Northern Ireland with Great Britain, at the same time admitting that this, of necessity, also gives rise to controversial political and constitutional questions. Finally, on the basis of the foregoing he looks to the future and concludes that the political, economic and other forces making for a change in the relationships between Northern Ireland and Great Britain are so strong and persistent that in the years ahead the likelihood of some alteration in the constitutional position of Northern Ireland cannot be completely dismissed. At the same time he stresses that it would be advisable to be highly flexible in our thinking about the constitutional, political and economic links which might emerge; also that it seems highly probable that any proposals or arrangements for future relationships between Northern Ireland, the Republic of Ireland and Great Britain which fail to take fully into account the hitherto absolutist nature of the collision of the two major identities are set for failure.

4: INDEPENDENCE
PAUL ARTHUR

Paul Arthur begins by telling us that independence is about interdependence: and 'any serious discussion of independence must recognise it as a retreat from the tyranny of history and as an exploration towards self-respect'. He stresses that he is concerned only with peaceful secession and that he is assuming that amicable arrangements can be reached with the two sovereign states, Great Britain and the Republic of Ireland. He points out that at present the independence option is being pursued seriously by only a tiny minority within the loyalist community in Northern Ireland and that it is viewed with suspicion by the major parties. He examines a number of case studies — 'straw men' — whose experience might have some relevance for Ulster. From these he suggests the following tentative conclusions: (a) that even in a favourable climate an independence movement needs time to assert itself; (b) that size *per se* need not be too important; and (c) that diffuse support (the nationalist myth) can help overcome an initially unfavourable economic climate.

He then argues that any group which propounds independence as an option must take account of Northern Ireland's lack of political cohesion and that it needs to think carefully of how it will be possible to integrate the two communities. It must also concern itself with two vital questions simultaneously — 'What is my nation?' and 'What kind of nation?' He concludes by raising some questions about the assumptions underlying the independence option but notes that as an exercise in the broadening of horizons and (just as importantly) in self-respect, independence as a solution should not be dismissed out of hand.

5: ALL-IRELAND PERSPECTIVES
JOHN A. BRISTOW

John Bristow assumes that Irish re-unification could not be a stable solution if it failed to attract the assent of unionists. He tells us that unionists have justifiable fears that their culture would be dominated in an all-Ireland state because the prevailing ethos of the present Republic is homogeneous and non-pluralist and argues that Irish unity has no hope of unionist assent unless political structures are devised which protect unionists from the things they fear. The best hope, he believes, would seem to lie in some kind of federal arrangement where the mark of success is not to eliminate regional differences or even tensions, but to contain the political effects of those differences so that the benefits of unity may be reaped. Having drawn on experience elsewhere of federations, in particular the United States, he suggests and describes a federal structure for Ireland based on two provinces.

John Bristow agrees that the acceptability or otherwise of a united Ireland will not be determined according to economic criteria but notes certain economic consequences of re-unification. He points out the following: (a) that Northern Ireland at present receives subventions from Britain amounting to over a quarter of her Gross Domestic Product and so the termination of such transfers would cause a dramatic reduction in Northern living standards; (b) that the present Republic could not afford to take over responsibility for these transfers which in 1979/80 would have required almost a 50 per cent increase in the Republic's tax bill; and (c) that the only solution would be for Britain to continue the subventions on a phased basis over a longish period.

He believes that if unification brings political stability there should be an acceleration of Irish economic growth and that the need for such transfers would decline. For him, in the longer term, unification may bring a greater degree of economic integration between the two parts of Ireland and more importantly the Northern economy would operate in a policy environment determined by local needs rather than in one designed in London for the United Kingdom as a whole.

3

Political and Economic Integration

Norman Gibson

The political and economic integration of Ireland with Great Britain may be said to have taken many different forms over the centuries. But the period from 1801 to 1921 provides a potentially rich background to examine, primarily from the point of view of Ireland, the experience of a particularly close form of political and economic integration; and since 1921 there is, of course, the Northern Ireland experience of devolution.

This paper begins by considering briefly some aspects of political integration. Next it examines significant features of economic integration as it affected first the whole of Ireland and subsequently Northern Ireland. Finally, on the basis of the foregoing, it looks towards the future.

Political Integration

The political and economic integration of Ireland with Great Britain reached its climax in the early nineteenth century with the Act of Union of 1800 establishing one parliament for the United Kingdom of Great Britain and Ireland. There followed in 1816 an act amalgamating the exchequers of Ireland and Great Britain and in 1825 an act assimilating the Irish and British currencies, or more accurately establishing a common British currency throughout the then United Kingdom. With unrestricted movement of labour and capital between the two islands the political and economic integration of Ireland and Great Britain could scarcely have been closer. But the fact is that integration of the form described was a failure. It did not lead to a sense of common purposefulness, to willingly shared interests; a United Kingdom nation did not emerge. Many reasons can be given for this, not least the failure to grant Catholic emancipation until twenty-nine years after the Act of Union, and the stimulus this failure gave to the movement for repeal. But the failure to grant emancipation is itself surely a sign of deeper and even more intractable differences.

The integration ostensibly achieved between Great Britain and Ireland by the Act of Union was finally fractured by the Treaty of 1921 which gave birth to the Irish Free State. Northern Ireland had, of course, come into being under the Government of Ireland Act 1920. But for some the establishment of the Irish Free State did not go far enough; dominion status within the Commonwealth remained repugnant to the Republican mind. And, as is well known, the process of diminishing the Commonwealth link culminated in the Republic of Ireland Act 1949 through which the last vestige of the Commonwealth connection of the twenty-six counties was severed. But Northern Ireland remained a part of the United Kingdom and this continues to be a deep-seated grievance for those with Republican and separatist aspirations.

Northern Ireland had, of course, come into being as a second-best solution as far as Irish supporters of the Act of Union were concerned. It seemed at the time to be the largest geographical entity that unionist power could effectively control and maintain within the United Kingdom. But the structure was threatened from the beginning, for it contained within itself intractably opposed forces. One-third of the population, more or less, looked to the rest of Ireland as the entity with which they primarily identified, whilst the remaining two-thirds increasingly saw the Irish Free State and later the Irish Republic as alien and foreign, and continued to cling to Britain as the source of their security and survival.

But, like the Act of Union, the Government of Ireland Act as it referred to Northern Ireland also failed, with the suspension of the Northern Ireland parliament in 1972. The experiment of a devolved government and parliament had come to a precipitate end; another form of integration for a part of Ireland with Great Britain had been tried and found wanting. Fundamentally, unionism in Northern Ireland found it impossible to share power with the Minority; for to do so was in the unionist view to put their very existence at risk. But no sizeable minority was going to accept such a subordinate position indefinitely.

In the years since 1972, except for the brief interlude of the Assembly and enforced power-sharing Executive for the first five months of 1974, which finally collapsed under the strain of the Ulster Workers' Council strike, direct rule from Westminster has become the form of government for Northern Ireland. This, of course, is basically a reversion to the principles of the Act of Union, only now applying to Northern Ireland rather than all Ireland.

Few observers of the position believe that direct rule in its current form can be a long-term state of government for Northern Ireland. Too many interests and power groups, both within and outside Northern Ireland, are, to say the least, dissatisfied with what it offers, other than perhaps as an interim arrangement. Moreover, successive United Kingdom governments have made it clear that they desire direct rule to be temporary, to be a means towards more permanent institutional arrangements. But this necessarily raises the question: what form or forms of more permanent institutional arrangements? This point is returned to later.

Economic Integration

What of the economics of integration? How did and do the forms of political integration satisfy the economic interests first of Ireland under the Act of Union and subsequently of Northern Ireland? These questions allow no simple answers and, indeed, in one sense are fundamentally unanswerable, as they beg the question: what would have been the alternative to integration and what policies and consequences would have emerged from this alternative?

Nevertheless, it can be said that there are signs of a growing agreement amongst economists and economic historians that the Irish economy (or economies) both currently and historically cannot at one and the same time reap the benefits of extensive external trade and insulate itself (or themselves) from the effects of world economic events. In other words economic interdependence is a kind of economic integration. Moreover, this interdependence would seem to have been as true of the past as it is of the present and is ably illustrated in L. M. Cullen's *An Economic History of Ireland since 1660.*

This point is not made in an implicit attempt to argue that the economic integration of Ireland with Great Britain under the Act of Union was in some sense ideal for Ireland's interests; that would certainly be difficult to sustain, though some would wish to argue that integration did suit the north east of Ireland. But the argument does suggest that whatever the plausible alternative to integration under the Act of Union might have been, Ireland in the nineteenth century would have experienced massive and painful economic, social and human adjustments as technological development and the effects of the industrial revolution spread throughout the world. In particular, it would have been extremely difficult to avoid large-scale emigration as the century progressed or alternatively to provide a tolerable standard of living for a population which had doubled from some four million to over eight million in the fifty years or so before 1841.

This is not to say, however, that the then government dealt with conditions of the time, the frequent famines and the appalling catastrophe of the Great Famine, with the desperate urgency that those events demanded. But even here, if some approximation to reality is our goal, it is necessary to avoid the superficial application of today's norms and capacities to yesterday's terrible problems.

The land, land ownership and security of tenure were the focus of bitter and recurring conflict throughout much of the nineteenth and early twentieth centuries in Ireland. To see the conflict only in economic terms would be to under-estimate the amalgam of economic, political and social factors, and the deep sense of oppression and injustice that went with the memory of conquest and land appropriation. Nevertheless, the economic dimension is important for the discussion of integration. As Lee has pointed out, 'The regulation and eventual abolition of rent did little to stimulate output'; and again, 'Price movements, not tenurial systems, dominated the volume and structure of agricultural output in the nineteenth century'.[1]

It would thus seem that the change in land ownership as such had little independent effect on agricultural output. However, it was, of course, of fundamental importance to the distribution of wealth, and presumably had profound effects on ameliorating widespread insecurity.

A repeated criticism of integration was that it imposed an unjust burden of taxation on Ireland. There would seem to be some substance in this criticism, at least in the years immediately following the Act of Union, when the long drawn out war with France put considerable strain on the finances of the United Kingdom. It would also seem that following the raising of taxation in Ireland to British levels, which occurred between 1853 and 1860, taxation was higher relative to income than in Britain. This would appear to have been primarily a consequence of a regressive taxation system which relied heavily on indirect taxes levied on products consumed extensively by the relatively poor.

But in any attempt to assess this matter attention also needs to be given to public expenditure and the share of it which occurred in Ireland. This, however, is not easy to determine though there is evidence that in the decade before 1914 government expenditure exceeded revenue, thus representing presumably a net transfer of resources to Ireland.[2] But even if the net transfer is a fact and, indeed, if it had been true throughout the whole period of the Act of Union this is clearly insufficient to establish that United Kingdom fiscal policy was in the best interests of Ireland. Autonomy in fiscal policy, reflecting the preferences, interests and standards of a particular society, is highly prized, and surely rightly so, though it too needs to be seen in a comprehensive context; for in certain circumstances fiscal autonomy might be worth foregoing and this may have been true, at least for a period, for Northern Ireland under the Government of Ireland Act. These are complex issues; there is no simple way to determine what constitutes an optimal entity for fiscal, political and other purposes. But it may well be that the economic integration of Ireland with Great Britain was not as damaging to Ireland in the nineteenth century as some have thought. An Irish government might not have greatly improved on the conditions of the time.

Under the Government of Ireland Act Northern Ireland had very limited fiscal powers as regards the raising of revenue. The power to levy customs and excise duties, income tax and taxes on profits was reserved to the United Kingdom government and parliament. The act did, however, make provision for Northern Ireland to grant relief from income tax but any payments so made had to come from its own resources. The outcome was that no repayment of income tax was ever made.

Northern Ireland had, however, more power over determining the forms expenditure should take. This was, of course, after it had met certain charges, the most well known being the imperial contribution. This was a payment towards those services which were considered to be a benefit to the whole United Kingdom and included national debt charges, defence expenditure, the civil list and the Royal Family. But the fact of the matter is that the finances of Northern Ireland were in difficulty right from its establishment. Among the reasons for this were the initial scale of the imperial contribution, the costs arising from the disturbances and political violence at the time, and heavy unemployment. The eventual result was that, after various enquiries and agreements, the parity principle was gradually accepted. This, in effect, provided that with parity of taxation should go parity of public services and that if the revenue paid by Northern Ireland was insufficient to meet the cost of the latter the difference would be subscribed by the United Kingdom Treasury. In other words, net transfers could be made to Northern Ireland and it need not be financially self-supporting. But it was not until 1938 that the parity principle became formally accepted. In retrospect this was a profoundly important development in the economic integration of Northern Ireland with the rest of the United Kingdom. But it will be argued below that economic integration has been a mixed blessing for Northern Ireland.

The acceptance of the parity principle and subsequently in 1954 the so-called parity plus principle, which allowed accelerated expenditure on certain public services in Northern Ireland in order to raise them closer to the standards available in Great Britain, suggests that fiscal integration provided Northern Ireland, at least in the period after the Second World War, with a standard of social services and other forms of support which it could not have sustained from its own resources if it had had fiscal autonomy. This judgment, even if accepted, does not, of course, establish that the financial and fiscal arrangements of the Government of Ireland Act were overall beneficial to Northern Ireland.

The introduction of direct rule in 1973 has led to a simplification of Northern Ireland's financial arrangements with the rest of the United Kingdom. Various special financial agreements were swept away and the major sources of support for Northern Ireland government expenditure, in addition to the revenue raised in and attributed to Northern Ireland, are a grant in aid from the United Kingdom Treasury and the vote of the Northern Ireland Office. The estimated amounts involved since 1973—4 are shown in Table I below.

Table I

Subventions to Northern Ireland, 1973—4 to 1979—80. £m.

1973—4	1974—5	1975—6	1976—7	1977—8	1978—9	1979—80
314	393	571	625	700*	859	956

*Excludes once-for-all payment of £250m. to cover redemption of some of the borrowings of the Northern Ireland Electricity Service.

Sources: House of Commons Parliamentary Debates, Oral Answers, Col. 1220, 24 May 1979, Weekly Hansard, 18 May—25 May 1979; and House of Lords Official Report, Written Answers, Col. 247—50, Hansard, 13 May 1980.

The figure of £956m. for 1979—80 is more than three times the 1973—4 figure of £314m. and, even after rises in prices are allowed for, indicates a substantial increase in real terms. It should also be said that the amount of £956m. is incomplete in a number of ways. It does not include what is described as additional army expenditure of £97m., attributable to the costs of its involvement in Northern Ireland. On the other hand it does not seem to allow for certain funds, largely to do with agriculture, received by the United Kingdom government from the European Economic Community but which are technically attributable to Northern Ireland. No official estimates are available for the sums involved and whilst the amounts are not insignificant they would probably not dramatically reduce the figure of £956m. for 1979—80.

These comments on the net financial transfers from the rest of the United Kingdom to Northern Ireland necessarily raise the general question of their definition and estimation. This is a difficult matter which cannot be pursued at length here. For example, should the benefits which Northern Ireland presumably receives from general defence expenditure, diplomatic and similar services be included and costed as part of the net transfers to Northern Ireland? This, of course, was the purpose of the former imperial contribution. On the other side should some of the earnings of the Bank of England from their note circulation in Northern Ireland be attributed to the latter? However, there is little doubt that if allowance were made for these and other items and even if expenditure directly arising from the violence and destruction were excluded, there would remain substantial net transfers to Northern Ireland.

Granted the scale of the transfers it should come as no surprise to find that the ratio of public expenditure to gross domestic product is very high in comparison with the whole United Kingdom; over 60 per cent as opposed to around 40 per cent. An alternative way of indicating the relative importance of public expenditure to Northern Ireland is to note that public expenditure on goods and services is now some 30 to 35 per cent higher per capita than in the whole United Kingdom. In 1970 it was some 4 per cent lower.[3] I am well aware of attempts by the Northern Ireland Economic Council and others to explain away the 30 to 35 per cent public expenditure differential in favour of Northern Ireland in terms of special factors or special needs. Such arguments are fundamentally political in form and in no way reduce the real economic cost of the net transfers required to make the expenditure possible.

In the short term the extensive public expenditure is essential to cushion Northern Ireland from even greater hardships, because of the world-wide recession and its effects on the local economy and because of the cumulative effects, direct and indirect, of over a decade of violence, destruction and political instability, on private sector economic activity. The combination of these influences together with continuing technological and other changes affecting relative competitiveness, and total dependence on imported and expensive energy fuels, have had profoundly adverse effects on the economy. Over the last ten years or so employment in manufacturing industry has fallen from around 180,000 to about 120,000, or by about one-third, a rate of decline about 50 per cent greater than in the rest of the United Kingdom. Per capita income has always been much lower than in Great Britain and for the last thirty years has been probably around 70 per cent of that for the United Kingdom as a whole and output per member of the working population has fallen from 89 per cent of the comparable United Kingdom figure in 1971 to 84 per cent in 1979. The decline is the result of many factors but the arithmetic of it has been importantly influenced by a large increase in the number and proportion of women in the working population.[4] Unemployment over the same period has on average been twice that of the United Kingdom. These are some aspects of the harsh economic reality that any political proposals for Northern Ireland has to meet.

Whatever may be considered as the benefits to Northern Ireland of its economic integration with the United Kingdom (and there certainly have been major real net government transfers to Northern Ireland, especially over the last twenty-five years or so),[5] it has in terms of production and personal disposable income remained by far the poorest part of the United Kingdom. This prompts the controversial question of whether or not economic integration, and particularly the implementing of the parity principle, together with the rapid growth of the public sector, has been in the best interests of the Northern Ireland economy. The numbers employed in public services grew from around 103,000 in 1959 to 207,000 in 1979 with the latter figure accounting for over 40 per cent of all those in employment. The corresponding figure in Great Britain is about 31 per cent.

A feature of these developments is the extension to Northern Ireland of wages, salaries and employment conditions generally, which evidently could not be sustained by Northern Ireland out of its own resources. These consequences of economic integration may be expected to have the general effect of reducing the ability of the private sector to generate income and offer employment opportunities. Similarly, the presence and power of British trade unions in Northern Ireland insisting on parity of wages and employment conditions with those in the rest of the United Kingdom may have worked in the same direction. British trade unions must presumably emphasise the interests of British trade unionists and these interests do not necessarily coincide with the interests of labour generally in Northern Ireland. Similar effects on the Northern Ireland economy may be expected from the activities of non-Northern Ireland companies who for internal reasons pursue more or less uniform wage and salary policies throughout their organisations.

If these surmises are correct, and they certainly require the most careful and detailed scientific study, then economic integration has in a sense distorted the Northern Ireland economy and contributed to a weakening of the private sector — notwithstanding all the regional and other forms of aid — making it more difficult for it to maintain commercially viable economic activity. Furthermore, as the private sector becomes weaker the forces demanding an extension of the public sector and an expansion of public expenditure, including further aid for the private sector, are understandably likely to grow in strength. Indeed, as already emphasised, in the short term the maintenance of public expenditure is essential in the current circumstances of Northern Ireland. But it must be doubted if a tolerable standard of living for a population of some 1½ million people can or will be sustained indefinitely by an expanding public sector and public expenditure. Such an expectation would seem to be politically and economically unrealistic. Indeed, it is imperative to begin immediately to determine a strategy for strengthening and expanding commercially viable economic activity in the years ahead. Ideally this would more than compensate for any scaling down of the role of the public sector. But the issues go far beyond the question of the size of the public sector.

It may be suggested that the preceding discussion has been too much influenced by the experience of the 1970s in Northern Ireland and that if only there was an end to the violence and destruction and a measure of political stability the public sector would contract and the private sector recover. This is certainly a plausible argument but it is, I think, to be doubted that it totally undermines the misgivings already expressed about the economic consequences of the political and economic integration of a relatively poor region with a substantially more affluent economy. This judgment is reinforced when integration involves the parity principle, as described previously, and also takes into consideration the many other forces making for legislative uniformity and administered wages and prices, largely common to the aggregate and much better-off economy.

To speak in such terms, casting doubt on the overall benefits of economic integration as it has evolved since the establishment of Northern Ireland, suggests that there might have been a better economic alternative. Might integration have taken, or still take, a different form which would have generated a more viable and self-sustaining economy? In principle this is possible but politically and practically it is probably unrealistic, since constitutional integration and parity of public sector services, including salary and employment conditions, would now seem to be almost inseparable; and the same is probably true as regards the penetration into Northern Ireland of British trade unions and similar institutions. It would thus appear that it may be necessary to look to other forms of economic relationship if serious doubt can be legitimately cast on the longer-term benefits to Northern Ireland of its full economic integration with Great Britain.[6] But clearly this conclusion also raises very controversial political and constitutional questions.

The Future

If political integration of Ireland with Great Britain in the nineteenth and early twentieth centuries failed in an important sense; if the same can be said about Northern Ireland and Great Britain; and bearing in mind the economic consequences, as sketched previously, first for Ireland and subsequently for Northern Ireland; what is the likely future for political and constitutional integration?

My own judgment, for what it is worth, is that the political, economic and other forces making for a change in the relationships between Northern Ireland and Great Britain are so strong and persistent that in the years ahead the likelihood of some alteration in the constitutional position of Northern Ireland cannot be completely dismissed.

The overall thrust of the forces in Great Britain, Northern Ireland, the Irish Republic, the United States and elsewhere may well be working towards a loosening of the political, constitutional and economic integration of Northern Ireland with Great Britain. To suggest that these forces might be countered, and that even paramilitarism would fade away, if only the integration of Northern Ireland with Great Britain were made in some sense absolute, seems to me, if not a tautology — a kind of definitional solution — to be so question-begging as to be utterly implausible.

Other contributors have been given the task of examining two of the forms which a loosening of Northern Ireland's relationships with Great Britain might take; some kind of united Ireland and an independent Northern Ireland. It is not for me to trespass on their themes. But it may be that in any contemplation of a loosening of the constitutional and economic integration of Northern Ireland with Great Britain that it would be advisable to be highly flexible in our thinking about the constitutional, political and economic links which might emerge within Ireland and between Northern Ireland, Great Britain and the Irish Republic; standard models dealing with federation, confederation and the like may be too stereotyped. It is clearly not without significance that the communiqué in December 1980 following the talks between the British Prime Minister and the Taoiseach contained the now famous reference to 'the totality of relationships within these islands'. Does this foreshadow some new form or forms of integration within these islands?

Whatever the likelihood of the latter may be, the reality is that the destiny of the people of these islands is inexorably linked together; extensive interdependence is an ongoing and unavoidable fact; this interdependence needs to be unreservedly recognised and accepted. This calls for agreements, arrangements and institutional structures which at one and the same time provide a means of handling matters of common concern as well as conflicts of interest and which also allow and sustain a diversity of cultures and identities. I leave it to others better equipped than I am to explore the possible shape of such developments. But if there is point in my assessment of the consequences for Northern Ireland of its economic integration with Great Britain then it is of the utmost importance that whatever developments occur they should be such as to enhance the economic viability of the Northern Ireland economy.

It is perhaps worth stressing that at the root of all the failures of our past experiments in political and constitutional integration, both in the nineteenth and twentieth centuries, has, I suspect, been a complex and unresolved collision of cultures and identities. There is a danger in attempting to label these cultures and identities, as the labels suggest a monolithic uniformity which is false and misleading. But for the want of better terms they can perhaps be loosely described as Gaelic Catholic, Irish Protestant and English; and more recently Gaelic Catholic, Ulster Protestant and English.[7]

The Gaelic Catholic culture and identity has for centuries and with varying degrees of success bitterly resisted the anglicisation of Ireland as well as the English appropriation of political and economic power. The Protestant settlers and planters and their successors, the Ulster Protestants, always a minority in Ireland, have, it would seem, for ever felt threatened and insecure, but being determined to survive clung tenaciously to political power and to a lesser degree to economic power. For long periods something like a coincidence of interests has, with some reservations, by and large united English and Protestant interests in Ireland. But it would seem that that period may be nearly at an end. If this surmise is correct then the current tragic dilemma is fundamentally a conflict between Gaelic Catholic and Ulster Protestant.

The use of the terms Catholic and Protestant in defining the collision of cultures and identities is deliberate and I submit that any constitutional or political proposals or other institutional arrangements that fail to make provision for the chasm that divides the two will have little or no hope of success. For that chasm in its extreme forms betokens a divide that has hitherto never been bridged. In the past it has effectively precluded voluntary compromise. The only ultimately acceptable position for each has apparently been one of dominance.

The consequences of this collision of Catholic and Protestant absolutisms has been enormous; politically, socially, economically and not least religiously. The inability of the Churches as institutions and organisations to accommodate each other raises deep questions about the nature and expression of religious truth and belief. In particular, is there a profound danger that absolutist formulations, whether sacred or secular, may become a kind of idolatry that takes possession of the human mind and wreaks havoc both on the individual and on society?

That idolatry and fanaticism are components in our conflicts, at least at the secular level, can scarcely be doubted. For only too often the end seems to justify the means, however foul. Violence, destruction and death are the natural outcomes; so too is the self-destructive hunger-strike; and also the ultimate in self-humiliation and in the humiliation of others, the spreading of one's own excrement on a cell wall. And absolutism, whether sacred or secular, when combined with power and influence, stultifies and intimidates searching criticism and intellectual enquiry; it undermines the due processes of law and provides a spurious justification for the evil of paramilitarism; in short, it tends to corrupt the whole society. These are, I suggest, some of the terrible fruits of our absolutist conflicts.

In conclusion, it seems to me that any agreements and arrangements involving political and constitutional relationships between Northern Ireland, the Irish Republic and Great Britain will have little likelihood of being workable unless they take fully into account the hitherto absolutist nature of the collision between Gaelic Catholic and Ulster Protestant and the residual antipathy between the Gaelic Catholic and English identities. Indeed if its absolutist form persists it is almost certainly unrealistic to think in terms of a peaceful and lasting resolution of the conflict between Ulster Protestant and Gaelic Catholic. The outcome of this conflict is then much more likely to be separation of the two identities and cultures — a repartitioning of Northern Ireland. It is hard to see how such an eventuality could be brought about peacefully. And if it did come about through violence and civil war a new source of bitterness would have been born to bedevil relationships for generations to come. Surely the only moral and, dare I say, Christian way forward is the way of reconciliation, a tempering of our absolutisms, a willingness to accept and sustain pluralist cultures and identities. This is the great task that remains unresolved.

REFERENCES

1. J. J. Lee, *The Modernisation of Irish Society, 1848–1918*, pp. 101, 102, Gill and Macmillan, Dublin 1973.
2. L. M. Cullen, *An Economic History of Ireland since 1660*, Batsford, London 1972.
3. See 'Urban and Regional Policy with Provisional Regional Accounts, 1966–78', *Cambridge Economic Policy Review*, July 1980.
4. Per capita Gross Domestic Product in Northern Ireland in the 1980s is estimated at some 75 per cent of the UK average but this includes economic activity directly due to the security position. For per capita data, see *Economic Trends*, Appendix, p. 115. HMSO, London, November 1980.
5. It is difficult to know exactly in what year after the Second World War net government transfers to Northern Ireland became positive but it may have been in the early 1950s. The difficulties arise because of how to determine the imperial contribution and the offsets to it, including various special payments, agricultural food subsidies and payments to Northern Ireland under the national insurance arrangements.
6. There would seem to be profoundly important implications in this argument for the development of the EEC. Any attempt to universalise throughout the EEC the highest standards of public services and the wages and salaries of the public sectors of the more affluent members would be likely to have seriously adverse effects on the less prosperous members. It may also be doubted that any feasible regional policies would offset these effects.
7. The term Gaelic Catholic is perhaps the least satisfactory, as historically many who have been interested in Gaelic culture have not been Catholic and, in so far as the term is taken to denote republican or nationalist — and these are not identical — it is also inaccurate; some of the great republican and nationalist figures of

the past were neither Roman Catholic nor identified with Gaelic culture. Notwithstanding these reservations about the term, it remains a useful shorthand for the amalgam of cultural, political and religious factors which distinguish by far the greater part of the people of Ireland from their Ulster Protestant neighbours.

BIBLIOGRAPHY

Cullen, L. M., *An Economic History of Ireland since 1660*, Batsford, London 1972

Lee, Joseph, *The Modernisation of Irish Society, 1848–1918*, Gill and Macmillan, Dublin 1973

University of Cambridge, Department of Applied Economics, 'Urban and Regional Policy with Provisional Regional Accounts, 1966–78', *Cambridge Economic Policy Review*, July 1980, Gower, Farnborough 1980

4

Independence

Paul Arthur

I'm an Ulsterman, of planter stock. I was born in the island
of Ireland, so secondarily I'm an Irishman. I was born in
the British archipelago and English is my native tongue, so
I am British. The British archipelago are offshore to the
continent of Europe, so I'm European. This is my hierarchy
of values and as far as I'm concerned anyone who omits
one step in that sequence of value is falsifying the situation.[1]

The poet's mosaic begins to illustrate the complexity of the
Ulster identity. He is as aware as the next man that there is
another tradition, one that, to quote Seamus Heaney, 'lives
off another hump as well', a hump which uses English
infected by the rhythms of another tongue. A putative solution as stark as independence must face up to this clash of
identities.

There are more mundane matters to be considered. Take a
small land mass on the north-western tip of Europe, devoid
of natural resources, remote from the major markets, created
on a narrow industrial base, displaying a history of endemic
violence, and suggest to its people that it should go it alone.
But that is too stark. 'Independence' is actually about 'interdependence'; and any serious discussion of it must recognise
it as a retreat from the tyranny of history and as an exploration towards self-respect.

It would be as well to begin with some general comments.
We are concerned here with peaceful secession, and, for that
reason, we shall not examine the implications of a unilateral
declaration of independence — that way lies Conor Cruise
O'Brien's 'malignant model'. We are assuming that amicable
arrangements can be reached with two sovereign states, Britain
and the Republic of Ireland, so that, ironically, we may be
examining 'the totality of relationships' between these islands.
We acknowledge that, at present, the independence option is

113

being pursued seriously by only a tiny minority of one community whose onerous task is, to quote John Hewitt again, '"to invent the myth, invent the metaphor" for Ulster, which will give our people, *at whatever stage in history they came here,* identity . . .' (my italics).[2] Finally, our study will concentrate on political solutions rather than economic prospects, since prosperity presupposes a stable political framework.

Agreed secessions are rare birds in the contemporary world. We are more attuned to the Irish war of independence, to East Bengal's violent resistance to the Pakistan federation, the two million dead arising out of the Nigerian civil war. Armed insurrection, terrorism, civil war or the emergence of states as a sequel to military defeat and dismemberment by conquerors seem to be the norm in the emergence of new political entities. To be sure, the white Commonwealth countries of Canada, Australia and New Zealand as well as Iceland achieved independence peacefully. But those were overseas possessions of empire. Some would put Northern Ireland in that category. There has always been, however, an ambivalence about its constitutional status,[3] so that at the very least we can see it as a deviant case in normal intra-state relationships.

Norway's secession from Sweden in 1905 may be the only example we have of a peaceable separation. Superficially, it may offer some interesting parallels with Northern Ireland. Sweden, which had ruled it from 1814, considered Norway to be a province. It was economically very backward and did not even begin to develop its own language or its own history and folklore until the 1840s. Even when it won its independence in 1905 it was still very poor with little manufacturing other than that connected with the shipyards. Its economic and political success since then has been built on almost no resources except persistence and ingenuity. Now Norway is represented as a model of 'small is beautiful', of separation not as disintegration but as birth and renewal of vigour. Significantly, too, in the 'course of developing their economy, the Norwegians have displayed an inventiveness and verve that it is hard to imagine they could have exercised had they and their government been preoccupied instead with bitter political grievances and associated economic grievances'.[4]

But parallels can be misleading. Norway's cultural nationalism is more akin to the cultural and literary revival of nineteenth-century Catholic Ireland than to anything which occurred in Protestant Ulster. True, there was a spirit of independence in both nineteenth-century Norway and in Northern Ireland after 1920. But they ran different courses. In Norway it took the form of two persistent themes: one was their fearlessness in taking financial responsibility for their own affairs, in establishing their own central bank and their own currency; the other was their strategy of seeking whatever piece or symbol of independence they could find. Ulster 'independence' asserted itself through the development of a form of Sinn Fein Unionism in which Stormont, rather than Westminster, became a potential focus for allegiance. Consequently it 'led politicians in Northern Ireland into illusions of self-sufficiency, of taking part in a sovereign parliament. It created unspoken separatist tendencies'.[5] Northern Ireland 'sovereignty' was an illusion; in fact the devolution experiment underlined Ulster's dependence on Britain and may have undermined her traditional self-reliance.[6] Finally, Norway and Sweden separated at a time when they were both vital — as their subsequent histories proved.

Norwegian secession was achieved in a relatively favourable climate. Swedish rule was benign and Norwegian determination was wholehearted. Nevertheless there were at least three occasions in the thirty years preceding separation when the shadow of conflict between them became alarming. Clearly, persistence and the infection of the 'national idea' are prerequisites for any independence movement. But we shall see that even where conditions are reasonably favourable it is impossible to set a time limit on the march of a nation.

The Scandinavian case illustrates another general point which has some bearing on Ulster independence: the size of a political unit is of less importance in a world of interdependent states. Norway has a population of four million people, and there are twenty-five member states of the

United Nations which have a smaller population than Northern Ireland and they all have a smaller national income. In this instance, Northern Ireland may be part of a

> general, though irregular, trend in the historical evolution of nationalism within Western Europe from larger to smaller ethnic elements . . . the Norse number less than the Catalans or the Scots. Ireland's emancipation was a further step in this direction, and Iceland's decision to acquire separate status during World War II offered existent proof that size was no barrier whatsoever to independence.[7]

A general explanation can be found in the obsolescence 'of "the Woodrow Wilson model" of a world divided into nation-states, each one sovereign within its area and independent of the rest'. In its place we should think 'in terms of an overlapping set of decision-making authorities, autonomous in some respects but interdependent in others'.[8] Hence, NATO replaces the British gun-boat, and the EEC and the IMF fulfill the role of the Bank of England.

The Grand Duchy of Luxembourg serves as an outstanding example of the success of a small state. With a landmass of barely 1,000 square miles and a population of about 360,000 it seems to break most of the general rules. Its status as Duchy was achieved in 1354 when it was four times larger than it is today. Thereafter each successive stage towards nationhood and effective independence was marked by a reduction in territory. Although Luxembourg is virtually self-sufficient in basic food supplies, it suffers from the obvious theoretical weakness that its economy is overwhelmingly dependent upon a single form of production: steel output accounts for 80 per cent by value of the total national production; at least 90 per cent of it is exported; and it employs well over half the total number of workers engaged in industry. Yet Luxembourg works. It has to be said that to work as well as it does it has needed the sanction of its larger neighbours. An astute foreign policy enabled it to join the Zollverein when it was created in 1842. That was renounced in 1918 following Germany's defeat in the First World War and was replaced by the Belgo-Luxembourg customs union in

1922. More recent arrangements have been the accession to the Benelux Union by specific stages in 1948 and 1953, a founder member of both the European Coal and Steel Community in 1952 and of the European Economic Community in 1957. In short, Luxembourg is 'a small fully-developed and highly prosperous sovereign state', exhibiting 'the full and complex organisation of a state many times its size'.[9]

Obviously Luxembourg bears little relation to Northern Ireland. Its geographical position at the crossroads of Europe has helped its prosperity and encouraged it to make fruitful alliances. It enjoys a high degree of social cohesion which never existed in Northern Ireland. A national language, a recognition of the monarchy as a symbol of national independence, a Roman Catholic Church organised as a single diocese under a bishop who by law must be of Luxembourg nationality, its very size, but, above all, an historical resentment of outside interference, all have contributed to its unity and prosperity.

One final case study will be used to illustrate the point that a small independent state born in less than propitious circumstances has managed to flourish. The Irish Free State was born with its national ideal unfulfilled, an embittered and armed minority within its boundaries, a humiliating economic reliance on its traditional enemy, and an economy which supported too many unproductive people. Yet it endured. It may well be in this case that adversity has been the mother of invention and that its one outstanding asset has been a richness in integrative resources. The Irish Republic is a truly homogeneous political entity, one of the few genuine nation-states in the contemporary world. Catholicism has been the badge of Irish national identity, an identity which transcended the social and economic rigours of its beginnings and allowed the nation to adopt the mode of thought which saw Ireland as having a peculiar destiny in human affairs. It was de Valera in February 1933 who expressed this internationalism in a broadcast from the new Radio Eireann station when he urged his listeners to undertake the new mission 'of helping to save Western civilisation' from the scourge of materialism. Now, that was a tall (and genuine) order for a tiny, underdeveloped nation to attempt. It conveys the power of the national myth, the infection of the national idea:

> ... What really and finally matters is the thing which is apprehended as an idea, and, as an idea, is vested with emotion until it becomes a cause and a spring of action. In the world of action apprehended ideas are alone electrical; and a nation must be an idea as well as a fact before it can become a dynamic force.[10]

To such kitsch as harps and shamrocks and sunbursts Irish nationalists endowed the 'idea' with 'a repository of myths, images and motifs, literary modes and conventions cultivated to a degree that might indeed have been the envy of most emerging states in this century of infant, fragile nationalisms'.[11] Some went even further and built a cultural wall around Gaelic Ireland; Douglas Hyde, for instance, in a famous lecture in 1892, 'The Necessity for de-Anglicising Ireland', stressed the very powerful myth of Ireland's assimilative capacities, its ability to absorb continuing waves of invaders since the seventh century. We have only to examine the genuine incomprehension of the average citizen in the Republic towards Ulster Protestants to realise the force of this particular myth.

But society cannot rely solely on the heroic ideal as a metaphor of political hope: 'bread and circuses' became necessary concomitants of stability. Again, the Irish Free State's economic policy indicates the politics of adversity which may be necessary for an independent state. Ireland did start with some economic advantages. It had no national debt to settle. It had overseas assets of £200 million, a very substantial sum for a small country. It has been calculated by the Banking Commission in 1931 that annual remittances from emigrants amounted to £4.5 million. Its defence expenditure accounted for less than 1 per cent of its GNP – £1.5 m. in 1929 – and it began its existence with some vitality. Capital was available for investment because the last years of the Union had been prosperous ones; of the £23 m. flotation of the various national loans £20 m. had been raised internally. In sum, the inflow of money from various sources enabled the Irish Free State to avoid what would otherwise have been a chronic balance of payments flow.

Independence necessitated deviations from British practices while the Irish currency remained tied to sterling. The Bank Rate was kept at 1 per cent above the British rate to encourage capital to remain in Ireland, and rates of income tax were reduced to a level below those levied in the United Kingdom to encourage the owners of much of the potentially fugitive capital. The result was a heavy reliance on regressive taxes and the growth of income inequalities. With a large proportion of public money already bespoken (for the welfare needs of the large unproductive sector), there was little available for schemes of economic expansion and social welfare.[12] The new state was able to live in this sad condition even beyond the interwar years because it enjoyed the diffuse support it inherited from its powerful national movement.

George Bernard Shaw, not a man to hide hyperbole under a bushel, once described a projected Ulster entity as 'an autonomous political lunatic asylum' with Sir Edward Carson as 'the chief keeper'. He may not have been too far off the mark. Any group which propounds independence as an option must take account of Northern Ireland's lack of political cohesion and needs to think carefully of how it will be possible to integrate the two communities. Richard Rose's loyalty survey[13] indicates that Ulster people share a 'sense of alienness from Englishmen and Irishmen of the 26 counties', and believes that this 'implies that Ulster is truly a separate political system'. Presumably it is this sense of apartness that motivates those who favour an independence solution. But little else seems to hold Ulstermen together. In what may well be the most stark sentence in his study, Rose writes, 'Nearly everyone in Northern Ireland has a sense of national identity, but there is no collective agreement about what the nation is.'[14] Catholics maintain a much stronger sense of national identity than do Protestants who divide their allegiance into three groups — British, Ulster, and those who feel wholly or partly Irish.

Commentators have been conscious of this lack of communal confidence among Protestants. David Miller, a sympathetic chronicler of 'conditional Loyalism' has maintained that since the end of the nineteenth century there has existed in Ireland one (Catholic) nation and one (Protestant) community 'upon which, for certain specific reasons, the general causes of nationalism did not take effect so fully as elsewhere'.[15] His explanation lies in a version of contractarian theory, a theme which was pursued by William Craig when he resigned from the cabinet in 1968. He challenged the right of Westminster to interfere in the Province's affairs and declared that Northern Ireland's constitution was 'more than a mere act of Parliament'; it represented 'an agreed settlement — the settlement made when our grandfathers and fathers made their historic stand'.[16] Within four years, with the imposition of direct rule, he was challenging Westminster more directly by addressing bodies of men drawn up in military formation with a 'Declaration of Intent and Covenant to Act': 'we shall assert our right to take whatsoever action we consider best to safeguard our loyal cause . . . such action to include, if there is no alternative, the establishment of an independent British Ulster.'[17]

Craig was adopting the rhetoric and some of the tactics of the original UVF. A Vanguard pamphlet, 'Ulster — A Nation', published two months later, adopted a sense of betrayal and of despair by regretting that the Protestant community was now despised by the British nation and that, against its wishes, it might be forced to consider independence. Significantly 'the authors of this pamphlet find it really difficult to give their nationalism a mythic dimension . . . they use not the language of the enthusiast, but that of the social scientist.'[18] All of this is reminiscent of events and of attitudes in Ulster after 1912. That period, too, witnessed a modest literature celebrating Ulster and defining its differentiating characteristics, not in terms of nationality but of moral virtue. One polemicist went so far as to compose a scoreboard of the 'Belfast Man's' qualities. 'Determination 98, business capacity 94, courage 91, trustworthiness 90, self-esteem 84, mental vigour 78, hospitality 70, general culture 55, artistic tastes 48, social graces 44.'[19] (It cannot have been much fun being a 'Belfast Man'.) This cursory comparison has been used simply to signify that there has been very little movement towards a sense of Ulster nationalism in the years between 1912 and 1972.

Many years ago Max Weber made the seductively simple point that the sentiment of ethnic solidarity does not by itself make a 'nation'. 'To the degree that it represents a step in the process of nation formation, it testifies that a group of people must know ethnically what they *are not* before they know what they *are*.'[20] Ulster Protestants knew that they were not Irish — or, at least, not part of that Irish nation which had been fashioned by nineteenth-century Catholicism and a recreated Gaelic mythology. Since 1972 many of them have been probing their conception of what it means to be British.

Some have hedged their bets; the Rev. Ian Paisley, for example, in characteristic fashion asserts ethnic solidarity. 'We ask only to be allowed to live as a free people with an uninhibited right to self-determination.'[21] Others, in some confusion but with considerable courage, have begun to construct their own hierarchy of values; Glenn Barr is quoted as saying,

> I don't know what I am. People say I'm British. The British treat me as a second-class citizen. I am not Irish. I am an Ulsterman.[22]

Since that date Glenn Barr and those associated with him in the New Ulster Political Research Group (NUPRG) have adopted more positive criteria in their search for a political solution.

Before we examine the case for independence we need to look at the climate in which its proponents operate. We are all aware of the pathological condition of the polity and indeed any putative solution must take that into consideration. Oddly enough, that may be a bonus for the independence lobby since despair and a sense of war-weariness may induce the population to move as far away from the status quo as is politically possible. Equally we are conscious of our security dependence on our two more powerful neighbours; for many in the community that is a psychological dependence as well. Hence the case has been made that, as with

Cyprus, part of our problem is this reliance on two fickle guarantors. (Unfortunately that argument cuts both ways. The Treaty of Guarantee, part of the package of the London-Zurich Agreements in 1959, which safeguarded the constitutional and territorial integrity of the Republic by prohibiting the union of Cyprus with any other state or the partition of the island, was not worth the paper it was written on – as subsequent events proved. Instead, as President Makarios observed, independence made Cyprus a *state* but not a *nation*.)

Our social and economic ranking within the United Kingdom makes the most depressing reading of all. A team from Strathclyde University examined the twenty-eight regions of the UK against twenty-one social indicators in the years 1951–76, and concluded that England 'tends to rank first, and Northern Ireland last in the hierarchy of nations [*sic*] within the UK. Northern Ireland brings up the tail on 14 of 21 social indicators . . . and ranks first only on a measure of need: public expenditure *per capita*.'[23] We have the highest infant mortality rates, the shortest life-expectancy, the lowest ranking in substandard housing, the lowest weekly earnings and the lowest proportion of students sitting for University type education.

> On average, the years since 1951 have seen a narrowing of social differences . . . Scotland and Wales on average have moved three per cent closer to the overall United Kingdom standard. Northern Ireland overall has moved three per cent away from the United Kingdom standard.[24]

Relative deprivation has often been cited as a factor stimulating nationalist sentiment. There is no *prima facie* evidence that it is having that effect on Northern Ireland – one reason may be that the Province combines extreme variations within it. That could be of fundamental importance in an independent Ulster since political leadership might find itself having to deal simultaneously with two vital factors: 'What is my nation?' and 'What kind of nation?'.[25] A more recent survey suggests that the above is in no sense an exaggeration. Gibson and Spencer conclude that there 'seems to be insufficient appreciation amongst the public at large or the public representatives of Northern Ireland of the extreme precariousness of the position of the Northern Ireland economy and the implications for its political future'.[26]

Finally we need to examine public attitudes towards independence. A survey of opinion polls comes to the unsurprising conclusion that a decade of political troubles has intensified differences between Ulster citizens, and that although 'Ulster Protestants and Catholics disagree about some political alternatives they show a high level of agreement, accepting direct rule and rejecting an independent Ulster'.[27] It is unlikely that more than 5 per cent of the Northern Ireland electorate would endorse independence at present, but it does receive much more support from citizens of Britain and the Republic.

The independence lobby might garner some comfort from the startling rapidity with which seemingly dormant ethnic solidarities can 'take off'. Jean Lesage's Liberal government which came to office in 1960 made determined efforts to construct a positive Quebec state as an instrument of social and economic transformation. His successors continued to manipulate Quebec for nationalist ends and employed increasingly nationalist slogans to describe their goals. Masters in Our Own House, Equality and Independence, Cultural Sovereignty, and, latterly, Sovereignty Association. The Parti Quebecois, led by René Levesque, was fashioned out of the movement and grew powerful enough to form the Quebec government in 1976. Its success rate has been stunted more recently, notably its failure to win the referendum of May 1980 which sought endorsement for sovereignty-association. The PQ sees this as only a temporary set-back and will continue the campaign: 'If I understood you correctly, till the next time!' is how Levesque interprets the result. Once again, however, we are forced to conclude that Quebec's Quiet Revolution has no direct relevance to Northern Ireland. We come back to the essential point that until the myth is invented there is little probability of independence gaining acceptance. *If* it does, then we can admit the possibility of a fairly rapid take-off.

There is no evident support from any of the major parties either. Mainstream Unionism appears to see it as a weak option, a 'present calamity' clause to be invoked only if and when Britain withdraws. The then Official Unionist leader, Harry West, for example, told the Constitutional Convention: 'If this system (devolution) is totally rejected by Britain, or if the British government no longer accepts Northern Ireland within the United Kingdom and desires to break the Union, a negotiated independence would have to be examined.'[28] His colleague, John Taylor, has given it more considered thought from as early as 1972. Then he condemned UDI and maintained that independence would have to be in a British context:

> one which was still loyal to the Queen and one which played its part both in the British Commonwealth and within the Western framework. Our sentiment to the British throne is not based on the fact that there is no family planning in the Republic.

In January 1975 he raised the spectre of an independent state in which 'you almost cease to have what we call Unionists, you almost cease to have what we call anti-partitionists and in their place you have Catholics and Protestants ... people who identify themselves with the same nation, who support the Constitution.'[29] We need to recognise that this is not a theme, or themes, that he and his colleagues have pursued consistently. It is more of a mental exercise, one of many options to be glanced at from time to time. Further, we should note his reference to the force of sentiment. That could be a major stumbling block for the independence lobby among the unionist electorate. Certainly none of the heavyweights have committed themselves publicly and unequivocally to the concept. Individuals have raised options ranging from Kennedy Lindsay's 'Ulster Dominion' to Desmond Boal's 'Amalgamated Ireland', kites that have been flown and either descended very quickly or took off into the stratosphere. The Orange Order, in a serious study of options within the context of British withdrawal, has decided that independence is not a viable proposition.[30]

Nor have the independence lobbyists received much support from Britain. The Strathclyde study indicates that during 1976 as many as 32 per cent of respondents on the mainland favoured independence as a solution but since the same survey records that British interest in Northern Ireland has declined steadily since 1971 we may assume that those people were motivated to some degree by a desire to get rid of the Ulster problem from British life. 'Withdrawal' might be a more appropriate term to describe British opinion, especially since Britain may no longer feel any moral obligation to stand by the Unionists ever since the UWC strike and the Convention failure. Officially the government cannot endorse independence unless and until it receives widespread support. Its ambitions are much more modest; it seeks no more than 'the highest level of agreement . . . which will best meet the immediate needs of Northern Ireland.' For that reason it excluded debate on Irish unity, confederation, independence or the constitutional status of the Province from the Atkins conference.

At one stage an influential section of the Social Democratic and Labour Party championed the independence cause, and succeeded in having a motion passed at the 1976 Conference instructing the SDLP executive to 'undertake an immediate study of negotiated independence involving all levels of party machinery'. The Cookstown branch of the party produced a document entitled 'Negotiated Independence as a Way Forward' which was similar in outlook to the document 'An Independent Ulster' published by the Ulster Loyalist Central Co-ordinating Committee. Both shared common ground on a number of issues. They agreed that Northern Ireland be an independent state within the Commonwealth as a result of negotiations between the parties in the Province and the governments of Britain and the Republic of Ireland. They recognised the need for a transitional period of fifteen years before the institutional structure of the new state be finalised, and that a British financial subvention would be necessary during this period. Finally they proposed, at least for an initial period, an inter-party government, and suggested that facilities for cross-border co-operation on matters of mutual interest be encouraged. The document was attacked by a former vice-chairman of the party as:

not a plan for independence at all. It is an amalgamation

of the concept of a federal Ireland with part of the SDLP's original proposals for joint sovereignty. It is a misnomer to call it independence and raise fake hopes of a convergence of SDLP and Loyalist attitudes.[31]

A more traditional objection was raised by Austin Currie who wondered how negotiated independence could be compatible with a party constitution which advocated Irish unity based on Northern majority consent. After a brief flurry the party closed ranks and reverted to a policy of 'An Agreed Ireland'. None of the other parties — Alliance, Sinn Fein the Workers' Party and Provisional Sinn Fein — have endorsed the independence option either.

Levels of hostility and levels of acceptance vary towards the concept: for example, Michael Farrell sees it is a recipe for a loyalist takeover, and describes it as 'the strategy of double frustration'; on the other hand, David Rowlands stresses its liberating potential, that since the feeling of dependence is so damaging politically, the concept of people having the right to negotiate their own status will help to restore their self-respect. Neither of these views, no matter how valid, represent the big battalions. Independence is an option which raises only the slightest murmur from time to time. It could die by default.

If we were to set a date to the launching of the independence movement we could probably agree that the UWC strike served as a catalyst. Victory, then, restored Protestant self-respect but not their parliament. Their paramilitaries, spurned by the politicians in the United Ulster Unionist Council and angered by the Prime Minister's reference to Ulster people as 'spongers', began to cast around for roles for themselves and solutions to the Ulster problem. The creation of the Ulster Loyalist Central Co-ordinating Committee, an umbrella organisation of paramilitary groups, was a short-term experiment in furnishing a role. Its major contribution was to float the independence option, and in July 1976 the first serious study of that concept was launched. Entitled 'Toward an Independent Ulster' and prepared by the Ulster Independence Movement, the document is a curious mixture of pique and defiance. It adopts a note of high moral virtue in its attitude towards Britain:

To our people in Ulster, Britain has long since ceased to be great. It has become more and more like an ideologically backward and morally bankrupt country with signs of decay prevailing all aspects of society.[32]

Stung by the epithet 'spongers' the document maintains that if 'the full story were to be told we might well find that the outward subventions equal or possibly exceed the widely publicised inflow from Westminster'. Emphasis is placed on the huge outflow of profits, created by Ulster workers, to England, and on the need for a proper planning policy, and on the consolidation of the Ulster economy in Ulster hands in an independent Ulster. Suggestions, ranging from the issue of commemorative stamps to an intensive campaign of recycling waste materials, are made as an indication of the direction in which the independent state would set its sights. Rhetoric is not entirely absent from the document — references to 'the beginning of a golden age for all our children' are to be found — but it is the sobriety of the language which stands out. The proposals did not receive wide publicity and the organisation has not had a notable impact on recent Ulster politics; in fact, with the exception of Glenn Barr and Hugh Smyth there are no obvious politicians with paramilitary connections who have been endorsed by the electorate at Stormont level. At local government level there are no more than four councillors identified with the independence lobby.

Another characteristic of this early phase of independence floating was a certain degree of naïveté. Speaking to two American Congressmen, for instance, a representative of the Ulster Independence Association asserted: 'We feel that 200 years ago we helped you in your war of independence. It is time you came and helped us to get our independence'.[33] The more consistent and constructive New Ulster Political Research Group also lean toward American support, although at a slightly more realistic, if desperate, level. They seek a psychological guarantor, one who would be acceptable to both sides, a Supreme Court Judge to head the new state's Supreme Court for the first eight to twelve years of its existence. They have written this requirement into their proposed Ulster Constitution but it has been challenged by a group of American lawyers who wonder whether it meets the need for a non-partisan judiciary. There would be, of course, tremendous practical and constitutional difficulties in implementing the scheme. One final comment on the American connection deserves mention: Ulster separatists have miniscule support in the United States in comparison to the Irish integration lobby. The Ulster Heritage Society has been founded for the promotion of Ulster American Friendship and 'increased consciousness of the Ulster identity and contribution to American life'. As yet it has made no notable impact.

Pique, defiance, naïveté — these are negative qualities. We must recognise as well the generosity of spirit and travels in self-exploration undertaken by the spokesmen of the NUPRG. Their proposals need to be examined with the utmost seriousness if only because they represent the most powerful loyalist paramilitary group seeking a political role. They have displayed a tenacity which could undo their political ambitions and they have forced us to recognise independence as a serious option. The NUPRG believes that the 'only future for Northern Ireland is political diversity in constitutional unity' and that negotiated independence

> is the only proposal which does not have a victor and a loser. . . . Without [it] there is no hope of progress on any of the other vital issues such as unemployment and bad housing.[34]

Their major contribution has been 'Beyond the Religious Divide', a set of constitutional ideas published in Belfast in March 1979. The document is divided into four sections, the first arguing persuasively that independence is the only option which offers a prospect of peace and stability. The second, entitled 'The People and the State' is a proposed constitution and political structure. It is based on the American Presidential system with sovereignty residing in the people rather than the monarch; it relies on a system of checks and balances, and on a separation of powers. The key post would be held by the Speaker of the House. He would be elected by a substantial majority of the members of the House and in turn would appoint the various committees of the House proportional to party strength. The Speaker would have to be someone who enjoyed the trust of both sides of the community. (We could mention the outstanding role of the Lord Chief Justice, Sir Robert Lowry, during the sittings of the Convention. An independent legislature would need someone of that stature.) This section of 'Beyond the Religious Divide' is very impressive as a putative constitution. Any tentative criticism would be levelled not at the details but at the constitution again. Sadly there are too many examples of model constitutions implanted in an unfavourable environment: one thinks of Weimar Germany, of Lebanon and of Cyprus. That is not to dismiss these proposals out of hand, only to make the obvious point that the constitution is only the first stage in the process of negotiated independence.

The final two sections are of more dubious value. The proposed Bill of Rights (Section Three) has been criticised by an ad hoc American legal committee as being 'much too limited and conditioned on legislative silence'.[35] Probably it reflects the troubled times in which it was written and emphasises too much emergency powers provision. No doubt these provisions could be renegotiated in the spirit in which they were offered. As the authors themselves put it in this supplementary introduction of September 1980:

> . . . our proposals are based on honesty, sincerity and goodwill and as we have no desire to be the legislators of the future, most of the decisions must be left to the elected representatives of the people. We have only intended to be a catalyst.

There is no need to accept such altruism totally but we can be impressed by the fact that the complete proposals have been put to every battalion and every member of the UDA over a six-month period and that only six members failed to support it.[36] Again we must recognise that paramilitary organisations have a certain volatility, and that the NUPRG realise that it will have to prove its political integrity and its electoral strength. Time is of the essence for its proposals. With this in mind, an Independence for Northern Ireland Association was created to promote the idea of an independent Ulster among people who would not wish to be associated with an organisation connected with the UDA.[37]

The section on the economy discussed the economic viability of independence. Here we enter a more speculative and controversial area. Glenn Barr has offered his blueprint of the proposed state operating a mixed economy and reflecting a 'small is beautiful' philosophy or, at least, a healthy scepticism towards reliance on multinational companies. Intermediate technology would be encouraged and the state would be less centralised and less bureaucratic than at present with the ability to go direct to the markets of the United States, Europe and the Middle East. (Mr Barr, of course, has already established contacts in North America and the Middle East.) A unified industrial development agency would replace the present rather cumbersome trilateral arrangement, and the establishment of a central state bank encouraging the judicious use of tax incentives would encourage the creation of a stable economy. All of this presupposes continuing membership of the EEC and the negotiation of a financial commitment from Britain for a minimum of twenty-five years.[38]

There is nothing particularly revolutionary about the proposals. They represent an act of faith in the potential of an Ulster economy, and it is not surprising that the general public is sceptical about its prospects. (René Levesque discovered to his cost that a much more healthy Quebec economy could not induce a conservative electorate to take the leap in the dark; nearer home, North Sea oil acted as an eruptive factor for Scottish nationalism but it was not sufficiently powerful to convert emotion into electoral strength.) Economic analysis ranges from the downright hostile to the tentative, and the economic argument is usually cast as the lowest common denominator: *if* we were forced towards independence we could manage somehow.

Certain unpleasant facts have to be faced. We belong to an open economy highly dependent on external trade: 'Few (if any) European countries are so dependent on external trade for the economic well being of their citizens'.[39] There is general agreement that an independent Northern Ireland would need the same trading relation as she enjoys now within the United Kingdom. We rely on the UK government as job-creator, risk-taker and entrepreneur, and while there may be some disagreement as to the precise value of the subvention, the figure of £1 billion seems to be accepted by most.[40] Even with our much more attractive industrial incentives unemployment is twice the national average,[41] and we have an unhealthy reliance on public sector employment.[42] Our job creation efforts have been upstaged by the Industrial Development Authority in the Republic, and our lack of energy resources combined with an electricity operation heavily dependent on oil-firing has taken its toll. As the Prime Minister pointed out,

> Today 87 per cent of the province's plant is oil-fired, compared with 22 per cent in Great Britain. That has inevitably led to the high tariffs of the last few years.[43]

There has been a contraction in employment in the industrial sector, approximately 87,000 jobs were supported by job and training support schemes in 1977–9, and 'there has been a depressing output performance in Northern Ireland industry in recent years'.[44]

Undoubtedly, the impact of the violence has been a major factor in producing such a dismal picture: the total lack of foreign investment between 1970 and 1978 is one indication of this.[45] Undoubtedly, too, most of these constraints would operate in any future model of political settlement in this area, save the status quo. Nor should we ignore certain attractive aspects of investing in Northern Ireland – a pleasant physical environment, a highly adaptable workforce, a long tradition of industrial skills, a low rate of industrial unrest and so on. But there is a finality about independence, allied to a sense of isolation, which is not to be found in the other models of co-operation. We may assume too much, for instance, in expecting generous financial assistance from Britain over a fixed period of time. We do not have evidence of such generosity towards other dependent territories, and she needs to avoid the triggering effects of her own policies – after Northern Ireland, why not Scotland and Wales? The most optimistic picture we can paint, therefore, of a negotiated Northern Ireland economy has to be very tentative:

> If an independent Northern Ireland were the only generally accepted way to secure a stable community, then the

economics would be better than those if the prospect is one of continuing instability. If independence came, in these circumstances, it would not be easy to maintain the complete range of government services and incentives. Some reductions in spending or supplementary sources of revenue would be needed and the structure of these would be very dependent on the goodwill, or otherwise, of the UK and the EEC. The degree of cutback would be very dependent on the level of external assistance and on the extent to which the local community was motivated to make the economy more efficient. The more efficient was the latter, the less would there be a dependence on the former.[46]

This paper has not set out to present a blueprint for an independent Northern Ireland. There are too many imponderables and there are too many suspicions to be allayed. Everyone is conscious of the fact that the Provisional IRA will not accept anything less than an Eire Nua. Even the proponents of an independent entity do not rule out the possibility that it may be only an interim solution. Such ambivalence in itself can undermine the concept of separatism. There are tremendous social and economic problems within the Province: a new state could well flounder in its efforts at nation-building because it was unable to provide specific benefits evenhandedly. The continuing goodwill of two neighbouring sovereign states could strain the loyalities of the citizenry. The pursuit of a positive common identity has reached only the gestation stage.

We have set our examination in a loose historical and comparative context. Our conclusion must be that the debate to date has been conducted largely within the loyalist community, that so far it has been about self-exploration and self-respect, and that the next stage must embrace the concept of a nation:

> the largest community which, when the chips are down, effectively commands men's loyalty, overriding the claims both of lesser communities within it and those which cut across it or potentially enfold it within a still greater society.[47]

Faith, charity and a rapid upturn in our economic performance are the minimum prerequisities for such a leap in the dark. The prognostications are not favourable.

REFERENCES

1. J. Hewitt in 'The Clash of Identities: 1', edited by Eavan Boland, *Irish Times*, 4 July 1974.
2. J. Hewitt, 'A Question of Identity', paper read at Conference on Independence, Corrymeela, 1976, p. 4.
3. See A. Lijphart, 'The Northern Ireland Problem: Cases, Theories and Solutions', *British Journal of Political Science*, Vol. V, 1975, p. 96.
4. J. Jacobs, *The Question of Separatism: Quebec and the Struggle over Sovereignty*, Random House, New York 1980, p. 49. This section relies heavily on Jane Jacobs' account of Norway's secession from Sweden, especially pp. 26–64.
5. B. Faulkner, *Memoirs of a Statesman*, Weidenfeld and Nicolson, London 1978, p. 26.
6. See G. FitzGerald, *Towards a New Ireland*, Temple Smith, London 1972, pp. 63–85.
7. W. Connor, 'Ethnonationalism in the First World: The Present in Historical Perspective', in M. J. Esman, ed., *Ethnic Conflict in the Western World*, Cornell University Press, Ithaca 1977, p. 31.
8. A. H. Birch, 'Minority Nationalist Movements and Theories of Political Integration, *World Politics*, Vol. XXX, 1978, p. 341.
9. K. C. Edwards, 'The Grand Duchy of Luxembourg', in B. Benedict, ed., *Problems of Smaller Territories*, The Athlone Press, London 1967, p. 78.
10. E. Barker, *National Character and the Factors in its Formation*, Methuen, London 1927, p. 173.
11. T. Brown, *Ireland: A Social and Cultural History, 1922–79*, Fontana, London 1981, p. 79.
12. See T. K. Daniel, 'Griffith on his Noble Head: The Determinants of Cumann na nGaedheal Economic Policy, 1922–32', *Irish Economic and Social History*, 1976.
13. See R. Rose, *Governing without Consensus: An Irish Perspective*, Faber and Faber, London 1971.
14. ibid. pp. 207, 214 and 215. See especially chapter VI.
15. D. W. Miller, *Queen's Rebels: Ulster Loyalism in Historical Perspective*, Gill and Macmillan, Dublin 1978, p. 46.
16. ibid., p. 123.
17. *Irish Times*, 14 February 1972.
18. D. W. Miller, op. cit., p. 154.
19. ibid., pp. 114–15.

20. W. Connor, 'A nation is a nation, is a state, is an ethnic group, is a . . . .', *Ethnic and Racial Studies*, Vol. 1, No. 4, October 1978, p. 388.
21. *Belfast Telegraph*, 3 March 1980.
22. *New York Times*, 16 November 1974.
23. I. McAllister, R. Parry and R. Rose, *United Kingdom Rankings: The Territorial Dimension in Social Indicators*, Centre for the Study of Public Policy, No. 44, Glasgow 1979, pp. 7—8 and *passim*.
24. ibid., p. 15.
25. E. Nordlinger, 'Political Development: Time Sequences and Rates of Change', *World Politics*, Vol. XX, No. 3, 1968, p. 501.
26. N. J. Gibson and J. E. Spencer, 'Unemployment and Wages in Northern Ireland', *Political Quarterly*, January 1981, p. 114.
27. R. Rose, I. McAllister and P. Mair, *Is There A Concurring Majority about Northern Ireland?*, Centre for the Study of Public Policy, Glasgow 1978, p. 48 and *passim*.
28. Cited by Conor O'Clery, *Irish Times*, 5 July 1975.
29. *Irish Times*, 17 July 1972 and 24 January 1975.
30. ibid., 23 February 1977.
31. ibid., Ben Caraher, 12 January 1977. See also David McKittrick, 11 December 1976.
32. Ulster Independence Movement, *Toward an Independent Ulster*, Belfast 1976, p. 22.
33. *Northern Ireland: A Role for the United States?*, report by two members of the Committee on the Judiciary, Committee Print No. 23, December 1978, p. 67.
34. New Ulster Political Research Group, *Supplementary Introduction to Documents for Discussion, 'Beyond the Religious Divide'*, Belfast, September 1980.
35. *Critique of the New Ulster Political Research Group Proposals on a Constitution and Bill of Rights for an Independent Northern Ireland*, New York, September 1980, p. 8 and *passim*. The members of the committee were James P. Cullen, Thomas S. Howard, Paul O'Dwyer and Robert S. Stitt.
36. From a discussion with Louis Scott of NUPRG, February 1981.
37. See C. Thomas, *The Times*, 12 September 1980.
38. G. Barr, 'An Independent Ulster — What Can It Offer Industry? A Personal View', *Trade and Industry in Northern Ireland*, Vol. 2, No. 6, 1979.
39. J. Simpson, 'A Critical Look at the Economics of an Autonomous Northern Ireland', paper read at conference on independence, Corrymeela 1976, p. 1.
40. See *The Guardian*, 19 February 1980.
41. See 'Northern Ireland: The Other Ulster', *The Economist*, 28 June 1980; also 'The Northern Ireland Economy: A Special Report', *Irish Times*, 22 May 1980.
42. See *The Guardian*, 22 February 1980.

43. *Belfast Telegraph,* 6 March 1981.
44. R. W. Hutchinson and J. Sheehan, *A Revision of Selected Indicators of Economic Performance in Northern Ireland and the Republic of Ireland during the 1970s,* Co-operation North, Paper II, Belfast and Dublin, December 1980, p. 32 and *passim.*
45. See R. Davies and M. A. McGurnaghan, 'Northern Ireland: The Economics of Adversity', *National Westminster Bank Quarterly Review,* May 1975 for a more optimistic picture of conditions between 1950 and 1969.
46. J. Simpson, op. cit., p. 6.
47. R. Emerson, *From Empire to Nation,* Beacon Press, Boston 1960, pp. 95—6.

BIBLIOGRAPHY

Barker, E., *National Character and the Factors in its Formation,* Methuen, London 1927

Benedict, B. (ed.), *Problems of Smaller Territories,* The Athlone Press, London 1967

Birch, A. H., 'Minority Nationalist Movements and Theories of Political Integration', *World Politics* XXX, 1978

Brown, T., *Ireland: A Social and Cultural History, 1922—79,* Fontana, London 1981

Connor, W., 'A nation is a nation, is a state, is an ethnic group is, a . . .' *Ethnic and Racial Studies,* 1, 4, October 1978

Daniel, T. K., 'Griffith on his Noble Head: The Determinants of Cumann na nGaedhael Economic Policy, 1922—32', *Irish Economic and Social History,* 1976

Davies, R. & McGurnaghan, M. A., 'Northern Ireland: the economics of adversity', *National Westminster Bank Quarterly Review,* May 1975

Emerson, R., *From Empire to Nation,* Beacon Press, Boston 1960

Esman, M. J. (ed.), *Ethnic Conflict in the Western World,* Cornell University Press, Ithaca 1977

Faulkner, B., *Memoirs of a Statesman,* Weidenfeld and Nicolson, London 1978

FitzGerald, G., *Towards a New Ireland,* Temple Smith, London 1972

Gibson, N. J. & Spencer, J. E., 'Unemployment and Wages in Northern Ireland', *The Political Quarterly,* January 1981

Hewitt, J., 'A Question of Identity', paper read at Conference on Independence, Corrymeela 1976

Hutchinson, R. W. & Sheehan, J., *A Revision of Selected Indicators of Economic Performance in Northern Ireland and the Republic of Ireland during the 1970s,* Co-operation North: Paper II, Belfast and Dublin, December 1980

Jacob, J., *The Question of Separatism: Quebec and the Struggle over Sovereignty,* Random House, New York 1980

Lijphart, A., 'The Northern Ireland Problem: cases, theories and solutions', *British Journal of Political Science*, 5, 1975

Miller, D. W., *Queen's Rebels: Ulster Loyalism in Historical Perspective*, Gill and Macmillan, Dublin 1978

McAllister, I., Parry, R. & Rose, R., *United Kingdom Rankings: The Territorial Dimension in Social Indicators*, Centre for the Study of Public Policy, Glasgow 1979, no. 44

New Ulster Political Research Group, *Beyond the Religious Divide*, Belfast, March 1979

————, *Supplementary Introduction to Documents for Discussion, 'Beyond the Religious Divide'*, Belfast, September 1980

Nordlinger, E., 'Political Development: Time Sequences and Rates of Change', *World Politics*, XX: 3, 1968

Rose, R., *Governing Without Consensus: An Irish Perspective*, Faber and Faber, London 1972

Rose, R., McAllister, I., & Mair, P., *Is There a Concurring Majority about Northern Ireland?*, Centre for the Study of Public Policy, Glasgow 1978

Simpson, J., 'A Critical Look at the Economics of an Autonomous Northern Ireland', paper read at Conference on Independence, Corrymeela 1976

5
All-Ireland Perspectives
John A. Bristow

Introduction

The major purpose of this series of papers is to consider various possibilities for the constitutional development of Northern Ireland. This problem can, in principle, be approached in a dispassionate and disinterested — if you like, 'academic' — manner and it may be argued that an outsider and a professional social scientist like myself is at an advantage in this respect. However, I am conscious of a major flaw in such an argument, a flaw which seriously jeopardises my credentials in this matter.

Nothing I have done enables me to participate in the *emotions* of unionism or nationalism. I was not born or brought up in a community whose national identity is in doubt or at risk: nor am I one whose country was until recently a colony and who feels that part of it is still in need of liberation. More generally, I personally have very little sense of nationality. I therefore find it very difficult to evaluate the strength of these emotions. Specifically, to make any progress at all with the topic on hand, I am obliged to ignore the possibility that, for unionists, there may be an over-riding loyalty to Britain, perhaps focussed on the crown. If there is this over-riding loyalty, then nothing can be done to make a united Ireland outside the United Kingdom attractive to unionists. Since the majority of Irish people probably have an equally strong counter-loyalty which would prevent the re-incorporation of Ireland into the United Kingdom, then re-unification by assent could not be achieved. In that sense, therefore, I am here dealing with an abstract state of affairs.

When contemplating the political structure of a united Ireland, an essential preliminary is to ask to what extent it is necessary that the arrangements attract the immediate assent of the majority in Northern Ireland. This question was answered affirmatively in the 1949 Government of Ireland Act and, indeed, the public stance of most Irish and British politicians in recent years has been that it is unnecessary (and rather bad form) to ask it at all.

The arguments for requiring this assent are of two kinds: philosophical and practical. The philosophical argument is that to change the political status of Northern Ireland without the assent of its people would be undemocratic and imperialistic. There are two interrelated retorts to this argument. First, democratic political theory normally supposes that the group in question has by some means (be it race, culture, warfare or plain historical accident) been predetermined. It is therefore not used to grappling with the question of national boundaries. Secondly, there is undeniable force in the traditional Irish nationalist point that the boundaries of Northern Ireland were actually defined artificially in a manner which had no historical precedent specifically to ensure that a majority would be unionist. Such a procedure is not unknown elsewhere, but it does destroy the *moral* authority attributable to the majority view on the boundary issue.

The practical argument is that no arrangement which does not have the assent of the majority can be stable; it will be resisted by force of arms or by civil disobedience to a degree which makes the place ungovernable. More insidiously, such an arrangement could produce a festering resentment which retards social and political development and which may, even after many years, break out in confrontation.

I am unsure how to evaluate these practical arguments. Short-term instability – or even violence – may be a price worth paying for an arrangement which maximises the chances of long-term stability. So, it is quite conceivable that unification could be a success even if it were initially resisted. However, there can be no denying that the long-term chances of success would be greater if unification were achieved through consent (by which I mean the consent of all but an insignificant minority) and I therefore proceed on the assumption that unification must appear attractive to a large majority in Northern Ireland if it is to be a feasible option.

What we now have to do is to try to infer what it is that makes unionists unionist. Economic arguments for and against the union I leave till later.

The most general and least tractable issue concerns the whole set of feelings that one belongs to a particular group, that other groups are in a usually undefined sense 'alien', that one feels pride in the achievements of members of one's group, that one has a duty of loyalty to one's group, and so on. In everyday life, one is not usually conscious of these feelings and they usually do not influence one's actions. They most obviously surface when one's group is challenged and one feels morally obliged to 'take sides'. Actual or imminent warfare is an obvious example, but for most of us these issues are most likely to arise in the context of less harmful competition such as sport.

It is of considerable interest that most unionists are ambiguous in this regard. If there were war between the United Kingdom and the Irish Republic, there is no doubt as to which flag would rally them and they certainly take more pride in the past military and imperial feats of the British than would the typical inhabitant of the Republic (or, indeed, of Britain). However, there is equally no doubt that in matters more germane to cultural identity, Northern unionists show themselves to be Irish rather than British. They flock to Dublin in the hope of witnessing the defeat of a British team in rugby football and at parties they take pride in knowing the tunes and words of 'rebel' songs, most of which must have very little political claim on their affection.

These points are not trivial: they reflect instinctive cultural identification with co-habitants of *this* island. It matters not whether this instinctive popular culture is at times apparently anti-British; what is important is that these attitudes imply a feeling on the part of Northerners that their fellow Irishmen are not invincibly alien and that for many of the things which give everyday life its richness and enjoyment Northerners have more in common with Southerners than with Britons (and *a fortiori* than with Englishmen).

If that is accepted, we now have to ask what features of life in the Republic make that country seem foreign to unionists. It is here that Southerners frequently fail to understand what is at stake. Thus, over the years, speakers at Orange rallies and those like Mr Paisley have thundered about the desire to protect the 'Protestant way of life', about Romish influences on social attitudes and legislation in the Republic, clerical domination of this, that and the other, condemnation of which is frequently delivered in the name of religious and political freedom. It is too easy, as frequently happens, for Southerners to characterise this as crude anti-Romanism dressed up as liberalism, pointing to the truth that, nowadays, if you really want to see clerical anti-liberalism in action you should go, not to Limerick, but to Ballymena. What I am saying is that the ease with which a Southerner can reject this kind of well-publicised neo-Knoxite ranting can disguise the fact that there is more than a grain of truth in it and that there are features of Southern social and political attitudes about which all of us — not just Northern unionists — are right to be concerned.

The Republic is only now fighting its way free of the suffocating influence of an amazing cultural homogeneity almost totally untouched by the nineteenth-century liberalism so important in the formation of values in our neighbouring island. Only now are we seeing the signs of change in a society until recently dominated by peasant agriculture and an ultramontane Catholicism of the most reactionary kind: the sort of society whose values gave little prominence to personal liberty and whose instinct was to make illegal those aspects of personal behaviour which the majority find uncongenial, be it contraception or the reading of the works of Edna O'Brien. Such a society is the antithesis of pluralist, excessively suspicious of minority views — to label something as an 'alien philosophy' is still regarded by many as an acceptable substitute for reasoned debate. The situation is changing at an accelerating pace, for the same reasons as those producing a liberalisation of social attitudes everywhere and because Ireland can no longer isolate itself from the cultural influences of the USA and Northern Europe.

The point of all this is not that the Southern majority

hold Jansenist views on sex, or that Northern unionists are the standard-bearers of liberalism, neither of which propositions is true. The point is that the dominant value-system in the Republic is still intolerant of what it considers deviance. Deviance from traditional Catholic sexual mores is but a topical example: the problem is much broader than that. Northern unionists, who may themselves be liberal or just as intolerant as Southerners, would present the most spectacular challenge yet to the moral and cultural homogeneity still prevailing in the Republic. They therefore have reason to fear that their own values and traditions would be denied freedom of expression in a united Ireland. They have reason to fear that legislation and other social institutions such as the educational system would deny them freedoms they currently possess or would strive to suppress attitudes which fit uneasily into the Catholic nationalist consensus. Anyone who would dispute this may care to consider the tortured and tortuous legislation on contraceptives introduced in the Republic as recently as 1980, the reaction produced there by attempts to challenge Church hegemony in the educational field, and the attitudes which politicians feel obliged to take on divorce.

I have spent some time on this because I am firmly of the opinion that Irish unity has no hope of unionist assent unless political structures are devised which protect unionists from the things they fear. It is no good Southern politicians making vague noises about liberalising this, that and the other as a *quid pro quo* for unionist acceptance of unification. In a united Ireland, there would be little incentive for such liberalism (Protestants would form less than a quarter of the total population) and, in any case, changes in existing legislation (something which politicians can bring about) would not remove the difficulty, which is that the dominant value-system is fundamentally intolerant of diversity. The key is to produce political structures which would protect the minority from that intolerance. The best hope would seem to lie in some kind of federal arrangement.

Federations in General
Federation is a widely used device for creating unity out of

diversity: even Great Britain still bears the traces of a past when it was more federal than it is today. The significant things about federations are, first, that they constitutionally accept existential differences between the member states or provinces — indeed, in many cases, thrive on them — rather than wishing they would go away and, secondly, they constitutionally protect minorities when they can be identified in terms of member states. Indeed, it is noteworthy that countries which have attempted to operate a unitary structure in the face of significant diversity have difficulty in maintaining the cohesion necessary to make any nation work.

It cannot be claimed that there are any obvious analogies to the Irish situation. In the bitterness and violence engendered by ethnic, cultural and, indeed, religious differences, Yugoslavia has similarities with Ireland, but its experience with federalism is difficult to interpret. The centripetal forces of its socialist ideology, of the military, diplomatic and economic pressures from the Soviet Union and of the massive presence of Tito have all helped to disguise any weaknesses in its internal political structure.

The USA seems to illustrate both some of the problems federalism is designed to deal with and some of the mechanisms adopted in response to those problems. The reason why the colonies wished to band together (the first Congress met *before* the War of Independence) was to present a united front in dealings with Britain — not an objective very relevant to Ireland today. However, what are relevant are the reasons why a federal rather than a unitary structure was established after independence. The sense of a common Americanness was perhaps even weaker than the sense of a common Irishness between the two parts of this island. People thought of themselves as Virginians or Pennsylvanians (and even Georgians, even though Georgia had had the status of a crown colony for barely twenty years when independence was declared). As separate colonies, the original thirteen states had had their own governing structures, quite independent of their neighbours. There was no prospect of their entering a unitary arrangement which would permit their dominance by other states.

These attitudes produced two absolutely central features

of American federalism. First, the states retained the powers not explicitly vested in the federal government. This reflected the situation in the 1780s when the object was to band together for *specific* purposes (external relations — including foreign trade — and currency control were paramount concerns) on the part of states which otherwise considered themselves independent. Although the objectives of federation may be different, this general approach may have some lessons for Ireland.

Secondly, in the strongest part of the federal legislature, the US Senate, all states have equal representation. This protection for small states was of crucial significance in gaining acceptance for the US constitution and explains why the smaller states ratified that constitution with much greater enthusiasm than did the larger states. This is of immediate relevance to us, given what I said earlier about the necessity of assuaging unionists' fears of being swamped in a united Ireland.

The history of German federation also throws up analogies for Ireland. It must be remembered that the states forming the first Austro-German federation in 1815 had boundaries determined by the Reformation Settlement — that is, on religious lines. Although no longer of major significance in German politics, religious differences still play a part in the attitude taken, for example, by Bavarians to northerners. The present Federal constitution of West Germany is similar to that of the United States in the two respects we identified — the Länder retain powers not explicitly given to the Federation, and in the Bundesrat representation of the Länder is more equal than population differences would require.

As a final illustration, let us consider Canada. Here we even have a province — Quebec — with strong cultural links (and some would say vestigial political allegiances) to another country. It is interesting to note that Britain was not prepared to do to the Northern unionists what it had done to the Quebecois.

The point of these allusions is to indicate that federal structures have been widely used to weld into nation-states groups which were in the past politically separate and culturally heterogeneous. Few have been unqualified successes in eliminating internal conflict, but such conflict is far from unknown in unitary states. The mark of success is not to eliminate regional differences or even tensions, but to contain the political effects of those differences so that the benefits of unity may be reaped. The key to this is to prevent the political or cultural domination of one region by another and this gives us a cue for considering more precisely what a workable Irish federation might look like.

An Irish Federation[1]

I assume without discussion that a federal Ireland would be a republic.

There would be two provinces. (Some — including, but not uniquely, Provisional Sinn Fein — have proposed a four-province system but I see no merit in that.) Each would have a parliament, which could be unicameral, and an executive branch which, given our common British traditions concerning the non-separation of powers, would probably be generated from within the legislature. Whether or not each province has a non-executive figure exercising Bagehot's 'ceremonial' functions is not important.

On top of this would be the federal government. There would be a parliament, which might appropriately be bicameral. The methods used to constitute this parliament are crucial to the whole system and I shall return to this point shortly. The federal executive would presumably be derived from this legislature.

There would be a president, with powers broadly similar to those of the President of Ireland at present. Again, the method of choosing him could be important. Finally, the governmental structure at both provincial and federal level would be completed by a judicial system.

The issues on which I wish to concentrate are:
(a) The division of powers between the provincial and federal governments.
(b) The structure of representation in federal institutions.

Provincial and federal powers

There is much to be said in the Irish context for the

approach used in the US and Germany, i.e., the constitution defining federal powers explicitly and provincial powers residually. Although nothing about the future can be certain (as witness the massive growth of federal activity in the US in the past fifty years), at least this would provide some kind of insurance for Northerners.

To save wasting time on the obvious, let us concentrate on a few issues which are peculiarly significant in the Irish context. In the first place I regard it as important that, initially anyway, each province retain a good deal of fiscal autonomy. Federal institutions could be financed either by federal taxes or by levies on the provincial governments, but provincial institutions should be supported provincially and not by grants from the federation. The case for leaving major fiscal powers with the provinces derives from two arguments.

First, in a fiscally unified Ireland with broadly progressive tax and social welfare systems, there would be automatic net transfers from richer to poorer regions. One might expect Leinster and most of Northern Ireland to suffer and Munster, Connacht and the border areas to benefit. I do not see how a change from a situation where Northern Ireland is a beneficiary of external transfers (I shall have more to say about this) to one where she is a net benefactor in such a process would be an attractive prospect for those suspicious of reunification. It is very important that Northerners should not feel that Southerners view their province as a potential milch-cow.

Secondly, there is the general democratic argument that powers should be withdrawn from lower-level jurisdictions only if a higher-level interest (i.e., in this case, the national interest) demands it. I see no clear reason why the national interest would demand interprovincial uniformity with respect to many instruments of economic and social policy. For example, although there would have to be federally determined minimum levels of public provision for things like education, health care, housing and social insurance benefits, it may be appropriate that, if a province wishes to impose, say, a tougher income tax to finance a higher level of public provision for these things, it should be permitted to do so.

There are two arguments against this. First, fiscal federalism notoriously creates problems for national macro-economic policy. So, for example, the Central Bank's role in relation to the external value of the currency would be made more difficult if the provincial governments had unrestricted powers to issue debt — and, in particular, to borrow abroad. An extreme position would be to grant the previously-mentioned fiscal autonomy, subject to the constraint that the provinces balance their budgets. An intermediate position would be to permit the provinces to borrow domestically but to restrict foreign borrowing powers to the federal government.

Secondly, there are activities which may be more efficiently performed at the federal than the provincial level. One example may be the governmental promotion of industrial development, exports and tourism. This also is something to which I shall return.

The other area in which the division of powers between the provinces and the federation seem to me of particular significance concerns matters where cultural and religious differences are important. To come up with specific proposals here would require the skills of a lawyer rather than an economist but what I have in mind are certain aspects of criminal law and certain aspects of social policy. Thus, for example, the argument I paraded at the beginning for a federal arrangement would come to nothing if the North were subject to the South's present law on contraception or if Northern public schools or hospitals had imposed upon them the same regulations and managerial structures as those currently prevailing in the South.

Again, the US — with its distinction between state and federal offences and with the large role played by state and local government in the public provision of social services — provides a model, not necessarily to be copied but to be learned from.

Representation in federal institutions

Even though one might hope that those issues which are likely to be culturally or religiously contentious would be left with the provinces, it is vital that federal institutions be designed to give as much protection as possible to minorities. The only perfect way of doing this is to require unanimity for federal decisions, i.e., to give each relevant group a veto. The trouble with this is that it makes effective decision-making difficult and that it pays inadequate attention to the rights of majorities.

A form of compromise is sometimes reached by having, say, a bi-cameral federal parliament with one house having representation according to population (there are innumerable ways of electing such a house) and the other having equal representation from each province or state (or more equal than population differences would imply). I should like to make the following points here.

First, whether one or both of the houses of the federal parliament is constructed by direct election or by representation from the provincial parliaments (as was the case in the European Parliament and is still so for the Bundesrat in Germany) is a detail I shall not pursue.

Secondly, it is important that the house constituted more equally than according to population should play an important part in the federal legislature. That is, it should be more like the US Senate than the British House of Lords or the present Irish Senate. Otherwise it may provide inadequate protection for the smaller province: it may be limited to publicising any grievances the smaller province may have regarding potential federal legislation and may be unable to influence that legislation. However, there is a problem here which is my third point.

If an Irish Senate, say, were constructed as and had the powers of the US Senate, *one* province would have a veto if its members acted in harmony. That is less of a problem in the US because there are fifty states and an effective blocking coalition by states representing a minority of the population is correspondingly difficult to form. With only two provinces, however, such a blocking group could be formed by a single province. How important this may be in practice depends on the likelihood of the representatives of any province acting in harmony. Also, it must not be forgotten that the whole purpose of a non-proportional structure is to allow, on occasion, minorities to frustrate the intentions of majorities. The optimal structure is something I shall have to leave to political scientists to discuss.

Other federal institutions such as the presidency and the

federal supreme court would similarly have to recognise a degree of equality between provinces with markedly unequal populations. Thus, as an illustration, the presidency might be elected by the provincial parliaments alternately and the supreme court composed of, say, two members from each provincial judiciary plus a fixed-term chairman alternately from each province.

All of this business about protecting minorities has to be qualified in two ways.

First, the differences in political and cultural identity which we wish to accommodate harmoniously are, in the Irish case, not perfectly reflected in provincial boundaries. That is, the minority we seek to protect is not the population of Northern Ireland but a sub-set of that population. Therefore, equality devices designed to protect the smaller province could not, even in principle, provide perfect protection for the relevant sub-set of that province.

Secondly, there is a conflict of objectives here. Institutions designed to recognise certain differences may encourage the perpetuation of these differences and hinder integration. Thus, institutions which permit minority obstructionism to be effective may provide too little incentive for co-operative attitudes: they can be said to enshrine constitutionally attitudes of 'we and they'.

This is a fair enough point in the abstract but I doubt whether, in the Irish case, it would outweigh the opposite considerations. In the first place, the over-riding requirement is to find institutions which would assuage the fears of unionists that their culture, in the broadest sense, would, through the political mechanisms of a united Ireland, be dominated and perhaps eventually obliterated. And secondly, cultural integration — or, worse, homogenisation — is not particularly desirable. It is integration in the sense of a feeling of a common nationality which is important and this could develop only in an institutional environment which gave Northerners confidence. As this emotional communality grows, Ireland may move towards a more unitary structure but until that happens the possibility of minority obstructionism is a small price to pay for the environment which gives the best prospects.

I have not mentioned problems at the provincial level, although these may be thought to be important — at least in the Northern province. First, it is to be hoped that, in a united Ireland, the major political differences between Protestants and Roman Catholics will disappear and that the problem of the perpetual minority (that is, the problem I have been dealing with at the federal level) will wither away. Secondly, any problems in this regard show up more clearly in the context of Northern Ireland as an autonomous state and therefore are better left to another contributor.

Economic Matters

A convenient distinction here is between what for want of better terminology I call the short and long term. The former is concerned with the fiscal implications for Northern Ireland of breaking the union with Britain and the consequential fiscal implications for the present Republic. The latter is concerned with the less precisely analysable processes of economic development and structural change.

Short term[2]

Over the past five years, annual subventions to Northern Ireland from the UK Exchequer have been at a level equalling 26 to 28 per cent of Northern Ireland's Gross Domestic Product. And this excludes military spending.

In the fiscal year 1979/80, the total was £956m., the components being a grant-in-aid of £590m. under the 1973 Northern Ireland Constitution Act, £245m. representing the cost of the Northern Ireland Office, £69m. transfer from the British National Insurance Fund, and various other bits and pieces. The total was approximately equal to total taxes paid by Northern Ireland residents: that is, if the public expenditure financed by this transfer had had to be covered locally without any increase in the current budget deficit, tax revenue in Northern Ireland would have had to be doubled.

If the link with Britain were broken and these transfers withdrawn, the effect upon Northern living standards would be dramatic. Assuming that the £245m. attributed to the Northern Ireland Office (i.e., that part of the cost of the civil administration of direct rule borne by Britain) would still have to be incurred as part of the cost of, say, a provincial administration in a federal Ireland, and assuming a multiplier of unity (which is probably about right, or even too high, given the extreme openness of the Northern Ireland economy), then the change would cause a decline in average living standards of somewhat over 20 per cent. It is doubtful, to say the least of it, whether any Northerner – unionist or nationalist – would find that a price worth paying for reunification.

So, what are the chances that the rest of Ireland could take over from Britain the responsibility for these transfers? To have accommodated an additional £956m. of public expenditure in 1979/80 without an increase in borrowing would have required the total tax revenue of the Dublin central government to have been nearly 50 per cent higher; or would have required income tax receipts to have increased by almost 125 per cent; or excise duty receipts by over 150 per cent; or VAT receipts by 325 per cent.

In case anyone thinks that this burden could be lightened in the short run by the Southern government borrowing what is needed, it should be noted that this would have doubled the Exchequer Borrowing Requirement in the 1979/80, giving the South a ratio of government borrowing to national income of around 27 per cent – or a total public sector borrowing ratio of over 30 per cent. Furthermore, it must be remembered that these transfers are a recurrent expense. The idea that they could be provided through borrowing is not realistic.

Whether Southerners would be prepared to accept such an enormous increase in their tax bill as the price for reunification is not for me to say. However, even if they did declare their willingness to bear this burden, Northerners would be wise to be sceptical. It is one thing to agree to pay a once-for-all bride-price: it is quite another to have to pay this recurrently, especially when the potential consort is already richer than you are.

Locally generated income (GDP) per head is about 20 per cent higher in Northern Ireland than in the Republic and the gap has not narrowed much in the past decade or so. In these circumstances, would Southerners agree to transfer around

12½ per cent of their income (or about 18 per cent of the income left after paying their present taxes) to keep Northerners in the state to which they have grown accustomed? It is unlikely: it appears even less likely if one considers the dynamic implications of such transfers.

Even if Southerners were so besotted with the vision of imminent reunification that they were prepared to mortgage their living standards to this degree, they would soon learn that the price is even higher than they thought. The 45 per cent increase in average Southern tax rates needed to provide these transfers is certain to have effects on Southern growth: there would be a large incentive for mobile skilled personnel to emigrate; there would be work disincentives for those who remained; capital would emigrate in search of higher post-tax returns; it would be more difficult to sell the Republic to international entrepreneurs; the price effects of higher indirect taxes would make Southern industry less competitive; and so on. The cost to the South would not simply be the value of the transfers themselves: it would also be the income which is not created because of these unfortunate effects of the higher taxes.

This scenario must sound rather depressing to anyone who both favours a united Ireland and recognises that Northerners cannot be asked to pay the price of withdrawal of British subvention (or, more realistically, knows that Northerners would not accept a united Ireland on those terms). The only ray of hope is the possibility that Britain would, as part of the settlement detaching Northern Ireland from the United Kingdom, be prepared to continue subventions — for a fair period of time — perhaps fifteen or twenty years.

This is not the fairy-tale it might sound at first. Northern Ireland costs Britain more than the subventions. Its army is at war, with all its material and personal costs; the Northern Ireland question, whilst not being currently as important in British politics as the Irish question was in Home Rule days, is at the very least an irritant to British politicians, distracting them from what to them seem more pressing issues; there is evidence that withdrawal from the North would be popular in Britain; and I genuinely believe that Britain would, for the sake of the Irish, be prepared to do a good deal to foster a peaceful future for Ireland. Other countries, notably the USA, may also be prepared to provide assistance in this context.

Furthermore, if reunification brings peace and a real prospect of lasting stability, it will have beneficial economic effects. The present troubles undoubtedly reduce earnings from tourism both North and South and, above all, make the task of industrial development appallingly difficult in the North. If reunification brings peace, and peace brings greater prosperity, the North's need for these subventions (and the extent to which she will feel deprived if they cease to exist) will decline and, to a degree, the ability of the South to provide some assistance will increase.

Perhaps I appear too sanguine about all this. No-one can avoid the fact that this is a vitally important problem which, if it is not solved, would make Irish reunification a non-starter in unionist eyes (and perhaps also in Northern nationalist eyes) quite independently of any political considerations. It seems difficult to see how it could be solved without a pretty generous helping of British goodwill and one can only hope that that will be forthcoming.

Quite frequently, discussions of the economics of Irish unity stop here. However, I should like to finish by reviewing very briefly some other issues — what I call the long term.

Long term

Because tariffs and other barriers to trade are no longer of much significance within this island, reunification *per se* is unlikely to have very noticeable effects on trade patterns, the degree of economic integration or the geographical distribution of economic activity. If unification and the establishment of a common currency took place tomorrow, there would be a devaluation of the Northern Ireland £ in relation to the present Irish £ and this may provide some stimulus for Northern exports to the South and have the opposite effect on trade in the other direction, but it is hard to believe that these effects would be significant.

In the longer term, particularly if industrial development policy operates on an all-Ireland basis, there may be some increase in the degree of economic integration between North and South. We know that, in 1978, Northern Ireland was the destination of 8½ per cent of the Republic's exports and the origin of 4½ per cent of its imports. If the Republic's trade with Britain is taken as a bench-mark, and remembering that Northern Ireland's GDP is only about 2 per cent of the United Kingdom's, that would suggest a non-random degree of integration, which is not surprising given the geographical contiguity of the two regions.

The Industrial Development Authority in Dublin is currently rather worried that new projects exhibit low linkages within Ireland. If there were an all-Ireland policy which stressed the desirability of linkages, then in the long run we might see a greater degree of economic association between North and South. Obviously specific 'cross-Border' development projects would contribute to this process.

This brings me to the other — and to my mind more important — possible long-term economic issue, and this is that unification would change the general policy environment in which the Northern Ireland economy operates.

At present, this economy has to operate under policies designed in London i.e., policies designed by a government whose first responsibility is for a mature, industrialised economy with for all recorded history a much lower level of unemployment and a more balanced economic structure than Northern Ireland. The North's structure and policy problems are much more like the Republic's than Britain's. Just four examples will serve to illustrate what I mean.

First, the overriding priority given to the reduction of inflation by the present British government has involved severe restraint in public expenditure and a high external value of the £ sterling. The punishment thereby inflicted on the level of economic activity in Britain has been magnified in Northern Ireland.

Secondly, the North's farmers are represented in Brussels by a government 97 per cent of whose electors are food-consumers rather than food-producers. In a united Ireland they would be represented by a government for whom food-producers (and, especially, small farmers) are electorally important. (One cannot escape the feeling, however, that by the time a united Ireland is achieved, the Common Agricultural Policy will simply be of antiquarian interest.)

Thirdly, if the United Kingdom government wishes to take account of the special economic problems of Northern Ireland, it usually has to do so within the constraints of UK regional policy. On the comparatively rare occasions when those constraints are broken — as for car plants in South Wales and West Belfast or shipyards in West Scotland and East Belfast — there is a hullaballoo.

Fourthly — and to generalise the previous point — industrial development is at the centre of the policy stage in Northern Ireland and the Republic, whereas it is more peripheral to the economic policy concerns of British governments. Industrial development is, in the policy sense, more of a *micro*-economic issue, whereas the dominant concern of British policy-formation is with *macro*-economic issues.

So, for example, development policy requires structural planning and considerable flexibility at the micro level; it involves giving industrialisation objectives a high priority in policies of taxation and public expenditure; and so on. Thus, it is worth noting that the Republic has, after twenty-five years of zero profits taxes on manufactured exports, this year reduced its profits tax rate to 10 per cent for *all* manufacturing activities. Can one imagine the British Treasury agreeing to that just because Northern Ireland needs to attract foreign industrialists?

These points can be made only qualitatively, whereas the short-term fiscal problems of a united Ireland can be quantified. However, it is difficult to believe that they are unimportant. Ireland being so small, there may be a case for making certain promotional activities in the industrial, tourism and exports areas a federal responsibility. But whether they are federal or provincial, Northern Ireland would have a much greater influence over such policies than she has now.

Conclusion

I do not consider economic issues to be of the essence of the problem of Irish reunification: if unity is accepted by the people of the North and by the government of the United Kingdom, I do not doubt that the short-term fiscal problems will be solved or that the longer-term potential economic advantages will be no more than the cherry on the cake. This is why I have spent more time on the politics than on the economics.

In this paper, I have tried to describe the political structures most likely to make reunification acceptable to unionists. However, I am very conscious that there is a prior, and much more difficult, problem to solve – that of getting unionists to contemplate reunification at all.

REFERENCES

1. Practically nothing has been published on possible political institutions for a united Ireland, though Fine Gael (1979) makes some reference to this question. This document is of broader interest in that it is the only recent, developed statement by an Irish political party on the issue of reunification.
2. Most of the figures in this section are derived from Hutchinson and Sheehan (1980). A wider and deeper comparison of the economics of Northern Ireland and the Republic can be found in Gibson and Spencer (1977).

BIBLIOGRAPHY

Fine Gael, *Ireland – Our Future Together*, Dublin 1979

Hutchinson, R. W. and Sheehan, J., *A Review of Selected Indicators of Economic Performance in Northern Ireland and the Republic of Ireland during the 1970s*, Co-Operation North, Belfast and Dublin 1980.

Gibson, N. J. and Spencer, J. E. (eds), *Economic Activity in Ireland*, Gill and Macmillan, Dublin 1977

PART III

MODELS OF POLITICAL CO-OPERATION

The six papers which make up Part III of this volume were commissioned to enable the reader to examine different models of political co-operation attempted elsewhere in the world.

6: CONSOCIATION: THE MODEL AND ITS APPLICATION IN DIVIDED SOCIETIES
AREND LIJPHART

Arend Lijphart tells us that consociational democracy is a type of government that is particularly suitable for a society that is deeply divided by religious, ideological, linguistic, regional, cultural, racial, or ethnic cleavages. It is characterised by four principles. The two primary principles are (a) power-sharing or grand coalition government and (b) a high degree of autonomy for the segments into which the society is divided. Power-sharing and segmental autonomy complement each other: on all issues of common concern, the decisions should be made jointly by the segments; on all other issues, decision-making should be left to each segment. The two secondary principles are (c) proportionality as the basic standard of political representation, civil service appointments, and allocation of public funds and (d) the veto power, which a minority may use in order to protect its vital interests. In all four respects, the consociational model differs sharply from the majoritarian (Westminster) model: the essence of the latter is the concentration of power in the hands of the majority. Instead of concentrating power, the consociational model's basic approach is to share, diffuse, separate, divide, decentralise and limit power.

Arend Lijphart points out that the consociational model is not just a theoretical concept: there are twelve countries which have been consociations during part of their recent political histories. (Moreover, at the regional and local level many additional examples of consociational democracy can be found.)

Lijphart accepts that in a few cases civil strife has erupted but points out that the failure of a few consociations merely shows that the application of consociationalism is not a sufficient condition for the success of democracy in divided societies. It is his main contention based upon the empirical evidence that consociational democracy can work well.

What is the relationship between the consociational model and the other models of political co-operation that have been proposed for divided societies and for the divided international system, such as federation, confederation, international organisation, and supranational organisation? He argues that consociation is the most general model and that the other models are not alternatives to consociation but are subsumed to a large extent under the consociational model.

The consociational model presents, Lijphart tells us, a sharp contrast to the majoritarian (Westminster) model: there is no single consociational blueprint and as the twelve examples show, the consociational principles can be implemented in an almost infinite number of ways. In order to bring some order to this multiplicity of possibilities he suggests, using the empirical evidence, answers to the following questions: (a) Should the different consociational rules be laid down in formal documents? (b) Should the segments be defined explicitly or should neutral terms be used? (c) How extensive should the rights and powers of the minorities be? (d) Should a parliamentary or presidential system be adopted? (e) Should segmental autonomy be implemented on a territorial or non-territorial basis?

Lijphart concludes by identifying a number of background conditions that are conducive to consociational democracy but tells us that these are only favourable factors, not necessary conditions. He argues that a consociational solution should be attempted even when the conditions for it do not appear to be promising.

7: FEDERAL AND PARTLY FEDERAL SYSTEMS, INSTITUTIONS AND CONFLICT MANAGEMENT: SOME WESTERN EUROPEAN EXAMPLES
A.-P. FROGNIER

After considering the differences between confederal, federal and unitary states, A.-P. Frognier essentially focusses on the problems of some Western European federal and 'partly federal' states, i.e., states with some federalist features accorded to all or some of their components. His paper then divides into two parts.

In his first part, which is largely institutional, Frognier describes and compares the following institutions of these federal and partly federal states: bi-cameration, the respective powers of national chambers, the national executive, the share of legislative competence between power levels, the specific administrative means of implementation of laws, the allocation of fiscal responsibilities, the specific legislative bodies of components, the judicial organisation; and finally the indestructible character of the 'political whole'.

In the second part of his paper Frognier turns his attention to the conflict management capabilities of these institutional arrangements. He does so by first analysing the specific effects of federal and partly federal regimes with respect to two essential aspects, the autonomist (or self-rule) aspect and the co-operation aspect (the federal/central level) respectively; and by secondly examining some specifics in their socio-political environment. The latter includes an analysis of 'personal' federalism in the context of a discussion of the relations between federalism and consociational democracy and of balance of power problems respectively, with special attention to systems, such as that in Belgium, which are in transition.

8: FEDERATION AND CONFEDERATION: THE EXPERIENCE OF THE UNITED STATES AND THE BRITISH COMMONWEALTH
MAURICE J. C. VILE

The object of Maurice J. C. Vile's paper is to examine the experiences of the working of federalism in the United States and in certain countries of the British Commonwealth in order to assess those factors which seem to have been significant in the success or failure of the federal structure in dealing with the economic and social diversities which characterise those societies. He does not attempt an exhaustive treatment of the experiments in federalism which have been made, but rather he tries to draw out those points which seem most relevant to an assessment of the proposals which have been made recently for a 'federal solution' to the Irish problem. Finally, he ventures an opinion of what seems to him to be a way forward in the present circumstances.

Vile begins by clarifying certain points about the nature of federalism, of how federations differ from confederations and from unitary states. He points out that confederations tend to be transient, unstable arrangements (and that we should not be misled by the way in which the term confederation is sometimes used to describe political systems which are essentially federal). Federal systems, he tells us, involve a division of governmental powers and an effective representative authority at both levels of government. Confederations usually concern themselves with such matters as defence and foreign affairs, but federal governments, in addition, become involved in internal policy questions such as law and order, the regulation of trade, commerce and industry etc. During this process of clarification he surveys the main features of the development of federalism in Australia and Canada, with reference also the problems of federalism in Nigeria and India; he also makes reference to 'failed' federations, that is those federal experiments in the Commonwealth which were unable to provide a satisfactory institutional framework for a viable state.

Vile then poses the question: 'What are the factors which have enabled certain federations to succeed where others have failed?' and suggests, based upon the empirical evidence, the presence of the following features: (a) fewer diversities; (b) the relative lack of communalism; (c) a reasonably large number of units; (d) no single member state in such a dominant position that it can dictate the policies of the federal government; (e) the absence of (b) but the presence of (c) and (d); (f) the boundaries of member states are drawn so as *not* to coincide with communal division; (g), and perhaps most importantly, the development of a party system which will provide those political linkages across the boundaries of the member states, without which the process of bargaining and compromise essential to federal politics cannot take place.

Referring to a number of proposals recently put forward for a federal solution to the Irish problem Vile concludes on the basis of the above analysis that it is difficult to take any comfort in Fine Gael's proposal for a two-unit federation (see J. A. Bristow's paper, pp. 144 ff.). It is his conclusion that federalism does not offer a short-term solution to the Irish problem and indeed that there are almost certainly no short-term solutions. He does, however, look to the general nature of the problem and isolates the basic elements in the situation in order, as he says, to talk sensibly about short-term situations.

9: THE SOVEREIGNTY OF PARLIAMENT AND THE IRISH QUESTION
BERNARD CRICK

Bernard Crick argues that the student of politics must start from these two incompatabilities: that Northern Ireland is part of the United Kingdom and also of the island of Ireland. He suggests that the apparent contradiction of the two extreme viewpoints – the unity of Ireland or the unity of the present United Kingdom – only involves a total incompatability on a traditional, but now very suspect and self-deluding view of the sovereign state. He believes that the theory that every state must be sovereign and possess absolute power is as suspect as the theory that every nation must be a state. He suggests that British constitutional history needs re-interpreting to show that the doctrine of and belief in 'parliamentary sovereignty' has been a response to peculiar political conditions, hinted at in the very formula United Kingdom, rather than a necessity of law and order. He argues that the 'united' kingdom, though it has pretended to be a sovereign, centralised state, has had in practice to allow a kind of informal federalism. If the sovereignty of parliament can be seen as a useful myth, helpful at times but dangerous if accepted as a general truth about minimal conditions of political order, both sides might begin to be impressed, he suggests, by the overlapping edges rather than the solitary extremities of their boxed-in positions.

For Crick toleration and reconciliation involve mutual respect for, and recognition of, differences and indeed make it possible to govern without consensus and amid a diversity of values. 'Consensus' for him is best reserved to point to the need for agreement about means, not about ends, about procedures, not about their results.

It is Crick's contention that talk of immediate solutions is fatuous but the possibilities of containing the worst symptoms exist. Acceptable frameworks might be established in which future changes could at least be accepted as fair. Talk, he tells us, should begin about whether new forms of government or of inter-governmental relations could not emerge to reflect the fact (not change the fact) that Northern Ireland faces two ways.

There might be, he tells us, something to be said for examining (a) how federal a state the United Kingdom is already; and (b) whether *de jure* institutionalisation of *de facto* practices might not be advantageous.

10: THE THEORY OF POLITICAL INTEGRATION
EMIL J. KIRCHNER

Emil J. Kirchner, having defined 'political integration', goes on to discuss the four main approaches which he tells us have dominated political integration theory since the early 1950s: the federalist, the functionalist, the transactionalist, and the neo-functionalist. He points out that in the late 1960s and early 1970s attempts were made to redefine and reformulate integration theory in general and the neo-functionalist explanation in particular.

He contends that each of the four main approaches advanced in the study of integration contributes to practical explanation of the phenomena of Western European states over the past thirty years, facilitated through such organisations as the European Communities, but none provides a satisfactory conceptual framework for the analysis of the European experience.

One aim of his paper is to show, by way of a progress report on European Community integration, effective or possible impacts on the reconciliation of the Irish problem. Perhaps there is a pointer in his conclusion that the pace of integration in Europe has been (and will be for some time) determined by the ratio between the increase in the benefits to the member states and the loss of political power on national sovereignty this involves.

11: THE NORDIC MODEL OF NEIGHBOURLY CO-OPERATION
BENGT SUNDELIUS

Bengt Sundelius points out that in historical perspective Nordic relations have been characterised as much by conflict and rivalry as by peaceful co-existence and co-operation. He describes the period between 1800 and the end of the Second World War as an era of Nordic political disintegration, as the two traditional entities in the region — Denmark/Norway/ Iceland and Sweden/Finland — were split apart into five separate nation states (which states are now referred to as belonging to the Nordic region). This development took place on the constitutional level and with the rise of nationalism. However, since 1814 the region has, despite serious conflicts, avoided internal military conflict due to, he points out, the fear of Great Power intervention. It was, he believes, the separate decisions in favour of compromise solutions between the neighbouring countries which established the tradition of regional peaceful relations. Since the Second World War Nordic relations have been characterised, he tells us, by a gradual but steady increase in inter-governmental co-operation. This co-operation has, it appears, two features: first, while the major proposals for increased co-operation failed, much of the substance of these proposals has been achieved through incremental developments; secondly, the driving force for Nordic co-operation today is perhaps not so much a desire to unite the region as a wish to keep it intact.

Sundelius accepts that the fundamental motive of Nordic co-operation is defensive. However, he identifies other 'internal' motives. First, the geographical proximity of the nations generates a number of common problems — transportation, migration, pollution, and social and judicial services — which in terms of domestic objectives cannot be attained without joint efforts. Secondly, co-operation is a useful mechanism to overcome limited national resources in the areas of education, science, energy, communications, regional and industrial development. Thirdly, co-operation enables the countries to at least avoid undesirable alternatives where one common policy posture — be it economic, foreign or judicial policy — cannot be found.

For Sundelius integration is thought of as a process that reaches across the various national entities rather than one that links them with a higher, centralised regional level of activity. He identifies and defines three conceptual types of integration (societal, attitudinal and political integration) and seven operational dimensions. He uses this 'framework' to identify the dynamics and to trace the developments of Nordic integration.

The sources of Nordic co-operation can, he argues, be found in the cultural heritage, social and political structures and in the prevalent values and norms of the countries concerned. Among the latter he identifies in particular consensus formation, compromise and (exhaustive if slow) fact-finding.

He accepts that these background conditions may be unique to the Nordic region and agrees that it is an open question as to what extent the Nordic model for neighbourhood co-operation can be applied to other regions.

6

Consociation:
The Model and its Applications in Divided Societies[1]

Arend Lijphart

The Consociational Model

It is widely — and correctly — assumed that it is difficult to maintain a democratic regime and domestic peace in a society that is deeply divided by religious, ideological, linguistic, regional, cultural, racial, or ethnic divisions. Consociation is a model of political co-operation which is more likely to achieve both democracy and peaceful co-existence in divided societies than the alternative models, in particular the majoritarian or Westminster model of democracy.

The consociational model is characterised by four principles. The two most important principles are grand coalition government or power-sharing and a high degree of autonomy for the different groups into which the society is divided. (These groups will henceforth be referred to as the *segments* of the divided society.) Two secondary principles are the minority veto and proportionality.

First, a grand coalition or power-sharing government is an executive in which the political leaders of all significant segments participate. Power-sharing may take various institutional forms. The most straightforward form is that of a grand coalition cabinet in a parliamentary system. In presidential systems, power-sharing may be accomplished by distributing the presidency and other high offices among the different segments. These power-sharing arrangements may be strengthened by broadly constituted councils or committees with important co-ordinating and advisory functions.

Secondly, consociational democracy delegates as much decision-making as possible to the separate segments. This segmental autonomy complements the grand coalition principle: on all issues of common interest, the decisions should be made jointly by the segments; on all other issues, decision-making should be left to each segment. A special form of segmental autonomy that is particularly suitable for divided societies with geographically concentrated segments is federalism. If the segments are geographically interspersed, segmental autonomy will have to take a mainly non-territorial form.

Thirdly, proportionality is the basic standard of political representation, civil service appointments, and allocation of public funds. The great advantage of the proportionality rule is that it is widely recognised as an eminently fair standard of distribution. Moreover, it facilitates the decision-making process because it is a ready-made method which makes it unnecessary to spend time on the consideration of other methods of distribution. As a principle of political representation, proportionality is especially important as a guarantee for the fair representation of minority segments. There are two extensions of the proportionality rule that entail even greater minority protection: the over-representation of small segments and parity of representation. Parity is attained when the minority or minorities are over-represented to such an extent that they reach a level of equality with the majority or the largest group. Minority over-representation and parity are especially useful alternatives to proportionality when a divided society consists of groups of highly unequal size. In federal states, these two principles are often applied to the composition of the upper house.

Fourthly, the minority veto is the ultimate weapon that minorities need to protect their vital interests. Even when a minority segment participates in a power-shring executive, it may be overruled or outvoted by the majority. This may not present a problem when only minor issues are being decided, but when a minority's vital interests are at stake, the veto provides essential protection. The minority veto is synonymous with John C. Calhoun's 'concurrent majority' principle: that is, for a proposal to be adopted, it needs not only an overall majority in favour of it, but also a concurrent majority in each segment. In Calhoun's words, the veto gives each segment

the power of protecting itself, and places the rights and

safety of each where only they can be securely placed, under its own guardianship. Without this there can be no systematic, peaceful, or effective resistance to the natural tendency of each to come into conflict with the others.[2]

Consociation Versus Majoritarianism

The four principles of consociational democracy can be clarified further by contrasting them with the characteristics of majoritarian democracy, exemplified most clearly by the Westminster model. The essence of the Westminster model is the concentration of political power in the hands of the majority. Instead of *concentrating* power, the consociational model's basic approach is to *share, diffuse, separate, divide, decentralise, and limit* power.

Grand coalition or power-sharing stands in sharp contrast with the concentration of power in a one-party, bare-majority, non-coalition cabinet which is typical of the Westminster model. In the Westminster model, the cabinet is composed of members of the majority party — which, in a divided society, is likely to be the party representing the majority segment — and the minority is completely excluded. In parliament, there is a confrontation between government and opposition, but the government has majority support and can get its proposals enacted even against strenuous objections by the minority. Instead of this majoritarian government versus opposition pattern, the consociational model prescribes shared, joint, and consensual decision-making.

In the Westminster model, the system of government is unitary and centralised; there are no restricted geographical or functional areas from which the parliamentary majority is barred. Instead of centralised government, the consociational model prescribes the decentralisation of power to regional and local governments and/or to non-territorial groups. In contrast to the unitary and centralised characteristics of the majoritarian model, segmental autonomy entails minority rule over the minority itself in a specified area — either a geographical or functional area — that is the minority segment's exclusive concern.

The basic electoral rule of the Westminster model is the winner-take-all principle; in the single-member district plurality or 'first past the post' system, the candidate with the majority vote (or, if there is no majority, with the largest minority vote) wins, and all other candidates are excluded. The consociational principle of proportionality abolishes this sharp distinction between winners and losers: both majorities and minorities can be 'winners' in the sense of being able to elect their candidates to office in proportion to each group's relative electoral support. In practice, the effect of the plurality method of election is to exaggerate the representation and power of the majority. It may be called '*dis*proportional representation' in favour of the majority. Proportional representation treats majorities and minorities equally, and does not discriminate against either small or large parties. The two extensions of the proportionality principle discussed above — minority over-representation and parity — are also methods of *dis*proportional representation, but here the disproportionality is not in favour of the majority, as in the Westminster model, but in favour of minorities and small groups.

Finally, a typical feature of the Westminster model is an 'unwritten' constitution which can be amended by a normal majority vote. This means that the majority has the right to change even the most fundamental rules of government — a right without restrictions except morality and common sense. The minority veto of the consociational model limits the power of the majority to disregard the interests and preferences of the minority when constitutional or other vitally important issues are at stake.

Examples of Consociational Democracy

The consociational model described in terms of the above four characteristics is not just a theoretical concept. There are several empirical examples of consociational democracy in various parts of the world. In Europe, the examples are Austria during the period of Catholic-Socialist power-sharing cabinets from 1945 to 1966; Belgium since the First World War and, as far as its linguistic division is concerned, especially since 1970; the Netherlands from 1917 to 1967; Luxembourg during roughly the same fifty-year period; and Switzerland from 1943 on. Empirical cases of consociational democracy in the Third World are Lebanon from 1943 to 1975, Malaysia in the 1955—69 period, Cyprus during the few years from its independence in 1960 until 1963, Surinam from 1958 to 1973, and the Netherlands Antilles since 1950. In addition, there are two cases of what may be called 'semi-consociational' democracy: Israel since its independence in 1948 and Canada — both the contemporary Canadian system and, even more clearly, the pre-democratic United Province of Canada from 1840 to 1867. These two countries have been characterised by a number of consociational features, but they cannot be regarded as fully consociational.

Most of the above twelve examples are sovereign states, but the consociational model can be applied both at the national level and at the subnational level. In fact, two of the examples do not fit the category of fully independent countries: the Netherlands Antilles and Surinam. The Netherlands Antilles are an autonomous part of the Kingdom of the Netherlands. Surinam became independent in 1975, but during its consociational period it still had the same autonomous status as the Netherlands Antilles.

Moreover, at the regional and local level many additional examples of consociational democracy can be found. For instance, most of the cantons in Switzerland have power-sharing executives like the Swiss federal executive. Power-sharing has also been the rule at the level of the *Länder* in federal Austria since the early days of the First Republic — that is, both preceding the 1945—66 Socialist-Catholic grand coalition and outlasting it. In the Netherlands, most of the municipal executives have traditionally been *afspiegelings-colleges:* collegial executives whose party composition mirrors that of the municipal councils electing them.

The empirical cases of consociationalism have a twofold importance. First, they show the various institutional forms and practices that can be used to implement the four basic elements of the consociational model. This aspect will be discussed at greater length below. Secondly, they show that consociational democracy can really work. At this point, it is important to rebut the opposite argument — that the consociational model should not be taken seriously because several consociations have not proved to be lasting solutions or have clearly failed. This is a specious argument, and it is also insidious and debilitating because its practical effect is to divert attention from promising solutions to the problems of a divided society.

It should be pointed out, first of all, that at most three of the twelve cases of consociational democracy can be regarded as clear failures: Cyprus, Lebanon, and Surinam. The attempt at consociational engineering in Cyprus ended in civil war; in Lebanon, it is still too early to conclude that the consociational system has ended, but it has clearly been interrupted by the civil war that broke out in 1975; and democracy in Surinam was upset by a military coup in 1980. The failure of a few consociations does not prove that the consociational model is unworkable. It merely shows that the application of consociationalism is not a *sufficient* condition for the success of democracy in divided societies.

Secondly, the termination of consociationalism must not be equated with its failure. Austria, for example, shifted from power-sharing cabinets to one-party majority cabinets in 1966, but this was not because consociational co-operation had failed but because it had been so successful in alleviating the tensions between the religious-ideological segments that further consociational measures had become superfluous. The same conclusion applies to the more gradual shift away from consociationalism in the Netherlands.

Thirdly, one of the cases of 'failure' — Surinam — represents the failure of majoritarian democracy rather than the failure of consociational democracy. The power-sharing cabinets composed of Creoles and East Indians, the two largest ethnic segments in Surinam, were unwisely and prematurely abandoned in 1973. The 1980 coup toppled a democratic government from which the East Indian segment had been systematically excluded for many years.

Fourthly, in the cases of Cyprus and Lebanon it is important to inquire *why* the consociational regimes broke down. It is true that the Lebanese power-sharing government was unable to prevent the outbreak of the civil war in 1975. But it should be realised that this civil war can be attributed largely to the intrusion of external forces: the substantial Palestinian involvement in Lebanese politics and Syrian intervention.

Fifthly, a number of internal weaknesses must share part of the blame for the consociational failure in Lebanon and also in Cyprus. One of Lebanon's problems is the inflexible institutionalisation of several consociational devices, in particular the legislative representation ratio of six Christians to five Moslems — which fails to reflect the changing relative sizes of the two groups. The Christians were the majority at the time of the National Pact of 1943, but the present majority is Moslem. A basic flaw in the Cypriot constitution of 1960 was the wide scope and inflexibility of the minority veto. These weaknesses represent failures of particular applications of consociational rules, and the only reasonable conclusion that is warranted is that these weaknesses should be, or should have been, remedied — not that the entire consociational enterprise deserves to be condemned.

Finally, if one believes that consociationalism is not a suitable solution for countries like Lebanon and Cyprus, one must be prepared to propose an alternative solution. One reasonable, but drastic and extremely painful, alternative is partition. The other major alternative is majoritarian democracy. It is utterly inconceivable, however, that the Westminster model would work in such deeply divided societies — or that anyone in his right mind would even propose it.

Consociation and Other Models of Political Co-operation

What is the relationship between the consociational model and the other models of political co-operation that have been proposed for divided societies and for the divided international system, such as federation, confederation, international organisation, and supranational organisation? It can be argued that consociation is the most general model and that the other models are not alternatives to consociation but are subsumed to a large extent under the consociational model.

Federalism is a possible solution for divided societies only to the extent that it entails a high degree of consociationalism. Federations must therefore fulfil three further conditions.[3] First, the autonomy that is given to the states (or cantons, provinces and *Länder*) in a federal system must be a method for letting the segments run their own affairs as much as possible. The boundaries between the states of the federation should coincide closely with the segmental boundaries. To put it somewhat differently, the federal boundaries should be drawn in such a way as to create states that are quite homogeneous, or at the very least considerably more homogeneous than the country as a whole. In Canada and Switzerland, this condition is largely fulfilled. Most of the Canadian provinces and most of the Swiss cantons are linguistically much more homogeneous and less divided than the Canadian and Swiss federations taken as a whole.

The second condition is that the federation should be decentralised. The reason is that segmental autonomy can be instituted by means of federalism only if the segments tend to be concentrated in separate states (the first condition, described above) *and* if these states can in fact make political decisions on many important questions. Again, both in Canada and in Switzerland, provincial and cantonal autonomy is strong.

Thirdly, the segmental autonomy that a federal system may provide must be supplemented by the other primary characteristic of the consociational model: power-sharing. (And it is helpful if the two secondary consociational elements are also present to some extent.) There are no formal rules mandating power-sharing in Canada and Switzerland, but Canadian cabinets usually include Anglophones and Francophones roughly proportionally to the sizes of these two segments in the population; the Swiss federal executive is a seven-member grand coalition in which the country's main linguistic, religious, and political divisions are faithfully reflected.

In models of political co-operation among sovereign states — international organisation, supranational organisation, and confederal arrangements — the four consociational principles are usually readily apparent. The sovereign member-states of such organisations are the equivalents of the segments in a consociational democracy. Let us take the supranational European Community as an example. Its two executive bodies, the Council of Ministers and the Commission, are grand coalitions in which all of the member-states are represented. In the Council of Ministers, there is parity of representation; in the Commission, the smaller states are over-represented. Although extremely important decisions are made by the Community organs, the member-states have retained a great deal of autonomy; in fact, they are still basically sovereign states. Most of the members of the European Parliament are elected by proportional representation, but here the smaller states are also over-represented. The European Community is a supranational organisation, and this means that the members do not have an absolute and unlimited veto power. However, on the most fundamental questions, unanimity is required — giving each member a veto.

Finally, it should be pointed out that the consociational model is also relevant in cases of partition or secession that entail population resettlements. If, for a particular divided society, the conclusion can be reached that the establishment of a consociational democracy is impossible, the next step may be to partition the society in such a way that the principal segments are transformed into sovereign states. Unless the segments are highly concentrated territorially, the process of creating new homogeneous states will require some population transfers. In order to effect such a process peacefully and with the consent of the people involved, it will have to be conducted by means of continual consensual consultation.

Basic Options in Consociational Engineering

The consociational model and the majoritarian (Westminster) model differ not only in a number of crucial substantive respects, but also in the number of ways in which their basic principles can be implemented. The Westminster model does not allow much variation. It prescribes the concentration of executive power in a one-party, bare-majority cabinet, a parliamentary system in which the cabinet is dominant vis-à-vis parliament, a unicameral parliament (or a bicameral parliament with a weak second chamber), a single-member district plurality system of election, a two-party system, a unitary and centralised government, and a written or unwritten constitution that can be amended by regular majority vote. The two major empirical examples that closely approximate these features of the Westminster model are the United Kingdom and New Zealand.

The consociational model presents a sharp contrast: there is no single consociational blueprint, and the consociational principles can be implemented in an almost infinite number of ways. In order to bring some order to this multiplicity of possibilities, let us examine the major options.

1. Formal vs informal rules The first choice that has to be made is between laying down the different consociational principle in formal documents and relying on merely informal and unwritten agreements and understandings among the leaders of the segments. The most usual and logical way to formally stipulate consociational rules is to write them into the constitution, but they may also be stipulated in other basic laws, such as electoral laws, or in formal agreements between political parties, such as the 'coalition pacts' between the Austrian Socialist and Catholic parties. As Table 1 shows, informal agreements have been somewhat more common in the twelve empirical examples of consociational democracy than formal rules (with the exception of the rules prescribing proportionality in the electoral system). However, formal rules should probably be recommended for those cases —

TABLE 1

Basic Options in Consociational Engineering:
Formal vs. Informal Rules

Variable / Country	Power-Sharing	Segmental Autonomy	Prop. in El. System	Prop. in Civ. Serv.	Minority Veto
Austria	Formal	Inf.	Formal	Formal	Formal
Belgium	Formal	Formal	Formal	Inf.	Formal
Canada	Inf.	Formal	Inf.	Formal	Inf.
Cyprus	Formal	Formal	Formal	Formal	Formal
Israel	Inf.	Inf.	Formal	Inf.	Inf.
Lebanon	Formal	Inf.	Formal	Formal	Inf.
Luxembourg	Inf.	Inf.	Formal	Inf.	Inf.
Malaysia	Inf.	Inf.	Inf.	Formal	Inf.
Netherlands	Inf.	Inf.	Formal	Inf.	Inf.
Neth. Antilles	Inf.	Formal	Formal	Inf.	Inf.
Surinam	Inf.	Inf.	Formal	Inf.	Inf.
Switzerland	Inf.	Formal	Formal	Inf.	Inf.

such as Northern Ireland – in which it appears to be difficult to establish a consociation and where there is a high degree of distrust between the segments and between the segmental leaders. The examples of Belgium and Cyprus, in which both the primary and secondary principles of consociational democracy are constitutionally prescribed, and, to a lesser extent, the Austrian and Lebanese examples are therefore of special interest when we try to think of possible solutions for difficult cases like Northern Ireland.

Let us take a look at the major examples of constitutionally prescribed power-sharing. After its amendment in late 1970, the Belgian constitution states that the cabinet has to be composed of equal numbers of Dutch-speakers and French-speakers. The 1960 constitution of Cyprus provided for a presidential regime with a Greek president elected by the Greek community and a Turkish vice-president elected by the Turkish community. This power-sharing arrangement was completed by the provision that the cabinet had to consist of seven Greek ministers designated by the president and three Turkish ministers designated by the vice-president. The Lebanese National Pact of 1943 prescribed that the president be a Maronite Christian, the prime minister a Sunni Moslem, the chairman of the legislature a Shiite Moslem, and the deputy prime minister as well as the deputy chairman of the legislature Greek Orthodox Christians. The numerical strength of the different Lebanese sects was reflected in the relative importance of these offices. A proportionally constituted cabinet was also part of this power-sharing executive.

Segmental autonomy may be merely an unwritten tradition to delegate certain decisions to the separate segments, or there may be a precise constitutional stipulation for such a delegation of decision-making power. As we shall see in more detail later, segmental autonomy may be instituted on a territorial (federal) and/or on a non-territorial basis.

As Table 1 shows, proportional election outcomes are usually the result of constitutional or legal rules that mandate or facilitate proportionality. The usual electoral system that is prescribed is proportional representation – usually the list system of PR but, of course, the single transferable vote is a method that serves the same purpose. In Cyprus and Lebanon, the plurality rule in multi-member districts was used, but with special provisions aimed at obtaining proportional results. In Cyprus, there were separate voter registers for Greek and Turkish voters, who separately elected their own representatives. Proportionality is achieved in Lebanon by forcing each voter to cast his votes for candidates belonging to different sects in proportion to the sectarian composition of each electoral district. In spite of the single-member district plurality system used in Canada and Malaysia, the elections yield roughly proportional outcomes as a result of the geographical concentration of French-speaking and English-speaking voters in Canada and as a result of bargaining among the Malay, Chinese, and Indian partners in the dominant Alliance Party of Malaysia.

As far as proportionality in the civil service, police, and armed forces is concerned, formal rules are much less common. Formal requirements are sometimes designed to over-represent minorities, as in Cyprus where the 1960 constitution set a seven-to-three ratio for the civil service and a six-to-four ratio for the army and the police although the population ratio of Greeks to Turks was eight to two, or to correct the under-representation of certain segments, as in Malaysia and Canada.

The veto power must be regarded as a kind of emergency brake, and the great danger is that it will be used too frequently, causing governmental deadlock and immobilism. The Cyprus constitution gave both the Greek president and the Turkish vice-president an absolute veto power over decisions by the cabinet or legislature in the fields of foreign affairs, defence and security. And all legislative decisions on taxes, the municipalities and the electoral system could be reached only by concurrent majorities among both the thirty-five Greek and the fifteen Turkish members of parliament. The overuse of the veto by the Turkish legislators on tax bills was a major reason for the failure of the Cypriot consociation in 1963. This is one good argument for not introducing the veto in the form of an absolute constitutional right.

Nevertheless, even a firmly anchored veto power may

work well, and it does have certain advantages when a new consociational democracy is being engineered. In Belgium, the linguistic segments are given a formal veto power by the constitutional provision that laws affecting the cultural and educational interests of the linguistic segments can be passed only if majorities of both the Dutch-speaking and French-speaking legislators express their approval. In Austria, the most important decisions were made by a small 'coalition committee', or super-cabinet, on which Catholic and Socialist leaders were equally represented and which followed the rule of unanimity.

2. *Explicit specification of the segments vs. neutral terminology* If we opt for formal constitutional-legal stipulation of consociational arrangements, the next question that must be resolved is whether to define the segments in explicit terms or to use neutral terms that apply to any segment or group. Our empirical cases tend to favour the clear and explicit specification of the segments that are given consociational rights and powers: Dutch-speakers and French-speakers in Belgium, Greeks and Turks in Cyprus, and Maronites, Sunnis, Shiites, and several other religious sects in Lebanon. Participation in the power-sharing executives in these countries is defined in terms of membership in these constitutionally recognised segments. The major exception is federalism: it gives autonomy to groups of people defined in terms of geographical areas instead of segmented affiliation.

It is logically possible, however, to establish executive power-sharing without formal recognition of the segments in the constitution. For instance, the Progressive Federal Party's proposals for a democratic constitution for South Africa include the election of a lower house (Federal Assembly) by proportional representation. In the deeply divided South African society, PR will encourage the development of segmental, ethnic parties. The Progressive Federal Party proposes the following rules for the formation of the cabinet (Federal Executive Council):

> The Federal Assembly will elect a Prime Minister, who will be the Chairman of the Federal Executive Council, and can express its lack of confidence in the Prime Minister by electing someone to replace him . . . The Prime Minister

will appoint members to the Executive Council proportional to the strength of the various political parties in the Federal Assembly. In doing so the Prime Minister will have to negotiate with the leaders of the relevant parties.[4]

Power-sharing is here defined in terms of political parties. Indirectly and implicitly, this also entails segmental power-sharing.

A similar proposal has been made by the Nobel Prize-winning economist Sir Arthur Lewis for the divided societies of West Africa:

> One can alter the constitutional rules for forming a government: for example, instead of the President sending for the leader of the largest party to form a Cabinet, the rule may tell him to send for the leader of every party which has received more than 20 per cent of the votes, and divide the Cabinet seats between them, or such of them as will co-operate. Law is not without moral influence; it sets a standard for both the public and the politicians . . . So to write the coalition idea into the rules for forming a government in place of the present government versus opposition idea would itself be quite a step forward.[5]

An even simpler method to ensure executive power-sharing is found in the constitutions of all of the Austrian *Länder* with the exception of Vorarlberg. The *Land* legislatures are popularly elected by proportional representation. These legislatures in turn elect the *Land* executives by proportional representation.

3. The scope of minority rights and powers The third set of questions that must be answered is how extensive the powers, rights and protective devices for minorities should be. For instance, should minorities participate proportionally in power-sharing executives or should they be over-represented? As Table 2 indicates, proportionality is the more common arrangement. Examples of over-representation are the Cypriot cabinet in which the Turks held three out of ten ministerial posts, although their purely proportional share would have been two ministers, and the Belgian cabinet in which the French-speaking minority is equally represented with the Dutch-speaking majority.

TABLE 2

Basic Options in Consociational Engineering:
Cabinet vs. Presidential Government, Federal vs.
Non-Territorial Autonomy, and Proportionality vs.
Minority Over-representation

Country \ Basic Options	Power-Sharing: Cab./Pres.	Segmental Autonomy: Fed./Non-Terr.	Min. Rep. in Legisl.: Prop./Over.	Min. Rep. in Exec.: Prop./Over.
Austria	Cab.	Non-Terr.	Prop.	Over.
Belgium	Cab.	Both	Prop.	Over.
Canada	Cab.	Fed.	Prop.	Prop.
Cyprus	Pres.	Non-Terr.	Over.	Over.
Israel	Cab.	Non-Terr.	Prop.	Prop.
Lebanon	Pres.	Non-Terr.	Prop.	Prop.
Luxembourg	Cab.	Non-Terr.	Prop.	Prop.
Malaysia	Cab.	Non-Terr.	Prop.	Prop.
Netherlands	Cab.	Non-Terr.	Prop.	Prop.
Neth. Antilles	Cab.	Semi-Fed.	Over.	Over.
Surinam	Cab.	Non-Terr.	Prop.	Prop.
Switzerland	Cab.	Fed.	Prop.	Prop.

The electoral system may also give minorities more than proportional advantages. Here again Cyprus provides an example: the Turks had the same 30 per cent representation in the legislature as in the cabinet. In the legislature of the Netherlands Antilles, Curaçao is under-represented and all the other smaller islands are over-represented.

The implementation of the segmental autonomy principle entails many difficult decisions: how many and which powers should the central government have and how many and which powers should be delegated to the segments?

As far as the minority veto is concerned, it is probably unwise to give an *absolute* veto to *every* minority, however small, on *all* issues. Only the two large segments were given the veto power in Austria, Belgium, and Cyprus. In Austria, the scope of the veto was potentially unlimited, but it should be remembered that it was merely laid down in the inter-party 'coalition pacts' with a maximum duration of four years instead of in the constitution. As indicated earlier, the veto in Cyprus had a broad but not unlimited scope: it could be applied to issues of foreign affairs, defence, security, taxes, the municipalities, and the election laws. In Belgium, the absolute veto is limited to legislation affecting the cultural and educational interests of the Dutch-speaking and French-speaking segments. In addition, the Belgian constitution provides for the so-called 'alarm bell' procedure which entails a suspensive veto especially important for the Francophone minority: if three-fourths or more of the minority legislators feel that their segment's vital interests are threatened by any bill, they may appeal to the cabinet, in which they enjoy parity of representation, to reconsider the bill; the 'alarm bell' immediately suspends the parliamentary consideration of the bill for a period of thirty days.

If a strong veto power is desired in spite of the danger of deadlock or immobilism, it is important to consider measures that may be able to prevent or minimise the danger of complete deadlock. One possibility would be the institution of an appeal to a neutral arbiter or commission of arbitration. Such a commission might be composed of impartial and respected foreign lawyers or other experts, perhaps nominated by interested foreign governments.

4. Power-sharing executives: cabinets vs. presidents The principal institutional alternatives for power-sharing executives are cabinets in parliamentary systems (often supplemented by broadly constituted advisory and co-ordinating councils) and power-sharing arrangements of presidents and other top office-holders in presidential systems. As Table 2 above shows, the latter alternative does not occur frequently: Cyprus and Lebanon are the only examples. A clear disadvantage of presidentialism is that the president is inevitably the single most important political leader and he is bound to represent one particular segment to the exclusion of other segments. Cabinets offer better settings for collegial power-sharing. It should be noted that Switzerland is included among the 'cabinet' systems although its executive is not a normal cabinet in a parliamentary system; it is elected by parliament for a fixed term and cannot be dismissed by parliament.

5. Federal vs. non-territorial autonomy The choice of

whether to implement segmental autonomy on a territorial or non-territorial basis is largely dictated by the geographical distribution of the segments. Non-territorial autonomy is usually an informal arrangement, but there are a few suggestive examples of constitutional provisions for the delegation of powers to non-territorial groups. The 1960 constitution of Cyprus set up two separately elected communal but non-territorial chambers with exclusive legislative powers over religious, educational, cultural and personal status matters, and it also prescribed separate municipal councils in the five largest towns of the island. In Belgium, a combination of territorial and non-territorial autonomy is being developed. The constitution provides for three autonomous regions (Flanders, Wallonia, and Brussels) and two autonomous 'communities' which are partly defined in non-territorial terms: the Dutch-speaking community comprises Flanders plus the Dutch-speakers in bilingual Brussels, and the French-speaking community consists of Wallonia and the Francophone *Bruxellois*.

A final example of non-territorial autonomy is the Law of Cultural Autonomy passed in Estonia in 1925. Under its terms, each national group with more than 3,000 formally registered members had the right to establish autonomous institutions under the authority of a cultural council elected by the minority nationals. This council could organise, administer, and supervise minority schools and other cultural institutions such as libraries and theatres, and it could issue decrees and raise taxes for these purposes. The councils also received state and local subsidies, and public funding was provided for the minority schools at the same level as for Estonian schools. The German and Jewish minorities quickly took advantage of the law and set up their own autonomous cultural authorities. As Georg von Rauch writes, 'these cultural authorities soon proved their worth, and the Estonian government was able to claim, with every justification, that it had found an exemplary solution to the problem of its minorities.'[6]

6. Other institutional alternatives When a new consociational democracy is being established, a host of other institutional details have to be settled. For instance, should the legislature be bicameral or unicameral? How large should the legislative chamber or chambers be? Which system of proportional representation should be adopted? Should the legislature be elected directly or indirectly? All these options are potentially compatible with consociational principles, but a bicameral legislature offers special advantages if one wants to combine proportionality with minority over-representation: one chamber can be elected on a purely proportional basis, while minorities can be given a disproportionally strong representation in the second chamber. In federal systems, such a dual system is commonly used to represent both the people as a whole and the states in the federation.

Consociation and Creative Statesmanship

What are the chances that a consociational solution will be found for a particular divided society, such as Northern Ireland, and what are the chances that such a consociation will be successful? The research on divided societies and consociational democracy has discovered several background conditions that are conducive to the establishment and maintenance of consociational democracy: a multiple balance of power among the segments of a divided society in which no segment has a majority and the segments are of approximately equal size, a relatively small total population, external threats that are perceived as a common danger by the different segments, the presence of some society-wide loyalties, the absence of extreme socio-economic inequalities among the segments, the relative isolation of the segments from each other, and prior traditions of political accommodation that predispose to power-sharing.

These favourable conditions cannot be discussed in detail here, but it is clear that many of them are lacking in Northern Ireland. In particular, the divided society of Northern Ireland is characterised by an imbalance of power with a clear majority segment and Northern Ireland lacks a strong tradition of political accommodation. It should be emphasised, however, that these conditions are neither necessary nor sufficient conditions. Most of the empirical cases of consociational democracy show a mixture of favourable and unfavourable background conditions, but the two cases of semi-consociational democracy are unusually valuable in demonstrating that these factors should not be credited with decisive influence. In spite of consistently optimal background factors, Israel has not developed a fully consociational democracy. Conversely, in spite of overwhelmingly unfavourable conditions in Canada, strongly consociational practices have developed in that country, especially during the period of the United Province. This means that consociational engineering may be attempted even when the conditions for it do not appear promising at all.

If the leaders of the different segments in a divided society are willing to try to find a consociational solution, there are a great many institutional forms and practices for consociational co-operation from which they can choose. Without this basic willingness to co-operate, of course, very little can be accomplished. But, conversely, an awareness of the many possibilities and examples of consociational co-operation may well be able to strengthen co-operative attitudes and hence to increase the chances of a constructive and creative response to the challenge of a divided society.

REFERENCES

1. Several of the ideas contained in this paper were drawn from, and are elaborated in greater detail in, my book *Democracy in Plural Societies: A Comparative Exploration,* Yale University Press, New Haven and London 1977; my articles 'The Northern Ireland Problem: Cases, Theories and Solutions', *British Journal of Political Science,* Vol. V, No. 1, January 1975, pp. 83–106; and 'Majority Rule Versus Democracy in Deeply Divided Societies', *Politikon,* Vol. 4, No. 2, December 1977, pp. 113–26, and my chapter 'Federal, Confederal and Consociational Options for the South African Plural Society' in R. I. Rotberg and J. Barratt, eds, *Conflict and Compromise in South Africa,* Lexington Books, Lexington, Mass. 1980, pp. 51–75.
2. J. C. Calhoun, *A Disquisition on Government,* Liberal Arts Press, New York 1953, p. 28.
3. See A. Lijphart, 'Consociation and Federation: Conceptual and Empirical Links', *Canadian Journal of Political Science,* Vol. 12, No. 3, September 1979, pp. 499–515.
4. 'Report of the Constitutional Committee of the Progressive Federal Party and Recommendations based on the Report for Consideration by the Federal Congress of the P.F.P. to be held in Durban, 17th and 18th November 1978', Cape Town 1978, p. 34.

5. W. A. Lewis, *Politics in West Africa*, Allen and Unwin, London 1965, p. 83.
6. G. Von Rauch, *The Baltic States: Estonia, Latvia, Lithuania – The Years of Independence 1917–1940*, University of California Press, Berkeley 1974, pp. 141–2.

BIBLIOGRAPHY

Aunger, E. A., *In Search of Political Stability: A Comparative Study of New Brunswick and Northern Ireland*, McGill–Queen's University Press, Montreal 1981

Barry, B., 'Political Accommodation and Consociational Democracy', *British Journal of Political Science*, Vol. 5, No. 4, October 1975, pp. 477–505

———, 'The Consociational Model and Its Dangers', *European Journal of Political Research*, Vol. 3, No. 4, December 1975, pp. 393–412

Boynton, G. R. and Kwon, W. H., 'An Analysis of Consociational Democracy', *Legislative Studies Quarterly*, Vol. 3, No. 1, February 1978, pp. 11–25

Calhoun, J. C., *A Disquisition on Government*, Liberal Arts Press, New York 1953

Daalder, H., 'The Consociational Democracy Theme', *World Politics*, Vol. 26, No. 4, July 1974, pp. 604–621

Dew, E., *The Difficult Flowering of Surinam: Ethnicity and Politics in a Plural Society*, Nijhoff, The Hague 1978

Hanf, T., Weiland, H. and Vierdag, G., *Südafrika: Friedlicher Wandel? Möglichkeiten demokratischer Konfliktregelung – Eine empirische Untersuchung*, Kaiser, Munich 1978

Huyse, L., *Passiviteit, pacificatie en verzuiling in de Belgische politiek: Een sociologische studie*, Standaard, Antwerp 1970

Koury, E. M., *The Crisis in the Lebanese System: Confessionalism and Chaos*, American Enterprise Institute, Washington, D.C. 1976

Kyriakides, S., *Cyprus: Constitutionalism and Crisis Government*, University of Pennsylvania Press, Philadelphia 1968

Lehmbruch, G., *Proporzdemokratie: Politisches System und Politische Kultur in der Schweiz und in Österreich*, Mohr, Tübingen 1967

Lewis, W. A., *Politics in West Africa*, Allen and Unwin, London 1965

Lijphart, A., 'Consociation and Federation: Conceptual and Empirical Links', *Canadian Journal of Political Science*, Vol. 12, No. 3, September 1979, pp. 499–515

———, *Democracy in Plural Societies: A Comparative Exploration*, Yale University Press, New Haven and London 1977

———, 'Federal, Confederal, and Consociational Options for the South African Plural Society', in R. I. Rotberg and J. Barratt, eds, *Conflict and Compromise in South Africa*, Lexington Books, Lexington, Mass. 1980

————, 'Majority Rule versus Democracy in Deeply Divided Societies', *Politikon*, Vol. 4, No. 2, December 1977, pp. 113–26

————, 'The Northern Ireland Problem: Cases, Theories, and Solutions', *British Journal of Political Science*, Vol. V, No. 1, January 1975, pp. 83–106

————, *The Politics of Accommodation: Pluralism and Democracy in the Netherlands*, 2nd ed., University of California Press, Berkeley 1975

Lorwin, V. R., 'Segmented Pluralism: Ideological Cleavages and Political Cohesion in the Smaller European Democracies', *Comparative Politics*, Vol. 3, No. 2, January 1971, pp. 141–75

Lustick, I., 'Stability in Deeply Divided Societies: Consociationalism versus Control', *World Politics*, Vol. 31, No. 3, April 1979, pp. 325–44

McRae, K. D. ed., *Consociational Democracy: Political Accommodation in Segmented Societies*, McClelland and Stewart, Toronto 1974

Milne, R. S. and Mauzy, D. K., *Politics and Government in Malaysia*, University of British Columbia Press, Vancouver 1978

Nordlinger, E. A., *Conflict Regulation in Divided Societies*, Occasional Papers in International Affairs, No. 29, Center for International Affairs, Harvard University, Cambridge, Mass. 1972

Obler, J., Steiner, J. and Dierickx, G., *Decision-Making in Smaller Democracies: The Consociational 'Burden'*, Sage Professional Papers in Comparative Politics, No. 01-064 Sage, Beverly Hills 1977

Paltiel, K. Z., 'The Israeli Coalition System', *Government and Opposition*, Vol. 10, No. 4, Autumn 1975, pp. 397–414

Powell, G. B. Jr., *Social Fragmentation and Political Hostility: An Austrian Case Study*, Stanford University Press, Stanford 1970

Steiner, J., *Amicable Agreement versus Majority Rule: Conflict Resolution in Switzerland*, University of North Carolina Press, Chapel Hill 1974

Von Rauch, G., *The Baltic States: Estonia, Latvia, Lithuania – The Years of Independence 1917–1940*, University of California Press, Berkeley 1974

Von Vorys, K., *Democracy without Consensus: Communalism and Political Stability in Malaysia*, Princeton University Press, Princeton 1975

7

Federal and Partly Federal Systems, Institutions and Conflict Management: Some Western European Examples

A.-P. Frognier[1]

Introduction

Political integration is rather like a two-way street. One way proceeds from simple confederations of states to federal or even unitary systems, like Switzerland since the confederation of three cantons in 1290 till the federation of 1848 (but passing through a short unitary system in the Napoleonic period). The second way proceeds from unitary systems to federal (or even confederal) ones, like the Federal Republic of Germany after 1945, or Czechoslovakia since 1969, or Belgium at the present time; all have a partly federal status. As we know, this second process is fraught with danger and can even lead to the breakdown of the state.

A unique definition of confederation is difficult to find. In a broad sense, confederation is the same as union or associations of states and, as stated by Duchasek, one '... may resort to the time-honoured device, saving all vague definitions, and refer to many of them (including perhaps the United Nations or the Cominform) as confederations *sui generis* and be thus neither wrong nor right'.[2] We might best define a confederal system as one where member states delegate some of their powers to a common authority which very often debates and deliberates unanimously. One characteristic of that system is that members can more or less freely leave the confederation. The same Duchasek lists eighteen examples of confederations, the majority of which share these characteristics (and it is possible to add some other cases).[3] At the present time, the best known cases are: the French community, the British Commonwealth, the Arab League, the Confederation of South Arabian Sheikdoms, the South-East Asia Treaty Organisation, the EEC, the United Nations, Puerto Rico's association with the United States, the Organisation of American States, the Warsaw Pact, and the North Atlantic Treaty Organisation.

Federal systems are more easy to define. From the constitutionalist point of view, they are states or other political entities which delegate some of their powers to a common authority. This authority is usually divided into two legislative chambers — which deliberate according to majority rule. Most often, federal powers are restrictively defined, whereas the states retain other powers, including residual ones. Certain powers can overlap. Federated states possess their own legislative and executive bodies but cannot leave the federation freely.

There are about twenty federal states in the world, including states called 'confederations' but which are in reality 'federations', like Switzerland. We can list the following: USA, Canada, Brazil, Argentina, Mexico, Venezuela, India, Pakistan, Burma, Malaysia, Australia, Nigeria, Cameroon, Tanzania, USSR, Czechoslovakia, Yugoslavia, Switzerland, Federal Republic of Germany and Austria. So while the overwhelming majority of states have adopted unitary systems, in terms of dimensions, federal states cover more than half of the earth's surface.

A unitary system is usually decentralised: authority is vested in a unique state, but local government exercises certain powers under central supervision, despite having its own legislative and executive bodies.

The distinction between federal and decentralised unitary systems is not always a clear-cut one. Certain unitary states have delegated to some or all of their subdivisions powers going beyond simple decentralisation, and sometimes exhibit partly federal characteristics. For example, Denmark has conceded a certain level of autonomy to Greenland and the Faroe Islands; Portugal has done so too, for Madeira and Acoras; Spain for the Basque country, Catalonia and Galicia (and it could be extended to other regions); Great Britain for Northern Ireland, Scotland and Wales. We could say that these are unitary states with autonomy status. However, Italy and Belgium are different in the sense that they have granted or are going to grant autonomy status to all their regions. We could speak here of regional states although Belgium is nearer to a federal system than Italy.[4]

Some of these cases exemplify the relatively 'disintegrative' process mentioned at the outset. This is clearly the case for Belgium, Spain and Great Britain.

Federalism, including federal and partly federal solutions, has had two distinct forms of historical expression. The first was mainly a kind of integration process, putting the emphasis more on co-operation than on autonomy. The second was related to a disintegration process, with the emphasis more on autonomy than on co-operation. The same institutional techniques can be used with very different political consequences.

Even the traditional federalist states of the first type can exhibit significant historical differences. In Western Europe, the Swiss federal constitution of 1848 can be seen as a compromise, the aim of which was to put an end to a sort of civil strife between cantons, mainly for religious and economic reasons (Catholics versus Protestants, and in a coincidental way conservatives versus liberals seeking to establish a 'unitary' economic space). But German federalism was not directly linked with the solution of internal conflicts of this kind. Until 1914, it imposed itself under the power of a dominant component, Prussia, following an evolution from confederation to federation without important internal conflicts. This federalism succeeded in introducing liberalism without real opposition from the states' 'Junkers' through a kind of agreement well described by Anderson.[5] It succeeded too in avoiding intense religious conflict despite the *Kulturkampf*. One of the reasons for this is that Catholics are more dispersed throughout Germany than is the case in Switzerland. The post-First World War period was more troubled. After the Second World War, the Allies reintroduced federalism, mainly in order to counterbalance strong centralist powers. We can conclude that federalism in the German tradition does not involve the pacification of internal conflict as in Switzerland. This makes the Swiss case more interesting for the study of conflict-management processes than the Federal Republic.

However, the aim of this paper is not to analyse historical differences between institutional forms. Mainly we want to study in a more or less formal way the characteristics of what we shall call the federal solution in a broad sense. This encompasses the 'orthodox' federal solution together with specific solutions of unitary states engaged in relatively large delegation of autonomy. We shall call the latter 'partly federal states'. This label can certainly be criticised by constitutionalists, but it is clearer. We shall mostly treat the cases of Switzerland and Belgium, but without excluding other situations, like the Federal Republic, Austria, Italy and Spain. As we are concerned with Western Europe, we shall not take into account the confederations, except in some cases the EEC, which is in fact a sort of mixed confederal-federal system.

In the first part, we shall be concerned with the formal repartition (or distribution) of powers in federal and partly federal systems. In the second part, we shall examine the relations of their systems to the conflict-pacification problem. This first part, dealing with the institutional repartition of powers, will be essentially descriptive and institutional.[6] I shall describe the different situations of the countries already quoted. I shall use the usual juridical distinctions of constitutional law.

Bicameralism

The Western European federal regimes contain a bicameral system at the level of the federal state: one chamber is elected by universal suffrage and thus is representative of the citizens as a whole, and the other is often equally composed of the federated states. This is the case in Switzerland where the cantons are represented at par (two representatives for each canton). But in the case of the Federal Republic and Austria, there is a certain inequality. In the German Bundesrat, the Lander have three to five votes according to their importance, whereas in Austria states' representation varies according to their population rate.

Partly federal states do not possess such a characteristic.

Belgium, however, is peculiar. In the present state of the constitution, Belgium has two chambers (Representatives and Senate, elected by universal suffrage) with a Flemish-speaking majority and a French-speaking minority corresponding to their demographic weight. Each chamber is divided in two 'linguistic groups', one Flemish- and the other French-speaking. When passing certain laws, a special majority is required inside each group. On the other hand, each group is entitled to oppose certain laws when the law is held to be contrary to the group's interest. The consequence is to force the government into making a ruling within thirty days over the measure complained of. Therefore, it is not a real veto power, but a suspensive or revisional power. This procedure is called 'warning-bell'. Finally, the projects of the present government which should be enforced by the next legislature provide for the senators to be at the same time members of the autonomous authorities, a fact which would enhance the Senate as a 'states' chamber'. (This label does not apply to confederation, of course, since the states do not have a central legislative body elected directly by the people. However, in the hybrid circumstances of the EEC, we find the European Parliament where member-states are represented on a relatively unequal basis according to their population quota.)

Respective Powers of the National Chambers
If we take into account the fact that federalism is a technique trying to combine, on an equal basis, a global representation of the constituency and a representation at par of the member states, we should logically conclude that the two chambers should have equal powers. This is the case in Switzerland. But here again, the Federal Republic and Austria differ. Indeed, in the Federal Republic, if the Bundestag and the Bundesrat are both entitled to legislative initiatives, the former has more important powers than the latter. Certain laws passed by the Bundestag must also be approved by the Bundesrat if they concern its interests. The latter's veto cannot be overridden. Concerning other laws, once passed by the Bundestag, if the Bundesrat does not approve of them, it can request the intervention of a conciliatory

commission. The latter can make recommendations which are not compulsory to the Bundestag. Should a new project be proposed, the Bundesrat can veto it by a majority ruling. This veto in its turn can be overruled by the Bundestag by a simple or a two-thirds majority vote according to whether the Lander's vote has been a simple or a two-thirds majority one. In the partly federal states, this kind of problem does not occur since there is no such 'states chamber'. Again Belgium stands alone, for the Senate and the Chamber are supposedly on an equal basis with the division in linguistic groups inside each one.

The National Executive

The problem of establishing a federal executive is a delicate one. Whereas the legislative federal system provides for a balance of power between the two types of representation, how could this apply to the executive? And moreover would it be necessary?

In the Swiss case, the participation of state members is assured. Switzerland has a collegial system. The executive power is bestowed upon a Federal Council of seven members, elected by the two chambers together, i.e. by the Federal Assembly. The Council members must come from different cantons. Custom keeps a minimum of two seats to the French-speaking cantons. Each year, the Federal Assembly elects one Council member as President of the Confederation. This function has a formal and representative nature.

In other cases, such a need does not exist, which is certainly due to simpler structures of societies. This is the case in the USA and the Federal Republic of Germany.

In the Federal Republic, the President is elected by a Federal Assembly composed of the Bundestag and representatives at par of the Lander. Here then the two channels of representation are associated. However the powers that the President can exert are mostly formal and representative. In opposition to this, when forming the government, the federal principle does not appear. The Chancellor is elected by the Bundestag and, in his turn, he forms the government. Both the Chancellor and the government are answerable only to the Bundestag. Consequently, the political weight lies with the federal government which also has the right to oversee the functioning of the Lander governments.

In the partly federal European states, national executives are diversely affected by regional problems. In Italy and Spain, the executive has no effect over it. In Great Britain, the government contains secretaries of state for the regions concerned. In Belgium, the system is distinctly more restrictive; the Council of Ministers is kept at par as between Flemish and French speakers, except for the Prime Minister. However the government includes some State Secretaries who are not subject to the par rule. I should point out here that, during a transitory period, the community and regional executives are parts of government and therefore answerable both to the national parliament and their own respective assemblies.

The Share of Legislative Competence between Power Levels

In federal states, the following areas are generally recognised as depending solely on the federal state's power: foreign policy, national defence, financial and monetary policy, posts and telegraphs and customs. The following are generally recognised as depending solely on state members: education, culture, police and local administration. The allocation of economic matters is more variable. From the formal point of view, powers are delimited for state control and are residual for the members (Switzerland, the Federal Republic of Germany etc.) or the contrary (Canada). Besides, powers sometimes overlap.

In Switzerland, the Confederation possesses executive authority over foreign affairs, national defence (essentially), civil protection, powders, railways, posts and telegraphs, money and alcohol. Overlapping powers are defined in several domains. Either the cantons issue dispositions in the framework of general principles decided by the federal power, or they can legislate in certain domains as long as no federal law is already enacted. Finally, the cantons have what is called 'residual powers', i.e. those which are not explicitly attributed to the Confederation. The system in the Federal Republic of Germany is rather similar. In the case of overlapping powers, however, where the Lander can legislate only if the federal power does not do it, the federal power is subjected to certain conditions: an existing need for federal regulation; the Lander's incapacity to regulate effectively a matter separately; and the necessity to maintain the country's legal and economic unity.

How do the powers of the two levels in both countries compare? An indicator offered by Lijphart is the percentage of all government revenues spent by the central government.[7] In 1959, it was 61 per cent for Switzerland and 74 per cent for the Federal Republic of Germany. (In comparison, it was 77 per cent for the USA, 65 per cent for Canada and 84 per cent for Austria.) In both cases, the federal level has the main revenues, which confirms the general movement towards centralisation in federal states.

In partly federal states, such as Belgium, Italy and Spain, there are exclusive powers for regions which receive some autonomy.

In Belgium, the central power is in some respects dependent on the linguistic communities via the linguistic groups of the Chamber and the Senate. Moreover, for the time being, the linguistic communities and the regions have each a list of areas where they can exert an exclusive power. Indeed, in Belgium we can determine the following three levels of power: the national level; the linguistic communities, mostly responsible for cultural and linguistic policies with some social affairs regarding individuals; and the regional level, mostly concerned with socio-economic affairs. One fact is worth our attention here: the Belgian system allocates certain powers to the communities in external policy, even offering them a wide autonomy in concluding treaties on cultural exchanges.

Italian regions also have exclusive powers. We have to distinguish the 'regions with special status' (Sicily, Sardinia, Valle d'Aosta, Trentino, Alto Adige, Friuli-Venezia-Giulia) which have exclusive powers in important socio-economic and educational matters, and the other regions which have more local powers, exclusive only in the framework of outline laws at the national level, if they exist. (The first kind of region also has these powers.)

In Spain, the Basque country and Catalonia have exclusive powers in some socio-economic, local and cultural matters.

Moreover, they also have exclusive powers for the development and implementation of some national legislation.

It is difficult to estimate the relative weight of the division of powers. In Belgium, the part of the national budget of 1979 allocated to communities and regions was about 10 per cent (but the regions levied specific taxes later). For Italy, Lorenzoni and Merloni[8] estimate the same measure to be 4 per cent in 1972 but it seems to have grown since then. For Spain, we have no such information. To know whether, in these three cases, the powers bestowed are sufficient is difficult. Indeed this problem is at the centre of political controversies, especially in Spain and Belgium. There is no doubt that they are fewer than powers allocated in federal countries, but are nevertheless going far beyond those given to decentralised units. The character of exclusivity given to these powers is also particularly distinctive. However, they are rather strictly determined and there is no idea of residual powers.

Confederations also bestow powers on their central authority. In the EEC, one can say that these powers are unequally distributed according to the matters at hand. The Common Agricultural Policy (CAP) is highly integrated and there the EEC power is akin to that of a federal one. Other policies, such as scientific policy for example, are notably less so. The importance of the power granted to the EEC depends on the vested interests of the member states and on their willingness to put certain domains in common. Here, the power relationship between components of the confederation appears more important than in a federal state.

Specific Administrative Means of Implementing Laws

A balanced distribution of powers must necessarily entail sufficient means of implementation. In this regard, federal states differ.

In the USA, the system leaves to the federal power the implementation of federal laws, whereas states implement their own laws. In Western Europe, administrative prominence goes to federal authorities. The Swiss cantons and the German Lander implement a great deal of federal legislation, either through their own prerogatives or through delegation.

In partly federal states, components often have specific administrative bodies of varying importance. These implement laws according to powers granted to them, but do not implement national law which does not touch upon their allocated autonomy. Therein lies the difference with federated states' administrations.

In Belgium, community and regional administrations are established by allocating to them exclusively services and agents belonging to the national administrations. However, in the future, these administrations will depend solely on community and regional authorities, operating in the framework of national provisions for public expenditure.

The Allocation of Fiscal Responsibilities

Among a state's powers, those dealing with the right to levy taxes are particularly relevant, as they determine the level of resources available.

In federal states, both the federal and the federated authorities have the right to levy taxes. The respective powers are often defined in texts of great complexity. Customs duties generally go to the federal state. In Switzerland, such duties were originally the only federal resource, together with half the duties received on military exemptions. Later, fiscal powers in important domains like revenues, estate property, tobacco, and stamp rights on legal documents were added. As a consequence, there is a complete division between federal and cantonal finances. In the Federal Republic, the system is more complex. Income taxes, corporate taxes and Value Added Tax are common to the Federation and the Lander, and they are equally distributed (except VAT). Moreover, taxes on capital transfers accrue exclusively to the Federation, whereas the Lander dispose of taxes on wealth, death duties and transport taxes.

In the partly federal states under study, we find an independent fiscal power only in the Spanish, Italian and Belgian regions, and this only for part of their resources. In these countries, the bulk of the regions' resources comes from the central state's contribution. This often takes the form of a mixture of transfer and discount on the product of certain national taxes. These regions, therefore, depend on the central state which must allocate resources to them. Theirs is, accordingly, a 'minor form' of federalism, for while they levy their own taxes, these do not constitute the bulk of their resources. In this regard, the Spanish regions appear less dependent on the central state than those of the two other countries. However Spain has built up a Fund of Inter-territorial Compensation, a typically federal institution, which aims at transferring resources from some regions to other less favoured. Such a 'horizontal' mechanism is not found in Italy and Belgium.

Components' Specific Legislative Bodies

Here the question is whether political components, in order to exert their allocated powers, possess their own legislative bodies, i.e. bodies 'distinctive' from the federal/central level. A component's own legislative body can be of two types: either a 'distinctive assembly' or an 'assembly composed of specific mandatories'. The logic of federalism points in the second direction. If one presupposes the existence of a specific and autonomous power accruing to one entity, it seems normal that it should have its own exclusively elected representatives.

This is the case in three Western European countries. The other countries enjoy particular situations. In Italy, the region's citizens elect their Regional Council, and the same is found in the two Spanish regions already analysed. In Belgium, the system is different: separate assemblies represent the communities and the regions. Actually, there is one Flemish Council competent for the Flemish community of Flanders and Brussels, and one Regional Council competent for Wallonia. These two types of organisation are thus assymetrical: one assembly on the Flemish side and two assemblies on the French-speaking side. However, the members of these assemblies are national MPs and senators who simply 'switch hats', and in a few years time these assemblies will be composed of senators only. Doubtless we have here distinctive legislative bodies but they are not composed of specific mandatories. It is a kind of 'personal centralisation' which tends to mix roles in a way designed to avoid centrifugal tendencies.

Components' Specific Executive Bodies

It is obvious that in federal systems, the federated states must have their own legislative and executive power. However, the case of the other states appears more relevant. In Italy and Spain, we find such an executive. The Italian regions have a 'junta' headed by a President elected by the Regional Council. In Spain, the two regions have equally a government and a President, but the latter is appointed by the King and chosen from members of parliament. The regional government is answerable to the regional council.

In Belgium, the different councils each have their own executive with an elected President answerable to the respective council. In a transitory period, the executives in each council are formed in proportion to the strength of the political parties. After the transitory period, this restriction will be lifted. During this transitory period, the executives are parts of the central government and are answerable both to their respective councils and to parliament. Afterwards, they will be independent.

Judicial Organisation

For some authors, the logic of a federal system supposes the existence of two independent sets of courts, one at the federal level and one at the federated level. The only perfect case of the latter is to be found in the USA. In the three European federal states, the system is modified: the different courts are incorporated into the federated states with a kind of Supreme Court at the federal level whose function is essentially that of arbiter or appeal.

In Switzerland, judicial organisation comes entirely under the cantonal competence for both federal and cantonal law. On top, we find a federal court as court of appeal, which arbitrates in cases of conflict between federal and cantonal law and/or between cantons, and finally as a court for public law claims. In the Federal Republic, we find a similar structure, but the federal codes introduce a kind of uniformity of courts and procedures inside the Lander.

This type of judicial organisation is not restricted to federal states only. In Spain, the two regions can organise their own judicial power. The central government and the

Council of State exercise constitutional control over the regional laws. In Italy and Belgium, the components do not have their own judicial power, thus preserving a national character in legal affairs. In Belgium, a special Arbitration Court will be created, with a mixed composition of lawyers and MPs.

The Indestructible Character of the 'Political Whole'

In a confederation, the right to secession is generally admitted as being evidence of that 'free participation' which is characteristic of this kind of political organisation.

In federal states as well as in the three Western European cases, the right of secession is not granted to the federated states. However, Yugoslavia, where this right is explicitly recognised, is an exception to this rule.

Obviously, the partly federal states belong *a fortiori* to the category of the 'political whole'. The case of Spain is relevant here. The autonomy law explicitly forbids the regions to federate among themselves. Even co-operative agreements must meet the approval of the Cortes if they have not been explicitly planned at the beginning. We can easily guess that these restrictions aim at preventing certain alliances which could imperil the Spanish state.

Conclusion

It is now possible to outline some conclusions about the diverse forms of power distribution at the different levels.

It is commonplace to recognise that federal systems have a more balanced system of division of power between central and component levels than partly federal ones. However, we have discovered some points of difference between them.

Switzerland certainly has the more balanced system. The structure of the federal level gives more place to cantons than does that of the Federal Republic of Germany or Austria. The two chambers have about equal powers. The executive shows a differential representation of cantons. Anyway the general movement of the overlapping powers goes towards the federal level. And the public expenditure indicator shows that only about 40 per cent of expenses are left to the cantonal level. In the Federal Republic of Germany, there is a clear asymmetry between the legislative and executive levels, and in the public expenditure indicator the Lander have about 15 per cent less than the cantons. Austria seems the least balanced, and the same indicator is near that for the unitary systems.

For the partly federal regimes examined, the situation is more complex. It would appear that Belgium has the least unbalanced system, due essentially to the impact of the linguistic components at the central level. Moreover, the Belgian reform affects the country as a whole. Spanish regionalisation does not affect the central powers, and Madrid retains a nomination power for the President of each regional assembly, while in Belgium the components' executives are completely dependent on their assemblies. However, the Spanish regions have more specific assemblies than Belgium, their regional councils being composed of 'specific' mandates. (In Belgium, the national MPs switch hats.) Moreover, these Spanish regions have judicial powers unknown in Belgium. Thus, at the components' level, it is difficult to assess a clear difference of importance between Belgium and Spain. Even going through the list of powers, it is hard to decide. But the external powers of Belgian communities, which is a sort of confederal device, also has to be considered. Italy also has a global regional system, like Belgium. But here, beyond the absence of the effect on the central level, the powers are much less important ones than in the two preceding cases (except maybe for the five regions with special status). But they share, with the Spanish case, the characteristics of specific councils.

The aim of this next section is to assess the efficiency of the different institutions, briefly described above, in dealing with social conflicts.

The theory implied here is that democratic political structures allow for the non-violent expression of conflict and offer procedures to resolve it. Among these structures, what is relevant is what may broadly be called the federal technique. This consists of trying to pacify a conflict by maintaining or offering political autonomy to opponents (or to one or several of those). This autonomy obtains in the context of a state which enjoys legitimacy together with specific powers. It is a political strategy which aims at self-government without breaking the political whole. In federal regimes, the power given to autonomous entities is certainly greater than in partly federal ones, but no doubt the problem is not substantially different.

In order to examine this conflict-management question, we shall first study the specific conflict-pacification characteristics of federal (or partly federal) solutions. We shall examine them with respect to both autonomy and participation in a political whole, both of which must be present in order to warrant this type of political organisation. If the former is too much stressed, the risk of dominant centrifugal forces increases; this in turn might be conducive to participation. If the latter is prominent, we face a false autonomy nearing the situation of a unitary state, *stricto sensu*. The capacities of a political regime also have to be seen in relation to other socio-political phenomena. For some countries these include their relations with consociational democracy. Finally we shall focus on a specific point: the effect of a balance of power between entities on a federal or partly federal system.

Specific Capabilities of Federal and Partly Federal Systems
Autonomy
One well-known facet of autonomy is its direct effect on conflict management. The division of a political whole into entities can 'compartmentalise' conflicts and thus contain them. This is generally established for Switzerland as Kerr concludes: 'In short, to the extent that political power is dispersed in an ethnically divided nation, the probability of cleavages finding political expression nation-wide across the many areas of party competition is reduced.'[9] Some Marxist authors see federalism as a means of dividing the working class and consequently restraining class struggle. An example of a special type of pacification was the anxiety of the Allies to give West Germany a federal constitution in order to avoid the resurgence of a strong central power, able to mobilise a large part of the German population.

A second effect of the strategy of self-government is the

division of a conflictive whole into non-conflictive (or less conflictive) entities, in the hope that this kind of internal pacification of entities will result in a pacification of the whole.

Lijphart has shown that this hope could be translated formally in the language used by Rae and Taylor to analyse cleavages.[10] They define 'fragmentation' according to a given cleavage as the probability of having a pair of individuals, selected at random, who belong to different groups on the cleavage. This measure F varies thus from 0 (all of them belong to the same group) to 1 (all belong to different groups). The problem then is to know whether the fragmentation F_W of a state considered as a whole could be mitigated by F_m which is the mean (and weighted) fragmentation of the autonomous entities inside that given state. The answer is yes, as we can prove that $F_W \geqslant F_m$.

In this regard, what do the cases of some previously analysed states show? Two federal cases have so far been under scrutiny: Switzerland and Austria. The measurements made by Lijphart give different results for the two countries.[11] In Switzerland, religious fragmentation is .49 for the country as a whole and .34 for the cantons' weighted mean; whereas linguistic fragmentation is .40 and .17 respectively. The two sets (religious and linguistic) fragmentation gives .68 and .23 as a result. In Austria, religious fragmentation is .66 for the state and .63 for the Lander's weighted mean. We can therefore conclude that federalism has a more pacifying effect on the type of conflicts measured in Switzerland than on those measured in Austria. In both cases, what is worthy of notice is that religious cleavage is important. In Switzerland, the federal constitution of 1848 was born, as already stated, of a civil war, having an essentially religious character (though also an economic one). On the other hand, Austria too has known a civil war, this time between the three ideological Läger: Catholic, Socialist and Nationalist.

Lijphart has also applied his measure F as far as religious fragmentation is concerned to the case of Northern Ireland in view of a hypothetical federal constitution.[12] The result is rather similar to the Austrian one: the counties' fragmentation and that of Northern Ireland considered as a whole are almost identical (F_w = .45 and F_m = .43). To be sure, very different social mechanisms intervene in Austria and Northern Ireland and have contrasting pacificating effects. We shall come again to the problem when discussing the consociational democracy theme.

One important problem with the 'division' strategy is how to implement it. It is possible to distinguish two ways. In Switzerland, the strategy is necessarily combined with a popular vote; the result is a strong form of legitimacy. In Belgium, the situation is much more complicated; Flemish and French speakers have a different view on the popular vote in this area. The former refuse it systematically in the name of *ius soli,* but mainly in order to avoid sanctioning the Francisation of Flemish populations. French speakers argue to the contrary and this divergence is one of the causes of difficulty in finding a solution to the Belgian community problem: the players do not agree on the rules of the game.

Participation

With respect to the other critical aspect of federalisation, co-operation at the level of national decisions, we consider here only the viewpoint of internal policy and not that of external policy. The latter is important, however, as the origins of some federal systems lie in the desire to increase external security.

The problem may be stated in the following way: two political logics must be associated at the central level. One is the classical democratic logic of one man one vote and the other is the logic of co-operation between political entities differently constituted. We have already seen the different systems which have been built in several countries. We have then been able to establish that there is a greater equality between the two channels of power in some countries (for example Switzerland) than in others (for example the Federal Republic of Germany) at the legislative as well as at the executive level.

It is generally admitted that, in federal states, the tendency is towards increasing powers at the central level. At the same time the classical democratic channel tends to overtake that of the constituent parts. The first phenomenon is well known and is the result of the increasing weight of state 'economic' intervention (since the Thirties and in the actual crisis situation). The second is partly linked to that. However, it is our belief that this second phenomenon seems also to stem since the turn of the century from the role of the classical parliamentary channel in integrating the socialist movement in a broad sense through universal suffrage. Both phenomena explain why, for instance, a research survey made in Switzerland among MPs shows that the more MPs are on the left the more they favour a greater centralism.[13]

The problem is different in non-federal states which undergo reform on a more or less federal line. Here we are facing reforms imposed by critics of unitarian structures of classical democracy. The general tendency towards more centralisation is therefore partly 'blocked'. This is the case in Belgium, whereas in Spain and Italy there is no institutional impact of regional reforms on the central level. In Belgium, where part of the problem has socio-economic roots, the survey research already quoted for Switzerland shows that mostly in Wallonia (but also partly in Flanders) the more the MPs are on the left, the more they are against unitarism (with the exception of the Flemish of the extreme right who are traditionally separatist).[14] We see clearly the contrast with Switzerland as well as the different direction taken by the same institutional situations in different social contexts.

The question which often arises in Belgium is to know whether the autonomy movement would not offer more dangers in socio-economic terms at a time of greater concentration of state powers. Some think, on the contrary, that this situation is to be wished for in the framework of the re-structuring of a state both at the infranational and supranational level. This is the old theme of a maladjusted state: at the same time too small and too big. Often too, in Belgium, the most federalist circles are the most pro-European ones, as shown by a survey research made by Ingelhart.[15]

Anyhow, whatever the power relationship between the two channels of central power, it is obvious that the success of a federal or partly federal solution depends on the legitimacy of the central power. The question is not a simple one.

It is particularly acute in the constitution of a federal executive or sometimes of an executive in a partly federal regime. In federal states like the USA or the Federal Republic of Germany, which have some homogeneity in society, rather 'homogeneous executives' are found, which make relatively fewer concessions to the representation of the entities. In states where there is strong pressure towards entities' representation, like Switzerland or Belgium, the executive is a more heterogeneous one. In fact, the Swiss system is exceptional, for its legitimacy is not affected by this heterogeneity. Rather, it takes the form of what Easton called 'support towards the regime',[16] a support which can be given independently of persons filling the positions of power. This form of legitimacy is no doubt the most stable.[17] Legitimacy can also be derived from 'support toward authorities' (also according to Easton) and one has in mind immediately Tito's Yugoslavia. Without sufficient legitimacy of one form or other, federal or partly federal executives can hardly survive.

In a more general appraisal, the problem can be seen as one of the behaviour and traditions of elites, that is, of the existence of recognised elites and in particular of their ability to negotiate. The problem is an acute one for systems in transition, which most often experience struggles between rival elite groups. In such cases, the existence of a supreme authority, like a monarchy, can play an integrating role if it can remain above the struggles (which is not easy). Elites' struggles can dangerously weaken the legitimacy of a system where that legitimacy is already under question.

Moreover, a system in transition can weaken the legitimacy of the elites themselves. This is certainly the case in Belgium. Since the Sixties, many negotiations have terminated in failure. Procedures as well as negotiators have changed many times. Discussions were sometimes held between parliamentary groups and other times involved outside interests (for instance in 'party summits'). Sometimes a mixture of both procedures was tried. Also, there were conflicts between negotiators on each side (mainly French-speaking ones), because some of them thought they had to offer a united 'front' while others did not want to 'freeze' the negotiations with such a front. Also, because governments had short periods of life, this meant frequent changes of negotiating partners, except for the Christians who were members of every government for twenty years. Even the federalist parties were included in some governments, but without success.

Concerning the broad level of mass politics in a federal system (or the political culture of the population), one can imagine that the central power must have a 'balanced' place in relation to autonomous entities. An empirical appraisal can be made by comparing similar research in Belgium and Switzerland. The question was on the classical theme of 'belonging'. People were asked to what they felt they belonged most: to the whole country or to a canton (or a community or region in Belgium). Curiously enough, the percentage of answers indicating the whole country is very similar: 45 per cent in Switzerland and 41.5 per cent in Belgium.[18] Have these percentages a more general meaning which should be empirically tested? Or is the percentage for Belgium, traditionally a unitarian state, peculiarly low, showing therefore a very deep crisis?

Federalism and Other Social Characteristics
Federalism and Consociational Democracy

Discussions on federalism and consociational democracy are closely related. Let us recall the definition of this latter concept by Daalder: '. . . the term "consociational" has been increasingly used to characterise a certain pattern of political life in which the political elites of distinct social groups succeed in establishing a viable, pluralistic state by a process of mutual forbearance and accommodation.'[19] The term consociational democracy was mainly elaborated by Lijphart.[20] Both concepts have several characteristics in common; above all they are means of associating potentially conflicting entities in a political whole. Dahl called consociational democracy 'sociological federalism'.[21] In fact, it is possible to distinguish three types of federalism: 'territorial federalism', which we have been discussing up to this point; 'sociological federalism' (consociational democracy); and somewhere between them 'personal federalism'.[22] The latter consists of allocating to a group such a mixture of autonomy and participation as characterises any federal solution. Sometimes personal federalism is simply considered as a type of consociational democracy. However, it is useful to distinguish the two. Personal federalism is a solution to the problem of coexistence between different peoples, whereas consociational democracy is the solution to the problem of coexistence inside one single people between different tendencies (religious, social, etc.). Nevertheless, such a distinction, relying on the definition of 'people', is sometimes difficult to make, and the two concepts can be very near, if not quite synonymous.

Since personal federalism may be useful when territorial solutions of peoples' conflicts are impossible, we shall discuss it further.

Personal federalism seems to have been first conceived by Austrian social democrats at the turn of the century. It has been applied several times since then, but only globally, to Cyprus (1960–63) and to the Lebanon (mostly from 1943 until the recent civil war). It is at present applied as a partial solution in Belgium to link the Flemish-speaking and French-speaking people from Brussels to their respective community councils.

The origins of personal federalism can be found in the Austro-Hungarian Empire.[23] Between 1867 and 1914, the conflict grew between those advocating the principle of nationalities and those opposing it. During that period, numerous solutions to the problem had been proposed. The social democrats put forward an original proposition. They built a system based on the principle of national autonomy. For Karl Renner, nationality was the attribute of each citizen, by the same virtue of his belonging to such or such a religion. Now, it was not always possible to attach nationality to a given territory. Therefore, in his view, Austria's organisation should be arranged, not along the principle of territoriality, but along that of nationality. Thus, the state should be divided into 'associations', each including only individuals belonging to the same nationality. In ethnically mixed countries, each nationality forming a legal entity has a council to which the administration of cultural affairs was entrusted. For political or economic questions of a common interest, mixed councils were formed with a proportional representation of the different nationalities on a territorial basis.

The Cypriot solution, even if it lasted only three years,

deserves to be described. The 1960 constitution built the state on the basis of the Greek and Turkish communities, more or less equal in number and separated by language and religion. The constitution sanctioned a diarchy of the Greek and Turkish communities and decided their composition. It stated that 'the Greek community includes all the nationals of the Republic who are Greek in origin and whose maternal language is Greek, who are of Greek cultural tradition or who belong to the Greek Orthodox Church', and 'the Turkish community includes all nationals of the Republic who are Turkish in origin, whose maternal language is Turkish, who are of Turkish cultural tradition or who are Muslims'.

Therefore, four criteria were used to determine members of the communities. The nationals who answered to these conditions had to opt for one or the other community. As for religious groups, they must exert this right of decision collectively. Besides this individual or collective right of decision, there was a right to break away: any national of the Republic had the right to stop belonging to the community on which he depended, and to join the other one, following a declaration on his behalf and upon his accepting the legislative body of the other community. Generally speaking, each national necessarily had to belong to one or the other community.

The communities' boundaries were therefore not territorial. Geographical partition had been excluded. The entities so defined were entitled to their own political organisation. The two communities were each represented in a specific assembly. The chambers of each community assembly enjoyed assigned powers. The constitution enabled them, regarding their respective communities, to exert legislative power over such domains as religion, culture and education. These community chambers constituted a rough equivalent, without any territorial basis, to the states' legislative chambers in a federal system. The constitution also organised the collaboration between the two communities; it added that the total or partial union of Cyprus with any other state whatsoever was excluded, as was secessionist independence.

The Cypriot state was a republic with a presidential regime and a representative chamber. Each citizen had the right to vote in all elections organised according to the constitution. But there was no unique electoral college. Separate electoral colleges, established on an ethnic basis, designated their own representatives. Therefore Greek and Turkish electors chose their MPs for the representative chamber separately. The President of the Republic was separately elected by the Greek electors and the Vice-President by the Turkish ones. The representative chamber was composed of fifty members, 70 per cent of whom were elected by Greek Cypriots and 30 per cent by Turkish ones. These percentages, said the Constitution, 'are independent from any statistical data'.

Lebanon's organisation up to the civil war was better known and will not be described at length. Lebanon is composed of several Christian and Muslim religious communities whose importance is more or less equal. These communities are mixed throughout the territory. The constitution of 1926 recognised the principle of sharing the legislative seats between the communities. In 1943, the National Pact recognised the fact that each of the main communities was entitled to have the number of parliamentary seats corresponding to its numerical importance. The representation of communities was equally to be found in governmental and administrative areas. The constitution, passed in 1943, determines that 'the communities could be equitably represented in the composition of public services and ministries provided it does not prejudice the state's interests'. The composition of governmental agencies is ruled by confessionalism. This explains why the Presidency of the Republic is always given to a Maronite and the Council's Presidency to a Sunni. The share accruing to the other religious communities inside the Executive depends on their importance.

The Cypriot example is a classic case of personal federalism. The Lebanese case borders on both federalism and consociational democracy. Although the Cypriot case was a failure, we cannot say the same about Lebanon for the experience lasted longer.[24]

In Belgium, the present state reform is based on the personal federalism principle for linking up Flemish and French-speaking inhabitants of Brussels to one community or the other, and is concerned mainly with numerous social and cultural matters. On the other hand, in 1978, a global solution was negotiated by political parties (including Flemish and Brussels federalists) then in power. This solution, the so-called 'Pacte d'Egmont' was resolutely federalist. But, soon after, this Pact was denounced by the Flemish Christian Party, which thus reversed its earlier decision, and the whole project fell through. In the framework of this solution, the French-speaking population — dispersed throughout the Flemish communes around the capital, where they sometimes make up to 40 per cent of the inhabitants — would have had the opportunity to choose a fictitious domicile in the (bilingual) capital and therefore would have been administratively dependent on it.

These examples show that if a strategy of territorial division does not work out, there are other courses of action for peoples' relations in the same country. To be sure, in states where internal borders have no particular historical weight, it is possible to design new borders which would reduce fragmentation. Should it turn out to be impossible, mostly in cases where there is no clear-cut geographical border between groups scattered throughout the territory, there always remain personal federalist solutions.

This being the case, federalism and consociational democracy can coexist inside the same system, as in Switzerland and Austria, and also in Belgium. This coexistence can assume various shapes. In Switzerland, both federalism and consociational democracy seem to reduce conflicts. In Austria, consociational democracy factors play a more important role than federal ones in ameliorating conflicts. In Belgium — and it is maybe typical of transition processes — there is to some degree an opposition between new partly-federal structures and nationally-based consociational structures. For example, employers and trade unions are organised on a national basis. Part of the difficulties encountered by a more federal solution results from the consequent restructuring of power; in short, these organisations resist any tendency to self-divide. It must be pointed out that in Belgium, political parties are more friable than the big social organisations. The parties (except the Communists who are too small) have been totally divided along community lines.

This question raises an important problem. Would a transition to a form of federalism in a historically unitarian state be smoother where federal division is institutionalised in the interest-group system? Some argue that a solution to the Belgian problem would be easier should all social organisations be divided *ex ante*. The result would probably be either that it would indeed favour federalism, or that it would be conducive to separatism pure and simple. It is to be expected that a federalisation whose tempo would be progressive could allow for a better harmonisation of the evolving political and social structures.

Problems created by a federal reform in a consociationalist state can be viewed as a struggle, not only between new elites and consociational ones, but also separately within the latter. From a consociational point of view, an ideal situation would be where a transformation occurs smoothly in the consociational structure at the same time as in the structure of the regime. But actually the federal or partly-federal divisions frequently change the balance of forces inside the interest-groups themselves, thereby creating conflicts.

The Balance of Power Problems

The strategy of self-government and co-operation between entities is linked — as in consociational democracy — to power relations between entities. It is generally admitted that the existence of a balance of power between entities can favour the system. This can be realised in several ways. Where the state is entirely divided there are two different cases: one where there are more than three entities and another where there are two or three at most. The case of states where one or several regions enjoy autonomous status without affecting the whole of the state is different because very often an imbalance of power is found. However, structural autonomy is granted to rather powerful regions, as in Spain.

Balance of power does not imply equality of power between entities but rather acceptance without too much frustration of a certain pattern of power between these entities. The case of the German Confederation between 1866 and 1871 is an extreme case in this regard. The Confederation was visibly dominated by Prussia, with a relative recognition of this domination by the other states which derived certain economic benefits from it.

It seems that a balance of power can be better established

with a system of more than three members, but not too many. Such a system allows for multiple coalitions, which generally increase the possibility of having real balance of power. The most difficult problems arise in cases where constituent entities are few and of unequal weight. If only two, the strongest entity dominates. If three, more possibilities do exist but they have no stable structure: we know, for example, the disproportionate advantage of a small entity alongside two big ones. It can tilt the balance of power. This is the *tertius gaudens* of the sociologist Simmel.

In this regard, Belgium's case is particularly relevant. One of the difficulties stems from the disagreement between Flemish and French speakers over the number of elements to be taken in consideration. Again the disagreement is over the rules of the game. For the Flemings, who are economically and politically predominant, Belgium should be mostly organised on the basis of two communities, Flemish- and French-speaking. For the French speakers, there should be three regions: Flanders, Wallonia and Brussels. Indeed Brussels is a bilingual region representing about 10 per cent of Belgium's population but with about 80 per cent of French-speaking inhabitants. This explains why French-speakers want to grant it autonomy, in order to allow their majority to play its role in Belgian politics. A compromise has been reached which distinguishes two levels of power, the communities and the regions (as already described) and organises the Flemish part in a different way to the French-speaking part. However, the Brussels problem has not been solved.

Moreover, Belgian history is one of imbalance between its two main regions, Flanders and Wallonia. During the last century and the first half of this one, Wallonia has assumed the leadership, thanks mostly to its heavy industries, coal and ironworks, whereas Flanders faced deep crises and was only slowly developing. Since the 1960s, on the contrary, Wallonia has entered a period of quick decline and Flanders has become more and more prosperous. On the political level, French speakers have long held power because of the francophilia of the high bourgeoisie and aristocracy of Flanders. The total Flemish takeover of Flanders, the demographic increase and the political impact of the Flemish movement have contributed to partly reversing this situation. Therefore, the imbalance of power is still there but reversed. This has created a very complicated situation where elements from past and present are mingled in the political culture. Some even talk of a situation where all in Belgium feel they belong to a minority. Therefore they are all frustrated and aggressive.[25]

Conclusion

We have seen that, in some cases, federal or partly federal institutions may have a specific buffer effect on conflicts. Concerning the 'autonomy' aspect of these institutions, this buffer effect can stem from the borders of these autonomous entities serving as limits to conflicts which otherwise might extend to the social whole. To this we can add the effect which cleavages division on this autonomy can carry. More homogeneous entities can be created where oppositions are less clear cut than in the political whole; such is clearly the case for Switzerland, but not for a country like Austria.

Concerning the 'co-operation' aspect of the systems we are studying, the problem of the effect on conflicts lies in the organisation of co-operation over matters of common interest. This co-operation can only have its pacifying effect if federal/ central elites have sufficient legitimacy to maintain a global political order. This can take several forms. The problem of the mechanisms of co-operation is more acute in transitional systems, where elites' struggles most often occur.

Political institutions have to be situated in the real political scene. Other socio-political mechanisms can interfere and give specific and contrasting aspects to formal institutions. For example in the USSR the centralist power of the Communist Party gives to the country's federal constitution a very centralised emphasis. We only examined this question from the viewpoint of the relations between federalism and consociational democracy. Both mechanisms can go together. One can be dominant or sometimes they can be in opposition. The tempo of federalisation can be of decisive importance.

Some attention was given to personal federalism, which means federalism with different peoples but without territories. Here, we are very near to consociationalism, and its successes or failures can be analysed in a theoretical framework. This technique can be useful when it is impossible to resort to a territorial self-rule strategy, because of very dispersed populations. Finally, autonomy and co-operation are dependent on the balance of power, which is more difficult to realise in a system with only two or three components. We must note the particular case of Belgium where the number of entities (two or three) is in itself a political contest and where these entities have known reversals of balance of power with effects historically delayed in the respective masses' reactions.

REFERENCES

1. The author wishes to thank Elizabeth Drory and Jean-Luc Roux for their co-operation in documenting this paper and Michèle Schiegelow for translating it.
2. I. D. Duchasek, *Comparative Federalism: The Territorial Dimensions of Politics*, Modern Comparative Series edited by P. H. Merkl, Holt, Rinehart and Winston, New York 1970, pp. 160–61.
3. op. cit., p. 161.
4. The expression 'regional state' is used by D. Mazzega and J. Musitelli, 'L'Organisation Regionale en Italie, Notes et Etudes Documentaires, No. 4553–4', *La Documentation Française*, Paris 1980, p. 11. In Belgium, the usual expression is 'regionalisation'.
5. P. Anderson, *L'Etat Absolutiste II – L'Europe de l'Est*, Maspero, Paris 1978, ch. 3.
6. For this section the principal references are: R. Bowie and C.-J. Friedrich, *Etudes sur le Federalisme*, 2 parts, Libraire de Droit et de Jurisprudence, Paris 1960; D. Mazzega and J. Musitelli, op. cit.; B. Touret, *L'Amenagement Constitutionnel des Etats de Peuplement Composite*, Presses de l'Université Laval, Quebec 1973; F. Delperee, *Droit Constitutionnel, T1, Les Données Constitutionnelles*, Larcier, Brussels, 1980; I. D. Duchasek, op. cit.; *Etudes sur le Regionalisme en Belgique et à l'Etranger*, Bruylant, Brussels 1973.
7. A. Lijphart, *Democracy in Plural Societies: A Comparative Exploration*, Yale University Press, New Haven and London 1977, p. 90.
8. See F. Lorenzoni and F. Merloni, 'Les Regions en Italie' in *Etudes sur le Regionalisme. . .*, p. 227.
9. H. Kerr, 'Switzerland: Social Cleavages and Partisan Conflict', *A Sage Professional Paper*, Contemporary Political Sociology Series, Vol. 1, London and Beverly Hills 1974, p. 31.
10. A. Lijphart, *Linguistic Fragmentation and the Dimensions of Cleavage: A Comparison of Belgium, Canada and Switzerland*,

report presented at IPSA meetings, Montreal 1973, p. 14; see also D. Rae and M. Taylor, *The Analysis of Political Cleavages*, Yale University Press, New Haven and London 1970.

11. Lijphart, *Linguistic Fragmentation*, pp. 94, 99.
12. ibid., p. 140.
13. A.-P. Frognier, 'Configuration générale des Parlements Belges, Italiens et Suisses. Parlementaires et Clivages Socio-politiques', report presented at conference entitled 'The Role of European Parliaments in Managing Social Conflicts', Stony Brooks, New York June 1979.
14. ibid.
15. R. Inglehart, *The Silent Revolution, Changing Values and Political Styles among Western Publics*, Princeton University Press, New Jersey 1977, p. 238.
16. D. Easton, *Analyse des Systèmes Politiques*, Part 3, A. Colin, Paris 1974.
17. See J.-P. Cot and J.-P. Mounier, *Pour une Sociologie Politique*, Part 1, Seuil, Paris 1974, pp. 217–18.
18. See N. Delruelle and A.-P. Frognier, 'L'Opinion Publique et les Problemes Communautaires', *Courrier Hebdomadaire du CRISP*, No. 880, 1980, pp. 19–20.
19. H. Daalder, 'On Building Consociational Nations: the Cases of the Netherlands and Switzerland, *International Social Science Journal*, Vol. 23, No. 3, 1971, p. 355.
20. See A. Lijphart, 'Consociational Democracy', *World Politics*, Vol. 21, 1968–9, pp. 207–25.
21. Quoted in S. Verba, 'Some Dilemmas in Comparative Research', *World Politics*, Vol. 20, No. 1, 1967, p. 126.
22. ibid., p. 211.
23. For the descriptions which follow and for the cases of Cyprus and Lebanon, see Touret, op. cit.
24. For a discussion of these failures from the consociational democracy point of view, see Lijphart, *Democracy in Plural Societies*, ch. 5.
25. These are the findings of a recent unpublished survey by N. Delruelle and A.-P. Frognier.

8

Federation and Confederation: The Experience of the United States and the British Commonwealth

Maurice J. C. Vile

The object of this paper is to examine the experience of the working of federalism in the United States and in certain countries of the British Commonwealth in order to assess those factors which seem to have been significant in the success or failure of the federal structure in dealing with the economic and social diversities which characterise those societies. I shall not attempt an exhaustive treatment of the experiments in federalism which have been made in the Commonwealth, but rather I shall try to draw out those points which seem most relevant to an assessment of the proposals which have been made recently for a 'federal solution' to the Irish problem. Finally, I shall venture to offer an opinion of what seems to me to be the only way forward in the present circumstances.

First, it is necessary to clarify certain points about the nature of federalism, of how federations differ from confederations and from unitary states. The discussion of definitions may seem to be a rather tiresomely academic activity, but it is essential that we should be quite clear about the concepts that we are using in this debate, for there is a great danger that people imagine that they are using words in the same way, only to find later that they have completely misunderstood one another. To use terms such as 'confederal' and 'federal' in a vague fashion in order to create a climate of opinion favouring agreement may well produce only disillusionment in the long run. This danger is already apparent in the pamphlet published by Fine Gael and entitled *Ireland — Our Future Together*.

The terms 'confederation' and 'federation' have in the past been used ambiguously. Thus both Switzerland and Canada have described themselves as confederations although most students of federalism would place them in the same category as the United States and Australia, which are normally described as federations. The clearest distinction between confederations and federal states lies in the way in which decisions are taken for the confederation or federation as a whole, and in the way in which those decisions are implemented. Essentially a confederation is a group of states which have come together for certain common purposes in order to act jointly in a restricted sphere of government responsibilities. The United States operating under the Articles of Confederation from 1781 to 1789 is the prime model of this system of government, and the European Community under the Treaty of Rome operates as a confederation across much of its sphere of action. In such an arrangement the component parts of the confederation consider themselves still to be sovereign entities, important decisions have to be taken unanimously, and the possibility of secession from the organisation remains open. In this respect a confederation is little different from an international organisation operating under a treaty. Furthermore, the decisions taken by the confederation fall to be implemented by the authorities in the member states, the confederation as such having no judicial or administrative machinery to enforce its decisions directly upon the citizens of those states. Confederations have normally limited their area of concern to defence, foreign affairs and economic *collaboration,* but have not become involved in the control or regulation of the internal affairs of the member states, the provision of social welfare or the maintenance of law and order. In this respect the Treaty of Rome, by providing for a degree of commercial and agricultural control, has blurred the distinction between confederation and federation; it operates in part like one and in part like the other. As far as the British Commonwealth is concerned it is difficult to find examples of confederations. One has to look to Scandinavia, to the Benelux countries, or to organisations such as NATO to find examples of this model. Confederations are, in effect, little more than treaty arrangements, and as such they tend to be unstable and transitory. They depend upon a perceived and continuing joint interest of the member states, but they are subject to the assertion of the overriding national interests of the member states, so that the attitudes of Gaullism, or *'l'Europe des patries'*, is the characteristic of the confederation. It is either a stage on the way to a federation proper, or else a transitory arrangement which will disappear when the circumstances which led the members to come together have disappeared.

The legal basis of a federation, however, is quite different. The member states merge their sovereignty into a new legal entity in which neither the central government nor the member states are sovereign. Sovereignty lies in the constitution and with the bodies which have the power of amending it. Decisions of the central government of the federation will no longer require the unanimous consent of the member states, and the federal government will have its own judicial and administrative machinery for the enforcement of its decisions. Of course the ending of the formal legal requirement of unanimity will not of itself remove the *political* restraints upon the actions of the federal authorities, who may still have to secure a very wide degree of consent before they can act effectively. I shall return to this point later. A federal system necessitates a division of powers between two levels of government, federal and state, each of which must have a high degree of autonomy, neither level being subordinate to the other. The federal 'bargain' or 'compact' which is made at the outset of the federation will set out the division of the powers of government between the two levels that is then thought to be appropriate, usually vesting in the federal government such powers as defence, foreign affairs, control of the currency, and the establishment of a postal service. The states usually retain control over such matters as education, local government and perhaps the civil and criminal law. However, it should be emphasised that in many areas of government action, such as the regulation of commerce, and taxation, both levels of government will be involved. Furthermore, a federal system is not a fixed and static entity. The division of powers between federal and state governments will continually change in line with changing attitudes concerning what is appropriate to be dealt with by one level or the other.

Federal systems of government have had considerable success, both within and outside the British Commonwealth. The United States, Switzerland, Australia and Canada are the most successful examples. India and Malaysia have also had a high degree of success in coping with problems arising from social and economic diversity, although certainly in the case of India the threat of a possible breakdown of the federal system has been present ever since it was established in 1950. But there have also been failures. The Central African Federation, the West Indian Federation, Pakistan and Nigeria have all in differing ways illustrated the limits to the use of federal structures as solutions to the problems of government in diverse societies.

It is the existence of diversity, ethnic, linguistic, religious or economic, which has led those who were creating new governmental structures to choose federalism rather than a unitary system such as that of France or Great Britain. Where people perceive differences of interest between themselves and other groups with whom they wish to form an institutional link more permanent than that of a mere treaty, then they look for a structure in which they will not lose their group identity completely, and in which they will still be able, as a group, to exercise control over those things which they consider essential to their community. Thus federalism is adopted as the system of government where the sense of a shared national identity is very weak or hardly exists at all. Such a weak sense of national identity would normally inhibit the evolution of a new, wider state altogether, were it not for the existence of an external military threat, or because of the desire to follow a common economic policy which would offer considerable advantages to the member states. Successful federations have usually evolved as the result of a combination of fear of aggression and a desire for economic advantage.

There are then two aspects of federalism which should be clarified: first, its relation to nationalism, and second, its relation to the concept of majority rule. Historically, federalism has been the solution which has been adopted when the sense of national identity needed to sustain representative institutions in a unitary state is lacking. The only alternatives are not to integrate at all, or to be integrated by an authoritarian regime. Once a federation has been established, however, and once it has successfully weathered its early difficulties, federalism becomes a device, a mechanism for the cultivation and development of latent or weak nationalism. As time progresses the attachment to the member states weakens, and the sense of identity with the wider, newly-formed nation develops; there is a progressive transfer of allegiance from the narrower to the wider community. Certainly this has been characteristic of successful federations such as the United States, Switzerland and Australia. It is less true of Canada where the reality of Canadian nationhood is still questioned today, reflecting some of the special features and problems of Canadian society. Where there has been a complete failure to develop such a wider nationalism in the initial states, the federation has failed, resulting in disintegration, as in Pakistan, or in civil war and the failure of representative government, as in Nigeria.

The second point to stress about federalism is that it represents a deliberate limitation upon the operation of majority rule democracy. It is a recognition that there are certain areas of action in which a government responsible to the whole people of the federation should make the decisions, but that there are other policy areas in which the majority in each state or province should have the decisive voice. Therefore, the division of powers between federal and state governments, and the safeguarding of the autonomy of each level by constitutional checks to the exercise of power by one level over the other. Nevertheless, a federal system, like other systems of government, is in a continual state of change, and the division of powers between levels of governments is not a static, fixed balance, but a shifting one, in which functions which were once thought to be the sole concern of the states become the acknowledged responsibility of the federal government. This pattern of change reflects the changing attitudes to national identity and to the nation referred to above. As the nation as a whole becomes more integrated, more united, the federation adopts responsibilities which at an earlier time its citizens, or at any rate a large proportion of them, would not have entrusted to it. Thus successful federations have been engines of centralisation, shifting power and authority to the centre in step with the growth of national sentiment. Thus centralisation of government power and responsibility has gone much further in the United States and Australia than in Canada with its weaker sense of national identity.

Success and Failure in Federal Systems

What then are the factors which have enabled certain federations to succeed where others have failed? Diversity is the hallmark of federations, but if the diversities are 'too great' then the federation fails to cope, at any rate in terms of genuinely representative governmental structures. How likely is it that the Soviet Union would remain as a governmental entity if complete freedom were allowed to its diverse peoples to determine their own fate? Representative institutions could not be devised to give a single framework of government to the West Indies, separated as they are by distance and local allegiances. Distance and cultural diversity made the federation of East and West Pakistan unworkable. Thus there are limits to the diversity with which federal institutions can cope. But how far can federalism cope with genuinely deep *communal* divisions within a society?

Two of the most successful federations, the United States and Australia, have not had to deal with communalism in the sense in which it is found in Europe and Asia. The United States, to be sure, has encompassed great diversities of ethnic origins, of colour, religion and of economic interest, but it has not had to contend with culturally different groupings based upon a historically identifiable homeland such as the Irish, the Basque, the Corsican or the Breton communities. The closest analogue we can find to these in North America are the Quebecois, which goes a long way to explain the frailty of Canadian federalism. The success of the most eminently 'Anglo-Saxon' federations can be traced in large part to the lack within their borders of communalism in the fullest sense of that term. In many cases where such communal divisions do exist, other kinds of solution, pluralist, consociational, have been tried rather than federalism, and, for the sake of clarity at least, we should keep these quite different structures conceptually distinct from federalism with its essentially geographical basis.

Other characteristics of American and Australian federalism point to the reasons for their success. In both federations there is a reasonably large number of units. No federation has survived with only two or three units of government at the lower level. It is indeed very unlikely that such a federation could survive, because federal systems operate on the basis of the bargaining between shifting coalitions of groups, bringing about compromises because no single group or coalition of groups is in a continually dominant position. The danger of an irreconcilable confrontation between the units in a two-unit federation is so great that sooner or later it would lead to civil war, secession, or both.

Another condition of successful federations would seem to be the requirement that no single member state should be in such a dominant position that it can dictate the policies of the federal government. There is certainly a considerable disparity in size and power between New York and Rhode Island, or between New South Wales and Tasmania, but in neither case does New York alone, or New South Wales alone, determine the fate of federal policies. Where one member state does have such a position of dominance the likelihood is that other member-states will attempt to secede, and through force or threats of force, the dominant state will effectively maintain a situation little different in reality from that of a unitary state.

Federal systems have been able to cope with the problems of societies in which deep communal divisions exist, such as in Switzerland, India and Malaysia, but in all these countries the conditions set out above, a large number of units, none of which dominates the federation, have been met. Furthermore it is clear that where the boundaries of the member-states are drawn so as to *coincide* with communal divisions the likelihood is that the problems of operating the machinery of federalism will be exacerbated. Thus in Switzerland there are religious and linguistic cleavages within the society, but the boundaries of the cantons do not coincide with these communal divisions; they cut across them, that is to say there is not a single German-speaking canton and a French-speaking canton. On the contrary, these linguistic groupings, and the religious ones as well, are broken up into a number of cantons, thus moderating the communal conflicts through the political and administrative structures. The problems of containing communalism in India have been more severe, and the fact that the Indian states do largely reflect communal interests has led to considerable conflict between the government of India and the governments of the states. Fortunately the large number of the Indian states and a relatively strong central authority has enabled India to survive.

The experience of India points up what is in the end probably the most important condition for the success of federalism – the development of a party system which will provide those political linkages across the boundaries of the member-states, without which the process of bargaining and compromise essential to federal politics cannot take place. The federal system necessitates a political structure in which each unit can assert its autonomy, but in which politics at the state level does not become disconnected from politics at the federal level. The Founding Fathers of the United States Constitution understood this very well. The Senate was established to ensure that the states had a voice in the decisions to be made by the Federal government, the President was to be elected by an Electoral College in the working of which the states exercised a considerable influence, and the states controlled the electoral laws for the federal, as well as their own, legislatures. In India the Congress Party, created initially as a national movement for independence, was able in the initial stages of the establishment of the federation to give the necessary degree of unity to India, whilst reflecting within its own structure the various regional interests which had to be respected if a head-on collision between the centre and the member-states was to be avoided. In this respect the failure of Nigerian federalism illustrates the problem only too clearly, and indeed before the outbreak of the civil war Nigeria met none of the conditions which I have suggested are necessary for the success of a federal system. The Nigerian federation began its life with only three member-states, and one of those, the Northern Region, was in a dominant position within the federal system. Furthermore, these three member-states reflected very closely the main tribal divisions within Nigeria, encapsulating within each region ethnic, religious and linguistic differences. The attempts of Nigerian politicians to bridge the gulf between these communal groupings failed, no national party system emerged to mediate conflicts between the regions or between the federal government, dominated by the North, and the other regions in the South. With hindsight at least, the Nigerian federation seemed doomed from the start.

Finally a word about the problem of civil rights in federal systems. There is no guarantee that in a particular federal system either the centre or the states will be deeply committed to the protection of individual or minority rights. However, there is a need for civil rights to be protected at both levels; against any attempt by the federal government to oppress minorities in any part of the federation, and to prevent the abuse of the rights of a minority within any of the member-states. Although there are plenty of examples of the abuse of civil rights by governments in highly centralised states, in genuinely representative federal systems, on the whole, the evidence points to the greatest danger of abuse coming from the attempts to use the authority of state governments to exclude from political power and influence those minorities within the state who do not conform to the values of, or belong to, the dominant political group in the state. Thus in the United States in 1791 the Bill of Rights was enacted to protect individual rights from abuse by the federal government, but in practice the greatest abuse of civil rights came from state governments, and it was not until in the 1950s that the Supreme Court, through the medium of the Fourteenth Amendment, directed the prohibitions of the Bill of Rights against the states that a real revolution occurred in the protection of civil rights in America.

Federalism and the Situation in Ireland

In recent times a number of proposals have come forward for a federal solution to the Irish problem. Dr FitzGerald has outlined such a proposal on behalf of Fine Gael, which would create a two-unit federal structure with Northern Ireland and the present Republic joined together. Sinn Fein has proposed a four-unit federal Ireland on the basis of the four historic provinces, in which Ulster would have a larger Catholic community than at present. More complex federal structures involving the Republic, Northern Ireland and Great Britain have also been proposed. From the analysis given above it is difficult to take any comfort in a proposal for a two-unit federation. Apart from some of the conceptual confusions to be found in the Fine Gael pamphlet, such an arrangement would seem to fly in the face of all the experience of federal systems, successful and unsuccessful. Two units, each dominated by a different communal majority, would seem almost inevitably to come into head-on conflict sooner or later, with none of the mechanisms available to mediate such conflict in federations with a larger and more varied collection of units. The problem of creating a federal government which would not be either totally dominated by one unit or totally deadlocked by the other seems to be insuperable. The Catholic population in the North would gain a great deal of confidence because of the association with the South, but the Protestant majority of the North would have no allies to turn to in the game of coalition-building and would therefore tend to maintain its present attitude of a total unwillingness to compromise.

It should also be stressed that the Fine Gael pamphlet does not really give the impression that the authors fully realise the commitment which would be involved in a federal structure involving, as it would, the dissolution of the Republic as at present constituted. On the one hand Northern Ireland would have to become, if only for an instant, independent of the United Kingdom, and then integrate itself into a new legal entity. Equally the Republic would have to amend its present constitution to make it appropriate for the status of a state in the new federation; it would have to accept that a new legal entity would exist with an authority above that of the new Southern state; and it would have to accept that constitutional provisions guaranteeing civil rights in the whole of Ireland would be necessary, guarantees which *might* conflict with some of the provisions at present applicable in the South.

Intellectually the Sinn Fein proposal is subject to considerably fewer objections in terms of its four-unit structure, and if the political basis for such a proposal existed, it would be well worth further discussion. At the moment I would imagine that few people would think that a constitutional convention could be called to give serious discussion to such an idea, and like the other long-term possibilities a great deal of political development would be necessary before such discussion could be initiated. Other long-term 'solutions' are conceivable, such as Northern Ireland as a unit in a federation of the British Isles, or as part of a European federation of regions, but at present these are all at least as remote as the realisation of a federation of the North and the South in Ireland.

Conclusion

The main conclusion of this paper would seem therefore to be a negative one: that federalism does not offer a short-term solution to the Irish problem, and indeed there are almost certainly no short-term solutions. That does not mean that federalism should not, in some form or another, be one of the long-run alternative frameworks for a peaceful solution. It would seem to me therefore that we must look to the general nature of the problem and isolate the basic elements in the situation in order to talk sensibly about short-term situations. These elements would seem to me to be as follows:

1. It is necessary to recognise that all the various aspirations that are held in Northern Ireland concerning its future are perfectly legitimate positions to hold. Complete integration into the Republic, a federal union with the Republic or with Great Britain, or within the wider framework of the European Community, independence for Northern Ireland, or complete integration within the United Kingdom, all these alternatives are ones which reasonable people can hold. Neither the United Kingdom nor the Republic is a hell-on-earth in which no reasonable person could be expected to live.

2. None of these alternatives, including the present situa-

tion of direct rule, is workable in the long run unless an overwhelming proportion of all the population of Northern Ireland is prepared freely to accept it. Therefore the first policy aim of the proponents of any of these alternatives must be to create circumstances in Northern Ireland where the population of the province can itself come to a collective decision which will be accepted by them all. At present this is impossible because the basic sense of trust, which alone could produce such a situation, is wholly lacking. The first requirement, therefore, for any of these outcomes is the restoration to the province of genuine political debate about the issues which the population should be concerned with — housing, education, employment.

3. At the present time it is the responsibility of the British government to make policy for Northern Ireland. It follows from (2) above that that policy must be in the first instance to restore a degree of self-government to the province so that the dialogue, from which alone the mutual acceptance of one community by the other can follow, can be initiated. Legislative devolution is an essential prerequisite for progress. Furthermore, such devolution would have to be in a form which ensured that a fair say was given to all sections of the community, and the only way in which that could be done would be a power-sharing executive, together with a system of proportional representation. There is nothing new in this suggestion, but it is a policy which, since it was abandoned in 1974, has not been taken up energetically by British governments although they have no alternative policy which could conceivably work.

4. In Northern Ireland it is necessary to develop a sense, in each individual, that his civil rights will be respected, whether by a government in London, in Dublin, in Stormont, in Athlone or in Brussels. The greatest need, therefore, is for some *constitutional* guarantees, properly enforceable. The need for such guarantees is greater in Ireland than on the mainland, but the need there is by no means negligible. Some means has to be found of breaking with the British abhorrence of Bills of Rights to give sufficient self-confidence to every individual that he will be given a reasonable hearing and fair

treatment. Such confidence certainly does not exist at present.
In some respects, as Irishmen of all colours seem determined to maintain, Ireland is a special case, a very difficult
problem. But of course there are many similar problems of
communal strife around the world, and Ireland is by no
means unique in this respect. In other ways the Irish problem
today is very different from the Irish problem of earlier centuries. No government, whether of the United Kingdom or of
the Republic, in its right mind, could wish to keep Ulster
within its borders unless the population of the province as a
whole wished to remain. The problem is to give to the people
of Ulster the ability to govern themselves in whatever context they themselves choose. It is to that long-term aim and
that alone that government policies should be directed.

BIBLIOGRAPHY

Black, E. R., *Divided Loyalties: Canadian Concepts of Federalism*,
Montreal 1975
Brady, J., 'The Meaning and Relevance of Pluralism in Northern
Ireland', *Studies*, Autumn 1979
Dikshit, R., *The Political Geography of Federalism: An Inquiry into
Origins and Stability*, Delhi 1975
Duchacek, I. D., *Comparative Federalism: The Territorial Dimension of
Politics*, New York 1970
Fine Gael, *Ireland — Our Future Together*, Dublin 1979
Franck, T. H., *Why Federations Fail*, New York 1968
Hicks, U. K., *Federalism, Failure and Success: A Comparative Study*,
London 1978
New Ulster Political Research Group, 'Beyond the Religious Divide',
Supplementary Introduction to Documents for Discussion, Belfast
1980
Simeon, R., *Federal-Provincial Diplomacy*, Toronto 1972

9

The Sovereignty of Parliament and the Irish Question

Bernard Crick

Much depends on how one perceives the problem. Certainly to see it as the relation of Ulster to the rest of Ireland is too narrow and begs the question. When it was seen that way by Liberal governments, however belatedly, as in 1886 and 1911, the Protestants of Ulster began to arm, effectively and respectably. Rival politicians have forgotten their history if they can seriously hope or seriously fear that Great Britain could either give or sell Northern Ireland to the Republic. The Republic could not accept such a gift without guaranteed free service in perpetuity: the British army could alone enforce it, even assuming (as it was assumed until the Curragh incident of 1913) that it would; and the Irish taxpayer might jib at the 30 to 50p in the Irish pound increase in the standard rate of taxation that it has been variously estimated would be needed to keep the North at its present highly subsidised welfare levels. Never to forget that the great constitutional lawyer, A. V. Dicey, expounder of 'the rule of law' and 'the sovereignty of parliament' as the two foundation-stones of the constitution, signed Carson's Covenant and put himself openly on the side of the 'respectable rebels'.

The true political problem, put in its most obvious and banal form, is that a large number of people will stick at nothing to achieve the unity of Ireland (or at least will tolerate violent actions by a smaller number), and that a large number of people will stick at nothing to maintain their homeland as part of the United Kingdom. Even that is too simple; Republicans do not seriously hope to achieve a lasting unity by force of arms, only to render Northern Ireland ungovernable by the British. And many, possibly most, Unionists would favour unilateral independence rather than loyally obey Acts of Parliament that appeared to move them constitutionally into a united Ireland, even a federal or confederal Ireland.

Perhaps only the two extreme positions are clear and logical, the unity of Ireland or the unity of the present United Kingdom. And these positions are surely contradictory. As a human being, I freely admit to feeling the intense plausibility of both positions, indeed to sharing the pain of being torn between not injustice and justice, but two rival views of justice. This is not unique to Ireland. Albert Camus was torn between the justice of the case of the Arabs in Algeria and that of his fellow *colons,* even though they were only third-generation settlers. Those who are committed utterly to 'One Ireland' or to 'No Surrender' can feel none of the moral agony of sharing two apparently incompatible perspectives. Sometimes, such people, for all their long, miserable faces, seem in fact to enjoy the storm and the conflict: violent deeds and violent words become a way of life, ends in themselves. But the student of politics must start from these two incompatibilities: that Northern Ireland is part of the United Kingdom and that it is part of the island of Ireland. Even if we accept fully the 'two nations' thesis, the Protestant nation of Northern Ireland seems in English, Welsh or Scottish eyes to have essential links with, and characteristics of, Ireland as well as with Great Britain.

Talk of immediate solutions is fatuous. But possibilities of political containment of the worst symptoms exist. If there are no agreeable solutions, there might be acceptable frameworks established in which future changes, even if not fully predictable, could at least be accepted as fair; or at least accepted. Any such frameworks have to face the fact that Northern Ireland does face two ways. Straightaway this ensures that there can never be any simple 'unity of Ireland', a straightforward extension, as some have imagined, of the jurisdiction of the 1922 Dublin government, with a few vague mutterings about 'guarantees' for the 'minority' (i.e., Ulster's majority). But we must also remember that from 1920 to 1972, Northern Ireland was by no means an ordinary part of the administration of the United Kingdom. If legally she was, political and administrative reality was very different, what I can only call quasi or *de facto* federalism. And even direct rule has not meant an integrated administration – no more for Ulster than for Scotland after 1707. I will suggest that the apparent contradiction of the two extreme viewpoints only involves a total incompatibility on a traditional but now very suspect and self-deluding view of the sovereign state. The theory that every state must be sovereign and possess absolute power is as suspect as the theory that every nation must be a state. People may want it passionately, that is a fact of political life; but it is not necessarily true. All sovereign power is understood by those who operate it at the time as being limited by well-known political and economic contingencies. This essay will suggest that British constitutional history needs re-interpreting to show that the doctrine of and belief in 'parliamentary sovereignty' has been a response to peculiar political conditions, hinted at in the very formula 'United Kingdom', not a necessity of law and order. If 'the sovereignty of parliament' can be seen as a useful myth, helpful at times but dangerous if accepted as a general truth about the minimal conditions of political order, both sides might begin to be impressed by the overlapping edges rather than the solitary extremities of their boxed-in positions.

Talk should begin about whether new forms of government or of inter-government relations could not emerge to reflect the fact, not change the fact, that Northern Ireland faces two ways. It is part of the role of the student of politics to talk or speculate, not to commit himself, and to talk freely in long time-scales, not to rival journalists in hard-headed realism about the next election, not simply to talk about possible federal or confederal relations. And as if such talk is not reckless enough, the dominant constitutional ideologies of both the Irish and the British state also need questioning to see if they are, indeed, general truths or simply responses to past political conditions. Has the Irish constitution reached its final form? Has the United Kingdom ever been as centralised and as unitary a state as its statesmen have claimed and its textbooks have loyally or thoughtlessly and uncritically repeated? My remarks are mainly limited to the United Kingdom.

Historically the very formula 'United Kingdom' was developed to stress the primacy, first of the crown, then of parliament, in the practical business of holding together the different historical communities of England, Wales, Scotland and Ireland (two of which, indeed, had themselves never had common government, any sense of being states, until conquest). The formula developed into a conscious exaggeration, for clear political purposes, of the unity and homogeneity of the realm. 'United Kingdom' implies that Great Britain is not a conventional state. The English may dominate, but their domination must take unusual forms. Perhaps there is an English state, but not a corresponding English nation. Some have seen this oddity as simply a colonial mentality, or 'internal colonialism', an imperial English heartland imposing not merely its military and commercial power but also a hegemony of all cultural values upon a Celtic periphery.[1] This is too simple, or it smacks of a racial anti-racial interpretation, for so long as English political conventions were accepted, Scottish, Irish and Welsh notables were readily allowed to make their careers on the Westminster and Whitehall stages, and to live, in various ways, in two cultures. And the colonial thesis ignores both the success of the English parliamentary ideology and the willing price it had to pay. No specifically English nationalism was developed; there was patriotism to United Kingdom institutions in the eighteenth century certainly, and imperialism towards the 'lesser breeds within the law' in the nineteenth century, but an English nationalism as a public ideology had to be foresworn. Indeed national sentiments were tolerated in Scotland, Ireland and Wales, even at times officially encouraged and preserved, even to the level of distinct local administration, so long as national sentiment stopped short of a nationalist claim to constitute separate states.

The doctrine of the sovereignty of parliament arose not merely in opposition to the powers of the crown as seen in 1688, but because after the Act of Union (that is the managed voluntary suppression of the Scottish parliament) parliament was intolerant of any other legally constituted authority but its own. Indeed, the legal doctrine of sovereignty (that no court or other assembly can override legislation passed by parliament according to its own rules of procedure) was almost consciously confused with an empirical, pseudo-historical doctrine: that political stability, indeed law and order themselves, depended on parliamentary sovereignty. The Irish parliament began to appear as a threat in theory more than as a practical and reasonably effective way of governing the country, even before Grattan's Parliament and the rebellion of 1798. Just as divided powers seemed impossible to practical men in 1775, so the 1798 rebellion must have seemed in large part at least a consequence of divided powers, not a case for reforming and trusting a subsidiary legislature.

The great Blackstone in his *Commentaries on the Laws of England* said that parliament

... hath sovereign and uncontrollable authority in the making, confirming, enlarging, restraining, abrogating, repealing, reviving and expounding of laws, concerning all matters of all possible denominations, ecclesiastical or temporal, civic, military, maritime, or criminal: this being the place where that absolute power, which must in all governments reside somewhere, is entrusted by the constitution of these kingdoms. All mischiefs and grievances, operations and remedies, that transcend the ordinary course of the laws, are within reach of this extraordinary tribunal. It can regulate or new-model the succession to the Crown; as was done in the reigns of Henry VIII and William III. It can alter the established religion of the land; as was done in a variety of instances, in the reign of Henry VIII and his three children. It can change and create afresh even the constitution of the kingdom and Parliaments themselves: as was done by the Act of Union and by the several statutes for triennial and septennial elections. It can, in short, do everything that is not naturally impossible.[2]

But is there really such absolute power? There is, but only in a legal sense: that no other body can make enactments. But politically no government or parliament can 'do everything that is not naturally impossible'. In any other sense but a narrowly legal one concerned with jurisdictions, the phrase is mere rhetoric. But politically it is not *mere* rhetoric; it is meant to impress, just as Thomas Hobbes' *Leviathan* state was meant to frighten people into obedience, but not to do very much else except keep the peace. And must such power, rhetorical or not, 'in all governments reside somewhere' (Blackstone clearly means in one determinate and sovereign institution)? Young Jeremy Bentham in his *Fragment on Government* famously mocked Blackstone. Did he not think that the Switzers had government in their federal cantons?

Even after the founding of the United States of America, even after the war of 1812, English statesmen and lawyers continued to assert that 'divided power', 'divisions of power', and federalism especially, were somehow inherently unstable, tending to breakdown and anarchy, from which we British (or English?) were preserved by sovereignty of parliament and the rule of law. This was part of Whig ideology: the regime needed to argue thus precisely because in political and economic reality the United Kingdom of Great Britain, Scotland and Ireland was anything but united. This cloak of legitimation had so many obvious holes in it that the practical need was recognised for a constant skilled management of Scotland and Ireland, both by and in parliament. If religion was often felt to be a major binding factor of civil order, this only made the problem more acute. Many Scottish historians now take the view that opposition to the suppression of the Scottish parliament was relatively muted because the Assembly of the Kirk was felt to be the true popular, national institution. And it is clear that Catholic Emancipation in Ireland was passed, much like the Reform Act of 1832, not out of principle or dislike of anomalies, but largely as an attempt to keep the country governable at all. (In the same way objections to proportional representation as incompatible with the basic principles of the British constitution did not override the political need for institutionalised PR in the elections for the Northern Ireland Assembly of 1974, the Convention of 1975 and the European Parliament of 1979; this alone created any realistic hope of these unusual institutions ever working). Even the mild ecclesiastical proscriptions in nineteenth-century Wales stirred up civil disobedience over Church taxes, and led to disestablishment as a political response.

The memory of the 1745 rising made management of

Scottish affairs from Whitehall and Westminster a conscious, constant and delicate matter. Even minor removals of Catholic disabilities to recruit Scottish highlanders for the American wars could have unexpected and formidable side-effects, stirring up a Protestant mob in the Gordon riots. The cabinet not merely ordered a reluctant George IV to Edinburgh for ceremonies of reconciliation stage-managed by Sir Walter Scott himself, but persuaded him to wear the kilt (once); and it was state policy that Queen Victoria should reside in Scotland for a noticeable part of each year, as well as changing her religion when she crossed the border. The establishment of the Scottish Office and substantial measures of administrative devolution to Scotland in the last quarter of the nineteenth century were conscious attempts to stop Home Rule agitation growing up there. The Scottish question was not felt to have ended with 1707 and then Culloden and the clearances: an historically minded political elite was conscious of the need for conciliation and special treatment of Scotland for longer than most twentieth-century accounts of practical politics would allow to be possible. An articulate doctrine of English nationalism had to be consciously restrained, unlike in all the other nation-states of Europe, as part of the actual politics of governing the multinational United Kingdom.

By the 1960s both Westminster and Whitehall seemed to have lost this skill in practising either a *de jure* quasi-federalism, as in the former colonies, or a *de facto* quasi-federalism, as in Scotland and Wales and in Ireland before independence. Each decade saw the old experience of imperial administration grow less and less tangible. If Northern Ireland still remained, and with a constitutional and political status wholly anomalous to sovereignty of parliament doctrine, it was resolutely ignored by parliament until the troubles of 1968. And in most student textbooks and elementary works of constitutional law, it vanished almost entirely.

The contradiction between theory and practice in British political opinion is almost schizophrenic when one considers that the cabinet and the Colonial Office in the nineteenth century seemed to accept as part of nature that Canada, Australia and South Africa, even, could only be governed with federal structures of public law. Almost unthinkingly a federal form of three-tier government was offered to the colonies in New Zealand, and astonishment was great when they rejected it as grossly extravagant. Many of the post-1945 new constitutions followed suit, notably India and Nigeria. But in the homeland the belief was strong that any relaxation of the sovereignty of parliament could lead to disintegration. Joseph Chamberlain feared in 1886 that 'Home Rule for Ireland' could lead to demands for 'Home Rule All Round', as by 1910 it did; and it was touch and go whether Liberals would proceed with a general act or a specifically Irish act first. After the First World War, the Irish rebellion and civil war, this was forgotten; but for a brief moment of power the Liberal Party had broken from the old Whig parliamentary ideology, now taken over by both Tory and Labour. Since Labour only came into government after the Irish question was held to have been solved, and since Wales and Scotland were distressed areas, needing central help, and heavily working-class and heavily Labour, the Labour Party has never developed a distinctive constitutional theory. The promotion of the Scottish Devolution Bill was an extraordinary piece of opportunism on Harold Wilson's part, and its drafting showed that it had been put together without any clear lines of principle by men who mostly did not believe in it and who certainly lacked the experience of thinking federally, as had the generation of Churchill, Amery, Milner and F. E. Smith in relation both to the Irish question and to the broader imperial 'great game'.

The dog that does not bark behaves most peculiarly. Specialised and now popular studies of objectivity and merit have been written on the Irish question, but most British textbooks on politics and law have simply ignored Northern Ireland (until after 1968) and Scotland (until the Scottish National Party polled 30 per cent in the two general elections of 1974). Even the President of Harvard, A. L. Lowell, said of Scotland and Ireland in the preface to his book, *The Government of England,* that:

> The British Constitution is full of exceptions, of local customs and special acts with which town clerks must be familiar. They fill the path of these men with pitfalls,

but they do not affect seriously the general principles of the government, and no attempt is made to describe them here. Even the institutions of Scotland and Ireland, interesting as they are in themselves, have been referred to only so far as they relate to the national government or throw light upon its working.[3]

And not much light did they throw apparently. Even our contemporary, Richard Rose, who has recently put us all in his debt with research work on Northern Ireland, called his first book *Politics in England*. Perhaps Rose could only make British politics appear as systematic as his social science models and frameworks demanded by ignoring initially the Celtic context of English politics. Members of his school tend, like Lowell, to see 'the periphery' as an exception to the normal practices of the English centralised, unitary state. Now local politics in Scotland, Wales and Northern Ireland are very different from local politics in England. But the separate identities of Scotland, Wales and Northern Ireland are not exceptional to the United Kingdom; they have posed major problems for the British state for hundreds of years and have radically affected the structure of the machine, as well as the states of mind of statesmen. Nationality problems are not exceptional to British politics: they are a characteristic part of it. Most of the great leaders of the past have been constantly aware of how integral was 'the Celtic fringe', and a large number either came from or made their reputations in the affairs of 'the periphery'. Only in the post-Suez generation of British politicians has this experience been lost. Among the old Tories this can still linger on, but among the new Conservatives the tradition is gone. And even in the Republic of Ireland, the British heritage (deliberately the wrong and the provocative word) still lingers on to an unexpected degree in many administrative and political practices.

All of this appears paradoxical only on two counts: firstly, if we try to write the history of the British state or even of the comparatively new Irish state as if they are wholly separate entities and experiences, as if the ideology and rhetoric were historical truth, and do not look at the political, social and economic relationships of — to use an historical and geographical expression — the British Isles as a whole; and secondly, if we adopt too rigid a language of 'parliamentary sovereignty' or 'the sovereign state' or (like some social scientists) develop abstract expectations that political systems, national and local, must be highly systematic and share a common 'political culture' or 'consensus' if they are to work at all. That states cannot work *at all* without a common political culture or consensus about basic values is observably false: think only of Belgium, Canada, Italy, Nigeria. What most people who say this must really mean is that they cannot work *well,* in evaluative terms, by modern Atlantic liberal, democratic standards. Even Northern Ireland can, after all, be governed, after a fashion, without consensus. And so can many other countries.

Self-deception goes deep. In a debate on the Government of Ireland Bill (1893) the Duke of Devonshire said:

> In the United Kingdom, Parliament is supreme not only in its legislative but in its Executive functions. Parliament makes and unmakes our Ministries; it revises their actions. Ministries may make peace and war, but they do so at pain of instant dismissal from office, and in affairs of internal administration the power of Parliament is equally direct. It can dismiss a Ministry if it is too extravagant, or too economical; it can dismiss a Ministry because its government is too stringent or too lax. It does actually and practically, in every way, directly govern England, Scotland and Ireland.[4]

My objection to this is not merely the familiar realist critique that parties try to do all this, if at all, not parliament. For the statement could simply be rephrased to speak of the need for working majorities of parties within parliament and governing through parliament, not literally government by parliament. I point to the flagrant falsity, long before that Duke of Devonshire's time and still not true today of his last sentence: he was perfectly aware that Scotland had its own ecclesiastical, legal and educational systems, which parliament might amend but would never abolish. Government administration in Scotland and Ireland (as now in

Northern Ireland) was highly devolved, peculiar and in indigenous hands. For obvious and well-known political reasons parliament was loath to interfere unless the local administration came near to breakdown. But for less obvious political reasons, the truth was always denied. Parliamentary sovereignty was the ideology of an imperially minded governing class, not a universal truth about or necessity of British politics (or of any other, for that matter).

British constitutional lawyers, reacting against Dicey, have been teaching their students for at least twenty years how narrowly legal a doctrine is parliamentary sovereignty, cheerfully regarding the claim to political sovereignty as absurd, noting the large number of bodies 'out of doors' that parliament handles most gingerly if at all.[5] But this critique has not penetrated far. Recently many advanced English socialists (who might have other reasons for scepticism about sovereignty theory) began to invoke it again, as if plucked from the folk unconscious, in their campaign against British membership of the EEC. They may have better reasons for suspicion of membership than a confusion of legal sovereignty (which parliament was in fact exercising) with political sovereignty which, in the sense of power, it notoriously lacked anyway, notably because of the declining economy, internal political factors and international realities and obligations. Indeed some of the left wing still talk both of 'parliamentary sovereignty' and of the authenticity of 'extra-parliamentary democracy', as sublimely unaware of the inherent contradiction as when Dicey went on and on about 'the rule of law' *and* 'parliamentary sovereignty'. And like Dicey, they are not above justifying direct action when some actual results of two contradictory beliefs and modes of behaviour appear.

I should make clear that personally, if slightly irrelevantly, I favour both more power for parliament and more power for extra-parliamentary representative institutions. But I talk about *power,* not sovereignty, that is, something to be balanced politically, uninhibited and unconfused by beliefs that there are any non-negotiable positions (such as, for instance, *the* constitution of the Republic of Ireland or *the* constitution or territorial integrity of the United Kingdom).

Political power has to be seen not as a unique institutional locus or as symbolic events, to which legal theory and romantic nationalism respectively can become attached, but as a process constantly responding to changes in the actual situation. Political power comes neither from the barrel of a gun nor from a lawyer's mouth: it always comes from compromise between continuity and change. Guns can sometimes wreck political power, or provide the marginal increment of destruction if a government is losing its power, in the sense of losing that authority which people ordinarily (in most respects) obey and respect or at least accept. But guns cannot govern. Quite simply, as Hannah Arendt remarked in her short book, *On Violence,* 'power is acting in concert':[6] public opinion has to be carried for orderly government to take place. Violence occurs when governments lose their power, it is seldom the cause of the loss of power; and it is obvious that most governments resort to violence only when their habitual political power begins to break down. Equally no amount of constitutional ingenuity ('politic words', as the poet said) can patch up an impossible situation, or provide more than a temporary patch pending long-term structural repairs and alterations.

To see power as a process should make us look at the widest possible context of a problem, and neither to be in awe of the gun nor inhibited by the lawyers. Certainly at some stage we need to begin to consider not just the peculiarity of the United Kingdom and of the Republic of Ireland as separate sovereign states, as in legal senses they obviously are, and in nationalistic senses too; but also consider the anomalies in British-Irish relations as so conceived. Patrick Keatinge's essay in this volume goes far in that direction. There are an extraordinary number of things in common between Britain and Ireland (quite apart from Northern Ireland) when compared to almost any other pair of sovereign states conceivable. It is not for me to comment on the interplay of English and Gaelic culture in the Republic, reaching even more widely than political and commercial institutions with common roots and practices. But consider only the most obvious anomalies on the British side, the openness of the ballot box as well as employment to Irish citizens. One would be hag-ridden by definitions if one used this as evidence that the United Kingdom is not fully a sovereign state, rather than simply noting that the actual state has responded shrewdly to unusual historical and political circumstances in specific ways. What are anomalies in light of sovereignty theory are, on both sides of the water, readily understandable in terms of both history and politics. And politically the case for building on them, quite apart from the problems of Northern Ireland, seems far more convincing, more likely to occur in fact, than the case for seeing them as purely residual anomalies that should be tidied up and out. And similar considerations apply to existing levels of cross-border co-operation, both formal and informal.

I must labour this point of theory. So many limitations of leadership arise because politicians pride themselves on being purely practical and do not recognise how much they view the world through theoretical presuppositions. Lack of self-consciousness can often lead, as J. M. Keynes famously argued, these practical men to carry with them out-of-date theory, not no theory. If power is seen as a process, then we must gradually abandon the old thick true-Brit way of looking at institutions and ideas as if never the twain shall meet, as if institutions are simply the inert carriers of ideas, never suffering any change of state by contact with the ideas themselves. Such a view is that parliament is sovereign and can do anything. Neither is its power politically sovereign; it can be predominant but never omnipotent; and nor has it ever been able to suppress the non-English national cultures of the United Kingdom. Acting inflexibly, it lost most of Ireland, but its flexibility has so far kept the constitutional connection with Wales, Scotland and Northern Ireland.

The conventional theory has not gone unchallenged. Harold Laski went so far as to argue in his once famous *Grammar of Politics* that all power is inherently federal, using that term in a broad sense where many would use 'pluralistic'. He argued, following Figgis on the role of churches and Deguit on the role of trades unions, that the theory of the sovereign state only had relevance to periods of state formation and nation-building: that otherwise any institution that claimed a monopoly of decision-making was both oppressive and unstable; that a realistic approach to order always meant recognition of a plurality of quasi-autonomous corporations or societies within the state — churches, trades unions, pressure groups and sub-cultures of various kinds. The state itself was a unique institution, but only in that it had the initiative to set the terms of processes of conciliation between other groups, not that it was absolute, able to make or break other groups.

To some such a view of the state as mediator or as 'group of groups', is inadequate. The emergency powers of the state, that to Laski are residual or only usable for the defence of the state itself, not for resolving problems within an inherently pluralistic society, to others are central and perennial. Even the sociologist Max Weber defined the state as that social institution which held a monopoly of legitimate means of violence. He at least stressed legitimacy, whereas some super-realists, like Hobbes, Mosca and Pareto, thought that the coercive power of the state could actually create legitimacy (a view that is as empirically dubious as it is morally dubious). On such a definition of the state some might hold that the United Kingdom is hardly a state at all, unable to enforce its monopoly of legitimate violence in Northern Ireland. Since it cannot govern, these realists might say, it should get out. But even Thomas Hobbes, while he argued that obligation ceases when the sovereign can no longer keep the peace and protect the lives of his subjects, carefully added that obligation is then only transferred to another sovereign if he can clearly do better. All conditions in between must be a matter of political judgment. In fact, none of these definitions are definitive. Beyond the traditional minimal functions of a state, the defence of the realm and the enforcement of law and order, and modern maximalist views of industrialisation and the welfare of the inhabitants lies a vast range of political alternatives, so little that is relevant can be inferred from such definitions. Even territorial integrity is negotiable and ideas of what it constitutes change through time. Unionists must be aware of that; indeed it is their deepest fear — though their fear need not be so obsessive when everyone (well, nearly everyone) can see the impossibility of coercing them. And as territorial integrity immediately leads to definition and control of borders, it is worth saying that there are borders and borders. 'Necessity of state' can sometimes close or tightly control borders, but sometimes states have to relax their borders, even turn a blind eye on the movement of, for instance, nomads or, in more complex societies, people with a dual culture or allegiance, with two passports in their pockets.

All states will defend themselves if threatened by armed force. Weber was right at that point. Americans fought to preserve 'the Union' when faced by military rebellion, but somehow 'the Union' (*ex pluribus unum*) was not, in a traditional European sense, 'the state'. My argument is that the 'United Kingdom', though it has pretended to be a sovereign, centralised state, has had in practice to allow a kind of informal federalism. It could be said that the Ulster worker's strike threatened the power of the state, but more precisely it threatened a policy of the government. I think that even the prevaricating and indecisive Harold Wilson would have let the police and army tear down the barricades had he felt the safety of the state to be threatened (he never seemed to care much for the integrity of his government so long as it survived). Many modern states have to show similar remarkable discretion where they attempt to enforce their 'sovereign power', in case it is challenged: many Emperors stay in bed for lack of clothes. Edmund Burke once asked the House of Commons over proposals to coerce the American colonists: 'I care not if you have a right to make them miserable, have you not an interest to make them happy?'

It would be easy if the concept of 'consensus' could replace sovereignty as the hypothetical, mystical cement that holds societies together. 'Consensus' and 'pluralism' are often linked, but if one is serious about pluralism, if one recognises that, for instance, Protestant and Catholic *do* hold different values, then what becomes of consensus as a necessary condition for government? Either one must say that good government is only possible where there is a consensus about basic values, which would lead to even more governments and even more instability and intolerance than nationalism has created as an ideology of government; or one must say that consensus is an ecumenical Hindu-Unitarian-Latitudinarian-Muslim-

Catholic-Protestant-Jewish-Humanist mishmash. Personally I think that toleration and reconciliation involve mutual respect for, and recognition of, differences, not excessive ecumenical fervour. It is indeed possible to govern without consensus and amid a diversity of values. Lord Acton actually thought (in his famous debate with John Stuart Mill) that government over different nations and religions was of a higher ethical order than national states, though one is bound to say that most such governments are of a more rough-and-ready nature. 'Consensus' is best reserved to point to the need for agreement about means, not about ends, about procedures, not about their results. Good government is impossible when people either cannot accept that decisions are made fairly or will not accept some decisions, however fair the procedures. Nobody in Northern Ireland is against elections, for instance, so long as they yield the desired and predictable result. Some people even favour institutional innovation to settle 'the problem': a referendum, says one, of all the people of the United Kingdom; or a referendum, says another, of all the people of Ireland.

Most actual government is to be found in the ground between the two extremes: Hobbes saying anarchy if no final and absolute sovereignty, or Adam Smith and Talcott Parsons saying that there is only a minimal need for government *if* values are shared and systematically related. There might be some sense, then, in taking Laski's admittedly vaguer 'all power is federal' as a starting point, rather than half hoping that Britain could be truly a state after coming to fear that the actual political system may not be that systematic after all.

It is thus necessary to destroy the myths of both 'sovereignty' theory and 'political systems' theory and their alleged empirical entailments, if any progress is to be made. To put it simply, the beliefs are widespread that basic order is always threatened if, says one theory, there is not a common culture or, says the other, a truly sovereign state. So the temptation is either to try to enforce the conditions to fit the theory (sometimes politely called 'integrated education' or elsewhere 'moral leadership') or deliberately to restrict the boundaries of the 'sovereign state' to correspond with the area in which norms can be enforced with minimum effort.

I favour an English state in the heartland of old Mercia, south of the Trent and east of the Wye. Some Ulstermen favour a Protestant state within redrawn, diminished and tight boundaries (though with Conor Cruise O'Brien as king). Sinn Fein presumably want a state of their own on the West Bank of the Gaeltacht. However, in the real world there might be something to be said for examining (a) how federal a state the United Kingdom already is and (b) whether *de jure* institutionalisation of *de facto* practices might not be advantageous.

If Mr Enoch Powell MP succeeds, for instance, in keeping the Official Unionists solidly behind an integrationist policy and they are not swallowed live by the DUP, the most likely result would be to increase radically British (that is English, Scottish and Welsh) opinion in favour of withdrawal. For the attempt to impose the British state on Northern Ireland, in Powell's sovereignty and unity sense, would simply over time prove too wearisome and bloody to be endured, even though nothing catastrophic might happen. And integration would reveal to Unionist supporters that once they forsake their peculiar institutions, they are but a small minority in the whole United Kingdom. But a federal recognition of likenesses/differences, common and rival interests, could work, might prove acceptable even if never fully agreeable. At least the White, Green, Buff papers of the last three years have moved from the Convention period language of 'agreement between the parties' to a more realistic 'solutions acceptable to the people of Northern Ireland'. The present British government could yet, if it acted with half of the zeal and firmness that some of us feel it is showing against the trades unions and the working class, impose an acceptable framework of parliamentary governing — certainly not on an unwilling majority in Northern Ireland, but probably only upon reluctant and hostile political leaders. What is acceptable and what is agreeable can prove very different in actual politics.

Both the *Working Paper* of November 1979 (Cmnd 7763) and *Proposals for Further Discussion* (Cmnd 7950) show a sudden, almost a frenetic, increase in what one can only call 'institutional inventiveness'. Some less inhibited minds, better educated about historical constitutional proposals, showing something of the old skills, have penetrated the Northern Ireland Office compared to the period of the Convention when the machine sat back and hoped that something would emerge from the *Sittlichkeit* and *Volksgeist* without external stimulus. But the old sovereignty myth dies hard: the exclusion of an 'Irish dimension' is obvious (and more apparent than real), but a Bill of Rights, entrenchment and judicial review are still obviously felt to be 'anomalous' if done for Ulster alone, likely to 'set a dangerous precedent' for the rest of the United Kingdom. This last point was very evident in 1974 and 1975 when any bilateral suggestions from the Northern Ireland Office of federalism or quasi-federalism for Northern Ireland were blocked by No. 10's fears that it would *encourager les Écosses*. Only a year later Wilson did his U-turn and went for Scottish devolution in the teeth of a then largely reluctant Scottish Labour Party.

Three years ago I tried to set this as a University of London 'A' level question, but the teacher assessors rejected it as too difficult: 'The concept of "devolution" was invented by Harold Wilson to obscure the hitherto reasonably clear distinction between Federalism and Local Government. *Explain and discuss.*' Top marks would have gone to the candidate who saw clearly long-term dangers of uncertainty. After all, if Stormont was *de facto* federalism for so long, an ordinary Act of Parliament, passed at great speed, could abolish it. That would not be bought again, either by majority or minority.

Even if inter-party talks were resumed in Northern Ireland, there may be very little hope for a genuinely federal constitution emerging there. What might have been *acceptable* to SDLP voters three or four years ago, even if never *agreeable* to their leaders, a Bill of Rights, committee chairmanships, the need for two-thirds majorities, etc., etc., even short of power-sharing, in other words a Pyrrhic victory for the Unionists and a noble defeat for the SDLP, all this now seems part of history, or a history that never was. The minority is more determined than ever on 'an Irish dimension'; indeed it is doubtful if the leaders of the SDLP could now carry their followers even into power-sharing in a purely United Kingdom context. So I only make the speculative comment that *if* Northern Ireland came into a clear federal relationship with the United Kingdom, implications would follow for the rest of the United Kingdom constitution such as Wilson feared but some might hope for: a Bill of Rights, Scottish and possibly Welsh devolution, proportional representation even. But these would not flow from liberal pressure of principle, rather from the need to carry on the Queen's government, a political response to a crucial recognition that the unity of the United Kingdom could now depend more on federalising power than on repeating historical formulas, however useful they were in their day in strengthening central authority amid the quadruple diversity of nations. Do Scottish separatists really want to separate? Do Ulster integrationists really want to integrate and lose their own institutions? Do Westminster opponents of devolution really fear the break-up of the United Kingdom or simply the diminishment of English dominance?

Of course *if*, equally if, the British Conservative government tired of trying to reach agreements, whether in Belfast or Dublin, and simply gave the Unionists what most of them want, the old majority Stormont, then it would be overwhelmingly likely that if the majority in the North felt secure in the conduct of what they hold to be their own affairs, that say in two generations time such a new Stormont would have become, if economics, geography and propinquity have any meaning, deeply involved in close working relationships with Dublin. This would probably stop short of any overall institutional expression, simply close inter-state functional co-operation in a dozen or so joint agencies. But it might be enough to satisfy and pacify — if only time would stand still in the meantime. But the minority will not wait. They want to see something change in their lifetimes, not those of their children's children. Functional co-operation seems, indeed, to have been the real substance of the Anglo-Irish talks, and the meetings of the civil servants. And it is fair to remind people in Northern Ireland that the United Kingdom does have other problems and interests in common with the Republic — people in Northern Ireland are understandably somewhat obsessive about the Northern Ireland problem. There is much to be done by way of regularising a special relationship quite apart from Northern Ireland. Nonetheless it must be hoped in Dublin and feared in Belfast that institutions of such functional co-operation would become imperceptibly constitutional (somewhat like the first theories of a way to European integration through the Coal and Steel Community), however much a Conservative government in London is determined that that should not happen. If such institutions were to emerge, who knows what the outcome would be? This might be a fair and sensible procedure to adopt, irrespective of different views of what the outcome would be. It would also be a very long process, whatever the outcome, but it is the remotest chance of this happening that stirs extemism in Unionist ranks.

If I speculate about a possibility of federalism in a United Kingdom context (which is as important for Scotland as for Northern Ireland), one must note a remarkable outburst of such speculation in an island-of-Ireland context by Irish politicians and what I will boldly call the more literate and reflective activists. What it has in common is a recognition that any possible unity of Ireland could not be a unitary sovereign state, as in the old Fianna Fail doctrine. Garret FitzGerald's argument for confederalism (with a 'British dimension') is only the most sophisticated of a large literature. In newspapers and in pamphlets there has been a noticeable growth in the last few years of, as it were, 'middlebrow' political speculation, not entirely unlike what Perry Miller once called 'the citizen literature' of the last few years of the American colonies and the early years of the Republic. It is written for activists by activists. It is neither philosophical nor usually explicitly theoretical. As yet nothing comes anywhere near the standard of *The Federalist Papers* nor seems especially likely to convince those it most needs to convince; but it is not all purely polemical. The end may be 'Irish unity' or 'negotiated independence for Northern Ireland', but the means are often moot and speculative; and some brave souls try to square these two circles. Both the publications of Sinn Fein and the New Ulster Political Research Group (the spiritual arm of the UDA) are now showing a sense of time scales, moving beyond next-electoral perspectives into much more realistic generational ones. Certainly most people now envisage 'a solution' less as an event in time (like a benign revolution) rather than as a long drawn-out process. Very few people in fact believe in the original content of the once most commonly argued 'solutions': that the six counties would become part of the Republic, or that they would simply be ordinary parts of the local government of the United Kingdom (what, after all, the Unionists originally fought for). The Provisional IRA proposed in its manifesto, *Eire Nua*, a federal Ireland of the four historic provinces with its capital in Athlone, not in hated Free State Dublin. The UDA has at least repudiated neither the official policy of its leaders, which is to seek negotiated independence, nor the remarkable content of their draft constitution: a kind of reinvention by themselves alone of the American constitution of 1787 replete with devices to ensure no effective government at all except with minority consent. The last bid of Her Majesty's Government in the late Atkins inter-party discussions, although it excluded talking to the UDA officially, at least moved on interestingly parallel lines: majority government with minority veto.

The SDLP also consider federalism: John Hume sees it as a way of reaching not the classic republican 'unity of Ireland' but an 'agreed Ireland', an 'Ireland of the future'; Seamus Mallon, their deputy leader, believes that, even so, some form of power-sharing would still be needed; and even Paddy Duffy has said that 'there would have to be some form of federal type of government, not a Republic-type of government as envisaged by former Republican leaders'. In June 1978, Mr Denis Haughey, the chairman of the SDLP, proposed a deal with the Northern Unionists: a federal union of Ireland but with a strong parliament still in Belfast, devolution of all local matters, a Bill of Rights and continued British citizenship. (Needless to say, this fell on politically deaf ears.)

Senator Kenneth Whitaker, the former Secretary of the Department of Finance and Governor of the Central Bank (often called 'the father of the Irish economic miracle') wrote an interesting article in the *Irish Times* (20 June 1978) in which he argued the impossibility of fully integrating Northern

Ireland into either the Republic or the United Kingdom in any foreseeable future: he too, therefore, argued for an intermediate solution in which two separate governments would establish a constitution creating a limited number of common institutions and the possibility of adding to them by mutual consent (shades of Calhoun). So from the *Irish Times* to discussion among and between the paramilitaries, the concepts of federalism and confederalism, even involving three 'states', has gained currency.

However vague much of this is, it is ahead of official thinking by the two governments most concerned and points to characteristics of some modern states, both in their internal and external relationships, that have been much obscured by the theory of sovereignty of the text-book writers.

The objections to a federal or confederal approach to Ireland are practical, not theoretical. With great respect to Professor Maurice Vile's paper, while I see the great difficulties of a federalism with only two units, I also see the great peculiarity of the problem. Federalism is not a pre-existent formula, but a dynamic response to situations of divided power. If the majority in Northern Ireland wanted such a bilateral or trilateral relationship, it should not defeat human ingenuity if the will was there. But it is not, and even strong advocates of Irish unity recognise this. Consider for instance, Mr Haughey's speech to the National Executive of Fianna Fail (as reported in the *Irish Times,* 27 March 1981):

> For my part, I have no hesitation in reaffirming openly and proudly that I am working actively for Irish unity. I have said before and I repeat now that progress towards the unity of all our people is my top political priority. I will not be deflected from pursuing that noble goal sensibly and patiently.
>
> In statements on February 10th and 25th last the Secretary of State for Northern Ireland spelt out what the British government mean by the constitutional status or position of Northern Ireland. He defined it as being that its position within the United Kingdom cannot be changed without the consent of a majority of the people of Northern Ireland and of the Westminster parliament.

Our position on this should be perfectly clear. As I have already brought out, the studies are part of a process initiated when I met Mrs Thatcher in London on May 21st last year. Reference to the communiqué issued after that meeting will show that I agreed that change in the constitutional status, the present factual state of Northern Ireland, would only come about with the consent of a majority of the Northern people. In my Dail speech on May 29th last I pointed out that this simply recognised the practical realities of the situation.

Ulster can no more be coerced in 1984, even, than it could be in 1914. Certainly he 'will not be deflected from' that 'noble goal' but he will proceed 'sensibly and patiently': shrewd political words indeed.[7] What could Dublin possibly do to gain the consent of a majority in the North to either a federal or a confederal solution? Can such a circle ever be squared? No Irish leader before Garret Fitzgerald has ever asked. It is hard to imagine why a Protestant majority should give up its British connection. And the matter would not be the least easier if Britain, which is most unlikely, were to give them up. As the SDLP realise, thinking of the 'troops out' movement, the matter might even be worse if the British army withdraws. Even the 'removal of the guarantee' would not alter the facts on which the guarantee is based. The IRA is a terrorist organisation that makes some aspects of government and ordinary life difficult; but the UDA, if unrestrained by the British army, would take the old UVF form of a militia that could actually take over first the streets and then the government.

Perhaps the circle can only be squared if a wider context is grasped and if we go back to our original point: that Northern Ireland *does* face both ways, and that many people in Northern Ireland do have dual allegiances: most Catholics have a clear dual allegiance and most loyalists would go for independence if Whitehall and Westminster ever tried to sell them out, even by nice stages and with baited hooks.

A *Guardian* editorial said in March 1980: 'it is more generally acknowledged in Dublin than is often realised that the two islands cannot be thought of as entirely separate units.' Who knows how true this is? But it could point to the wider context. What if political leaders could eventually grasp a sense of these islands as a whole as they have of Europe as a whole? Talk of the Republic rejoining the Commonwealth seems utterly unrealistic (when it will not even join NATO), even if the slow stages by which she left it are a salutary reminder that final constitutional solutions are often remarkably fluid in long historical periods. Everything I have masochistically argued about the British need to think again about the 'sovereignty of parliament' could also be turned against some aspects of constitution-worship in the Republic. Even the territorial clauses of the constitution are, any scholar knows, far vaguer and less commital than both Nationalists and Loyalists make out.

The Guardian's remark points in a different direction: speculation about the possibility of a Nordic Council-like institution, or the slow growth of one: not a federal constitution for Northern Ireland with an Irish dimension, nor a confederal constitution of all Ireland with a British dimension, but a Council of Britain and Ireland whose component members would be at least the Republic of Ireland, Northern Ireland, England and Wales, and Scotland. Even this is near fantasy, for it begs the question as to whether even in the context of such a definite but minimal framework (the Nordic Council demands unanimity of its component nations before proposals can go to the national parliaments), an acceptable representative institution could arise in Northern Ireland; and it adds the additional dimension of Scotland if only as a make-weight to the size and dominance of England and Wales (and Wales?). What common institutions would arise would depend on the agreement of the nations, but it would not in any sense govern the separate nations, whether they were themselves separate states or federal entities.

All this is speculation. But speculation is needed. There are no short-term or final solutions. Once it is realised that the sovereign state is not sovereign, new and flexible forms of political relationship could emerge. A confederacy of these islands is almost utter fantasy, but a Council of the Islands seems at least a reasonable speculation.

If Northern Ireland cannot come to find some form of mutually acceptable representative institution, the only other hypothesis is that neither the Haugheys nor the Thatchers would get their way, but that the full complexity of accepting that Northern Ireland faces two ways would begin to be mirrored in dual citizenship (which many Catholics already exercise), inter-governmental administrative agencies, even alternative jurisdictions. It is just possible that the only practical response would be the two governments creating what to tidy-minded constitutional theorists would be sheer muddle, unworkable anywhere else (but where else is there quite such a problem?). I could imagine setting in 2000 (though more likely someone else in 2020) those same 'A' level candidates a rather different question: 'Is Northern Ireland constitutionally more a part of the United Kingdom or the Republic of Ireland?' I am not talking about 'condominium' which would need a far more comprehensive and deliberate agreement and exercise of power at one time by the two governments together than either seems capable of even alone. I am suggesting that a slow evolution of a thorough but tolerable muddle could occur. The line between the institutional and the constitutional could be thoroughly blurred and bi-lateral or tri-lateral functional agencies replace much national and territorial administration. Speculatively I slightly favour *The Guardian's* hypothesis, however.

All this essay has really tried to do is to remove some conceptual obstacles to facing a situation that cannot be conciliated in terms of either traditional state sovereignty theory or nationalist theory. And for the meantime more people must analyse and speculate, not take sides. I think of what Albert Camus wrote of the Algerian crisis:

> The truth, alas, is that a part of French opinion vaguely holds that the Arabs have in a way earned the right to slaughter and mutilate while another part is willing to justify in a way all excesses [against the Arabs]. To justify himself, each relies on the other's crime. But that is a casuistry of blood, and it strikes me that an intellectual cannot become involved in it, unless he takes up arms himself. When violence answers violence in a growing

frenzy that makes the simple language of reason impossible, the role of intellectuals cannot be, as we read every day, to excuse from a distance one of the violences and condemn the other. This has the double result of enraging the violent group that is condemned and encouraging to greater violence the violent group that is exonerated. If they do not join the combatants themselves, their role (less spectacular, to be sure!) must be merely to strive for pacification so that reason will again have a chance.[8]

REFERENCES

1. See M. Hechter, *Internal Colonialism: the Celtic Fringe in British National Development*, Routledge & Kegan Paul, London 1975.
2. W. Blackstone, *Commentaries on the Laws of England*, London 1776, Bk I, p.82.
3. A. L. Lowell, *The Government of England*, Macmillan, New York 1908, pp. v-vi.
4. House of Lords, *Hansard*, 5 Sept. 1893, cols 33-4.
5. As most brilliantly argued by R. F. V. Heuston, *Essays in Constitutional Law*, 2nd ed., Stevens & Sons, London 1964, in the first chapter on 'Sovereignty'.
6. H. Arendt, *On Violence*, Allen Lane, London 1970.
7. The British Labour Party has now joined him, in their policy statement approved at the 1981 annual conference — but with similar reservations and realism.
8. A. Camus, quoted by N. Jacobson, *Pride and Solace: the Functions and Limits of Political Theory*, University of California Press, London 1978.

10

The Theory Of Political Integration

Emil J. Kirchner

This paper does not claim to provide ready-made solutions to the problem in Northern Ireland. Rather it looks at integration in a wider Western European context and examines critically those theoretical attempts which have tried to explain the phenomenon of Western European integration. Hopefully, a treatment of these theoretical attempts will provide some lessons in the search for solutions to the Northern Ireland problem.

Another aim of the paper is to show, by way of a progress report on European Community (EC)[1] integration, effective or possible impacts on the reconciliation of the Irish problem. This part of the paper will also consider the current European Community situation and outline the forces which at present encourage integration there.

Since the Second World War and especially since the formation of the European Coal and Steel Community (ECSC), much theorising has been going on about the phenomenon of integration. The aims of these attempts have been to discover the conditions, mechanisms and processes which underlie the occurrence or non-occurrence of integration in specific instances (regions) and which determine its form and evolution.

Integration theory consistently treats integration as the dependent variable. Theoretically, there is no reason this need be so. For instance, the level of integration could be used to explain the level of inter-societal violence (assuming, of course, that a conceptualisation of integration as something other than the level of violence were used). Nevertheless integration is always seen as the variable to be explained, and not as a cause. Integration theory seeks the causes or bases of integration.[2]

The use of the term 'theory' in this paper will be extremely generous. As both de Vree and Pentland maintain, compared with philosophy of science definitions of theory, integration theory proves quite inadequate. A more appropriate label which will be used in this paper would be to speak of theoretical approaches.

Though various definitions exist, political integration can be described as the process whereby nation-states voluntarily transfer their capacity to formulate policy and make binding decisions to some common central institution(s), thus losing the factual attributes to sovereignty. This transfer of capacity from the nation-states to the central (or supranational) institution(s) represents the integrative process. Integration differs therefore from inter-governmentalism in that the former seeks to transcend the nation-state whereas the latter tries to maintain it.

Four main approaches have dominated political integration theory since the early 1950s. These four approaches are the federalist, the functionalist, the transactionalist, and the neo-functionalist. The first two approaches are basically prescriptive in nature and the latter two are more empirically based.

Federalism

Federalism is a well-established concept in legal theory and is concerned with the form of government characterised by two or more layers (states) of semi-autonomous political authority. It represents a means of achieving unity where necessary, while allowing diversity where possible. In federalist thinking a 'desire for union' on the part of the national governmental actors is considered as the essential requirement for the creation of common supranational institutions, which either immediately or progressively absorb the sovereignty of the national governments. The end-result of this process — which is not supposed to be a protracted one — would be a method of government which divides political power between central and local institutions, each acting autonomously within its own sphere. What is envisaged here, therefore, is the creation of a federal government co-ordinating the sub-units for optimum efficiency and local institutions safeguarding democratic control and autonomy.

Federalism has had a chequered history in Europe. In December 1946, the European Union of Federalists was set up to promote integration along these lines, but with the defeat of the European Defence Community (EDC) in 1954 and the tough stand taken by De Gaulle in 1965–6 the maximalist position, with its unequivocal emphasis on the primacy of constitutional settlement, suffered a major setback from which it has yet to recover. Integration in the EC has progressed since 1954 but it has been more in scope (number of common policies) than in strengthening central institutions.

Federalists (such as Spinelli) have put much faith in the directly-elected European Parliament and see it, together with the Court of Justice, as the possible motor of federal integration. At the present time, however, these aspirations remain substantially unfulfilled. The directly elected parliament would have to tackle head-on the national governments sitting in the Council of Ministers in order to gain any significant powers. It is hard to imagine how, at present, this could be done.

While full-blown federalism, as the early US experience (civil war) demonstrated, has drawbacks as a model for European political integration, the acts of statesmen, stressed by federalists as an important integrative force, deserve further consideration. We shall return to this point later. Generally, federalists do not provide us with a dynamic explanation of the mechanism of the federalising process. Rather they tend to make mainly normative assertions about the efficiency derived from a federal structure and fail to inform us of how and why the national governmental actors would voluntarily transfer the national sovereignty to the common central institutions. For the federalist approach to become more relevant, it must try to delineate the multiplicity of forces that intervene between the initial 'desire for union' of the political actors and the end-result.

Functionalism

Functionalism is concerned with the reorganisation of political life on an international level, restricted initially to specialised and technical fields of economic and social life.

Unlike federalism, functionalists consider sovereignty and governmental authority as conditional upon a process of legitimisation expressed through the approval of the mass of the citizens. According to this approach, therefore, common central institutions cannot become sovereign or increase their authority merely by an act of political will on the part of the national governmental actors. The transfer of sovereignty from the national governments to the central institutions can only follow from the appearance of socio-psychological community[3] and a transfer of popular loyalties from the national to the international level.

A basic and necessary assumption made by this approach is the existence, among the integrative units, of a consensus on social questions. There are many politically neutral functions and non-political issues which individual governments cannot effectively carry out at the national level and therefore international co-operation is both necessary and desirable for effectively dealing with them. These functions can be delegated to functionally specific international institutions which carry them out more efficiently than the national institutions.

Capacity, therefore, is of crucial importance to the dynamic process of functionalism and the whole idea of this approach is to continually increase the capacity of the central institutions so that they will be able to satisfy the demands made upon them by the people. This functional process should continue until a homogeneous and strong socio-psychological community is created.

How relevant has functionalism been to an analysis of European integration? Pentland suggests that the thesis can be tested in two areas. Firstly, whether the technological and economic pressures, which functionalists such as Mitrany suggested would bring about the eventual withering away of the nation-state, have led to the development of transnational research, development and investment agencies. Secondly, whether international organisations have been set up to promote functional co-operation.

Pentland draws fairly pessimistic conclusions about the first area, pointing out that (in 1973) only 11 per cent of public research money in the EC area was allocated to bilateral and multilateral research. He points out further that the slow development of such functional agencies as Euratom would not appear to bear out the functionalist argument that the logic of technological development would prove to be the motive force behind the transcendence of national boundaries.

Pentland's conclusions about the second area are tentatively more optimistic, suggesting that organisations such as the Council of Europe and OECD may make a subtle contribution to a reorientation of values from the national to the international level. The International Energy Agency, for instance, may make a contribution to the functionalist development of international society.

In the functionalist model it is taken for granted that the functions and activities of the national governments can be separated into two distinct categories. This model, however, fails in the first place to provide us with a methodological answer to the problem of distinguishing between a 'political' and a 'technical' issue. More importantly, the idea that issues can in fact be divided into such clearcut categories is not entirely convincing. In the words of Puchala

> ... functional task-areas in international economics, communications, science and technology, which the functionalist model stipulates are immune from international politics, have in fact turned out to be the central issue-areas in the lively international politics of regional integration. There are simply no non-political issues in the relations among states.[4]

But even if one could isolate certain purely technical issues, there is no guarantee that a consensus exists among the people as to their solutions. In the majority of cases — if not all — the emergence of consensus is the result of hard fought compromise and not something that could be taken for granted as the model would have us believe.

A further shortcoming of the functional process model is that the dependent variable, i.e., the end result of the integrative process, is not formulated in any coherent sense and remains vague.

Having examined the two prescriptive theoretical attempts let us now look at the more empirically based theories.

Transactionalism

Karl Deutsch can be considered as the founder and chief exponent of the transactionalist approach. Deutsch's conceptual views of integration have changed somewhat over the years. His earlier definitions stressed central institutions and expectation of peaceful change. By the mid-1960s Deutsch de-emphasised the concern with institutions and the absence of violence. Together with other transactionalist theorists he now stresses interdependence and sense of community.

The transactionalist approach is based on the assumption that increases in the degree and level of all forms of communications within individual nations will result in the emergence of common values and a sense of community[5] among these units, provided that the system is at all times capable of responding favourably to the demands made upon it.

According to this approach, the success or failure of integration depends largely on the background conditions prevailing within and among the integrating political units. Deutsch lists four such conditions that can determine the integrative process: (a) mutual relevance of the units to one another; (b) compatibility of values and some actual joint rewards; (c) mutual responsiveness; and (d) some degree of generalised common identity or loyalty. (These conditions could also be considered for a possible union between the South and the North of Ireland.)

Regional interdependence – as distinct from global interdependence – is therefore of central importance to this approach. Interdependence, which can be established by a network of mutual transactions, can only lead to integration if it is also accompanied by a corresponding sense of community spirit, which in turn would depend upon the existence of mutual responsiveness and an increasing degree of mutual relevance.

Deutsch maintained in 1967 that according to his measurements '... since 1957/58, the structural unification of a Europe of the Six has halted'.[6] In contrast Inglehart and

Fischer submitted evidence indicating that this process began to develop significantly during the 1960s. One of the problems with Deutsch's approach is that the link between the dependent and independent variable is never made clear. He argues about political integration but concentrates his empirical research on social and economic communications (mail and telephone traffic, trade flow).[7] It appears that Deutsch uses transactions as the independent variable. Deutsch clearly argues that transactions create salience and response capabilities and thus in some sense both indicate and cause integration. Deutsch also concentrates on quantitative analysis without considering the content of communication flow, which after all may be hostile.

Keohane and Nye have suggested the use of the following two indicators for measuring economic interdependence and integration: (a) the 'sensitivity' of economic transactions between two or more nations to economic developments within those nations, and (b) the 'vulnerability' of the actors or units to changes in the rules or to a drastic reduction in the level of transactions in the system. The main disadvantage of these indicators is that it is difficult to operationalise and measure them in an empirical way. Measurement difficulties would also arise when accounting for not only actual, but also for perceptual interdependence.

Neo-functionalism

The neo-functionalist approach is based on the pluralist model of society, thus rejecting the functionalist assumption of popular consensus on social and welfare issues. According to the neo-functional analysis, on the supranational level we can at best find co-existing but differing interests. As Haas observed, there is no common good 'other than that received through the interest-tinted lenses worn by the actors'.[8]

Instead of relying on the appearance and strengthening of a 'sense of community spirit' as the main criterion for the success of integration, the neo-functionalists emphasise the importance of the politically relevant actors (interest-groups, political parties and supranational bureaucracy) and their influence on the institutionalisation of the integrative process. Accordingly, Haas defined political integration as the process whereby political actors in several distinct national settings are persuaded to shift their loyalties, expectations and political activities towards a new centre, whose institutions possess or demand jurisdiction over the pre-existing national states.[9]

Haas developed his model with particular reference to Europe. He was primarily concerned with the process of integration rather than the conditions under which the process can begin and proceed.

Neo-functionalism can be seen both as part of the 'end of ideology' thesis, in which a consensus on 'problem-solving' of welfare and economic needs develops as serious political conflict declines in saliency; and also as part of the 'group theory' of politics in which interest-groups assume a prime importance in the process of political developments and the articulation of demands. In this setting, Harrison suggests the role of government is 'creatively responsive rather than forceful and autonomous.'[10]

The central concept of neo-functionalism is that once the necessity of certain economic functions crosses national boundaries (such as a rationalisation of the coal or steel industry), interest-groups and political parties will become involved and will push for more integration. This will cause a 'spillover effect', whereby, as Haas says, policies made pursuant to an initial task and grant of power can be made real only if the task itself is expanded. Thus there is an 'expansive' logic to integration. Implied is the notion of a continuum from issues concerning the economic to the political sphere. Along this continuum integration in one area 'spills over' to affect another area where, consequently, integration also takes place, and so it goes on until eventually political community is achieved. Haas did not rule out the possibility of the process causing crises along the line but claimed that their resolution would lead to integration at higher level. The obvious implication of this proposition is that there is a continuous chain-effect or dependence between the functions performed by the regional organisation.

In 1966 Haas qualified the automaticity of the spillover process when he stated that: 'Integrative forces which flow from one kind of activity do not necessarily infect other activities, even if carried by the same organisation.'[11] He thus also accepted the criticism that the original theory did not sufficiently accommodate the role of political leaders

Haas' modification of the process, although it constituted an improvement to the model, did not in any significant way alter the basic mechanism through which integration is supposed to progress. It merely differentiated between issues which have the potential to cause 'spillover' and issues which do not.

This modification did not satisfy Hoffman's criticism. Hoffman argues that firstly one should not look at Europe or any other region in isolation but only within the framework of the international system. Within the international system, Hoffman argues, there is a logic of diversity which acts in the opposite way to Haas' logic of integration. Secondly, according to Hoffman, the process of integration in Europe predicted by the neo-functionalists has failed because it concentrates too much on the process of integration and not on where the process is leading. Thirdly, Hoffman maintains that there is a separation between those issues concerning economic welfare politics (low politics) and issues concerning the vital interests of national security and diplomacy (high politics). The barrier to integration lies between the two. The criticism that there is no economic/political continuum is sound but Hoffman's distinction between high and low politics is not. Economic questions often have political implications and vice versa, for example, the use of economic sanctions as a political weapon or the 1973 oil crisis. As Kaiser points out, the concepts of high and low politics can only refer to attitudes and not fixed objects of politics, with the result that no clear line can be drawn between the two.[12]

Modification or Rejection of Integration Theory?

In the late Sixties and early Seventies attempts were made to redefine and reformulate integration theory in general and neo-functional explanation in particular. In 1968 Nye argued that integration was not a unitary concept and suggested a set of subconcepts (economic, social and political). The problem with such a disaggregation arises when one tries to relate one subconcept to the others. Studies by Lindberg, Nye and Hughes have suggested some tentative relationships between these subconcepts by indicating that:

(a) integration at the level of mass publics (community) is not closely related to integration at the level of central institutional development. If a causal relationship exists at a lower level, it will run from central institutions to mass community.

(b) integration at the level of non-institutional governmental co-operation is quite highly related to integration at the level of central institutional development. Governmental co-operation may act as a necessary but sufficient basis for institutional development.

(c) integration at the level of mass publics (community) is not related closely to integration at the level of non-institutional governmental co-operation.

Whilst the attempt of disaggregation is analytically sound, more research is required to substantiate and elaborate on these proposed relationships, otherwise one is left with a disjointed picture which blurs the general framework of integration theory.

Another attempt introduced by Lindberg and Scheingold involved the notion of log-rolling and side payments to the integrative process. In addition, they, as well as Nye and Schmitter, modified the neo-functional logic of integration to take into account the possibility of a state of equilibrium or even spillback in this process. Nye also pointed out that more emphasis should be given to the influence of external actors.

In their reformulation of the neo-functionalist approach, these writers have maintained the basic philosophy of the theoretical approach but with a more long-term and less formalised perspective.

In line with a less formalised perspective but without any precise indication of further developments, Donald Puchala suggested that the integrative process might not, after all, be anything more (especially insofar as institutionalisation was concerned) than the system which we now actually observe in the EC. If this is true, then all efforts to conceptualise a theory that would predict a future and different outcome are bound to fail. He sees regional integration as a 'concordance system' which he defines as 'an international system wherein actors find it possible consistently to harmonise their interests, compromise their differences and reap mutual rewards from their interactions'.[13] However, the basic characteristic of this system is that nation-states are among the major component units of the system and national governments remain central actors in it.

It is essentially different from orthodox Realist analysis in that 'conflict' within the concordance system follows from divergent views about 'ways to co-operate' rather than fundamental incompatibilities in the interests of the various actors.'[14] Puchala expects that this type of conflict within the concordance system will terminate in agreements acceptable to all actors. However, he does not tell us anything about the scope or extent of these agreements or, as the case might be, disagreements. As such, it is basically a static model.

A more drastic verdict on the future of regional integration theory was reached by Haas in 1976. In his article, 'Turbulent fields and the theory of regional integration', he rejects most of the major assumptions of neo-functionalism as being obsolete for Western Europe, and completely abandons the notion of the expansive logic of economic integration. Haas suggests that theories of regional integration are becoming obsolescent because three core assumptions of these theories have not been evident over a period of eight years (between 1968 and the time of writing) and are therefore becoming less relevant. The core assumptions are: (a) that a predictable institutional pattern will be the outcome of the process of integration; (b) that the resolution of conflict within the regional unit and between members and non-members should be to the advantage of members; and (c) that decisions are made on the basis of disjointed incrementalism.

Haas claims to be dealing with regional integration theories in general but in fact he is concerned with his own theory of neo-functionalism. According to Haas, during the early period of European integration neo-functionalism adequately explained the European experience. Increased policy integration occurred within the fields of customs union and competition policy. However, new developments in international society, Haas points out, 'involve those aspects of industrialised societies that do not respond readily to the incentives of a customs union.'[15]

Keohane and Nye suggest that 'the usefulness of integration theory, shorn of its teleological and regional orientation, lies in the set of insights into the politics of complex sets of interdependent entities.'[16] This is somewhat similar to Haas' conclusion that the study of integration should be subsumed under the general study of interdependence, turbulence and systems-change.[17] This then breaks the necessary link which the traditional theories of integration made between increasing interdependence and increasing integration. The disaggregation of the two concepts is necessary because they are not always interchangeable. As Keohane and Nye point out, though they are interchangeable within the context of 'social interdependence/social integration, they certainly are not within a discussion of policy, where policy integration may be one among many strategies to cope with policy interdependence, or turbulence, as Haas labels it. This is in marked contrast to the neo-functionalist prediction which saw a clear causal link pointing towards the joint management of interdependence. Yet, as it has become fashionable to talk of interdependence rather than integration, there is also a danger of emphasis on the former at the expense of the latter.

As Puchala argues, Haas and others have 'relegated to exogeneous categories much of what is actually integral to the politics of European integration' and that 'interconnectedness of policy inputs and outcomes and hence the interdependence of politics at national and European levels gets less attention in the integration models than its importance warrants.'[18]

In similar vein Nau notes that 'what we have lost, most unfortunately, in the transition from integration to interdependence theories is the hierarchy of issues, interests and institutions that guided earlier integration studies'.[19]

Whilst it is true that the three assumptions mentioned by Haas are less relevant today than they were in the 1950s and early 1960s (and they were never entirely relevant then) this does not tell us anything about long-term trends, as it is based on such a short period. It can also be argued that the relevance of these assumptions has only declined in certain areas – those affected by turbulent fields. Certainly the first assumption concerning the development of an institutional pattern is still relevant in the wake of direct elections to the European Parliament and the institutionalisation of the procedures for drawing up the Community budget. Direct elections have also provoked activity in the sphere of political parties resulting in the formation of the European party federations. The upgrading of the role of the European parliament could also lead to increased activity of interest-groups at this level and will help to redress the imbalance of the institutional structure which Caporaso describes as 'a system with a weak executive that lacks legitimacy and political authority'.[20]

Moreover, even an area affected by turbulent fields, the monetary area, has shown central institutional developments with the establishment of the European Monetary System (EMS) in March 1979. Though comprising only eight of the ten EC countries, it would appear to be a step in the direction of Economic and Monetary Union (EMU).[21] However, it is also true to say that, when experiencing temporary monetary imbalances, member countries of the EMS tend not to turn to each other but rather to non-EC countries for loans. The envisaged creation of the European Monetary Fund will most likely become a decisive factor in the realisation of EMU.

Prospects for Integration Theory

Where does this leave regional integration theory today? Europe had certainly not developed according to the patterns that federalist, transactionalist, functionalist and neo-functionalist models predicted, and yet European integration has developed if only equivocally and falteringly. What then can be said about the validity of regional integration and regionalism as an analytical tool? What factors are most likely to encourage integration in Western Europe?

Each of the four approaches treated above contributes to a practical explanation of regional integration, but none provides a satisfactory conceptual framework for the analysis of the European experience to date. As Nye and Keohane point out, novel facts continue to appear, unanticipated, or at least not predicted by existing theoretical models. Should we conclude then that thirty years of theorising have produced not enough results or is it truer to say that thirty years is not long enough a period over which to formulate such a theory? Before we give a verdict on the relevance of integration theory let us examine some of the main actors and forces which relate to the process of integration.

Whilst multilateral actions and collaboration among countries of the EC are increasing it does not mean member governments resort automatically to EC formulas when they are faced with common problems.[22] The threat to cut off European oil supplies in 1973 and the ensuing energy crisis led to serious failures to respond within the EC and can hardly be said to be conducive to the integrative process. For an external threat to further integration, as Nye and Keohane point out, 'there must also be a prospect of gain for each important party to the scheme: that is, it must be possible to upgrade the common interest within the framework of a positive-sum bargaining situation.'[23] The relative infrequency of this eventuality is largely due to the perception by politicians that international diplomacy is usually a zero-sum game. Within the wider international environment, the 'realist' explanation of power still dominates political thinking.

As a consequence governments will pursue national and EC policies more or less simultaneously. In short, they will keep their options open for as long as possible. The pace of integration has been (and will be for some time) determined by the ratio between the increase in benefits to the member states and the loss of political power or national sovereignty that this involves. The establishment of a customs union involves relatively less loss of national sovereignty than the formulation of common policies in, for example, energy or monetary fields. One can also argue that integration up to a certain point has resulted in a revival of national self-confidence and consequently a resistance to further integration at the supranational level. Political co-operation rather than integration is now the dominant trend in the EC and this has been institutionalised in the form of a European Council.[24] The nation states of Western Europe remain viable actors in international relations. This will remain so, in my opinion, until serious steps are undertaken for a common European defence, largely independent of the USA. The need for such a policy to be adopted would largely depend on external events (involving Russian and American actions or pressures) and on the general progress the EC is making in co-ordinating economic policies and promoting political co-operation.

This has led to a number of consequences. Firstly, rather than creating the 'deliberate linkage of issues', the Commission has been reduced almost to the level of a secretariat awaiting the initiative of the Council of Ministers and paradoxically, as Nye and Keohane point out, 'as European affairs have become more important states have tended to withdraw responsibility from the Commission'.[25] The former monetary exchange alignment known as the 'snake' and the attempts to introduce 'political co-operation' among EC member states are examples. The experience of the Commission, therefore, does not provide evidence favourable to neo-functionalist predictions of integration. Rather, as suggested by Harrison, a concerted act of political will is necessary to stimulate the integrative process. Decisions to hold direct elections to the European Parliament and establish the European Monetary System lend credence to the federalist strategy[26] rather than to the automaticity and incrementalism of the neo-functionalist theory. The leadership tandem of Giscard-Schmidt was one of the main factors related to these decisions.

Secondly, the activities by interest-groups were seen by neo-functionalists as a main force for change in the integrative process. But the 'learning of new interests and attitudes' has not always supported a European perspective. Of transactional interest-groups Keohane and Nye say, 'their common interests tend to be less intense than the special concern for the satisfaction of which members still find it most profitable to lobby their governments.'[27]

Therefore, as Helen Wallace argues, it would be misguided to continue to press for a highly centralised super-government in Brussels. According to Wallace 'the rules of thumb should be that the European Community concentrates its scarce resources on reforming a smaller number of tasks rather more efficiently . . . on issues that governments cannot handle alone or where concerted action by a European block could be an asset to international bargaining.'[28]

There is no current fervour among the countries for closer ties — neither integration nor such policies as defence rank high in popularity with people in Europe. Member governments find it difficult to introduce a joint policy of economic stabilisation to cope with high unemployment, high inflation and low growth rates. There are even indications that the countries are further apart than ever from convergence of economic policy development. Yet the EC has nonetheless taken steps which are building blocks for further integration. The establishment of the EMS in March 1979, the first direct elections for the European Parliament in June 1979, the entry of Greece as the tenth Community member in January 1981, as well as current negotiations with Spain and Portugal are recent evidence of this building process for further political integration.[29] In doing so — and this is an often forgotten appreciative factor nowadays when considering the historical conflicts in Western Europe — the EC is contributing to the preservation of peace in this area.

The phenomenon of integration in Western Europe which we seek to identify and explain becomes more interdependent and difficult to assess.[30] However, as yet we have no theory of regional integration that can predict future development with any acceptable degree of accuracy.

Though the integrative process in Europe has not maintained the self-generating impetus that earlier theorists and practitioners alike expected, regional integration remains a relevant focus of political attention and a legitimate unit for research and analysis. It may, however, have to reorientate itself not only in the direction that Haas suggests and become increasingly aware of its own theoretical interdependence with other theories of the international political system, but also pay more attention to what Puchala calls the interdependence of politics at national and European levels. Thus, in the words of Nau, 'we need to continue in search of broader explanations, something more than eclecticism but less than all-encompassing global designs.'[31] Our aims must remain to define what integration is, to describe intermittent and end phases of the integrative process in Western Europe and to explain why and when the various stages will be reached.

REFERENCES

1. The term EC is hereafter to be the symbol for the combination of the European Economic Community and Euratom, set up in 1958, and the European Coal and Steel Community, established in 1952.
2. For a review of the epistemology of integration theory, see J. K. de Vree, *Political Integration: the Formation of Theory and Its Problems*, Mouton, The Hague 1972, pp. 1–48; and C. Pentland, *International Theory and European Integration*, Faber and Faber, London 1973, pp. 13–20.
3. Underlying this term is the distinction Tonnies made when referring to *Gemeinschaft* as distinct from *Gesellschaft*. The former is characterised by a sense of belonging among its individuals who have common loyalties and values, e.g. the nation. In contrast *Gesellschaft* is characterised by contractual relations and competitiveness. F. Tonnies, *Gemeinschaft and Gesellschaft*, translated and supplemented by C. P. Loomis, International Library of Sociology and Social Reconstruction, London 1955.
4. D. Puchala, 'Of Blind Men, Elephants and International Integration', *Journal of Common Market Studies*, Vol. 10, 1971–2, pp. 265–84, at p. 274.
5. Deutsch and his co-authors arrived at the following conclusion regarding the meaning of 'sense of community': 'It appears to rest primarily on something other than verbal assent to some or many explicit propositions. The populations of different territories might easily profess verbal attachment to the same set of values without having a sense of community that leads to political integration. The kind of sense of community that is relevant for integration ... turned out to be rather a matter of mutual sympathy and loyalties, of "we-feeling", trust and mutual consideration.' (K. W. Deutsch *et al.*, *Political Community and the North Atlantic Area in International Political Communities: An Anthology*, Anchor Books, Doubleday, Garden City 1966, p. 17.)
6. K. W. Deutsch *et al.*, *France, Germany and the Western Alliance: A Study of Elite Attitudes on European Integration and World Politics*, Charles Scribner's Sons, New York 1967, p. 218.
7. For a critical review of Deutsch's conceptual framework, see W. Fischer, 'An Analysis of the Deutsch Sociocausal Paradigm of Political Integration', *International Organisation*, Vol. 23 (2), 1969, pp.254–90

8. E. B. Haas, *Beyond the Nation-State — Functionalism and International Organisation*, Stanford University Press, Stanford 1964, p. 35.
9. E. B. Haas, *The Uniting of Europe — Political, Social and Economic Forces, 1950—1957*, Stanford University Press, Stanford 1958, p. 286.
10. R. J. Harrison, *Europe in Question*, George Allen & Unwin Ltd, London 1974, p. 80.
11. E. B. Haas, 'The Uniting of Europe and the Uniting of Latin America', *Journal of Common Market Studies*, Vol. 5 (4), 1967, pp. 315—43, at pp. 328—9.
12. See K. Kaiser, 'The US and the EEC in the Atlantic System: the Problems of Theory', *Journal of Common Market Studies*, Vol. 5 (4), 1967, pp. 388—425.
13. D. Puchala, op. cit., p. 277.
14. ibid., p. 280.
15. E. B. Haas, 'Turbulent Fields and the Theory of Regional Integration', *International Organisation*, Vol. 30, 1976, p. 173.
16. R. O. Keohane and J. S. Nye, 'International Interdependence and Integration', in F. Greenstein and N. Polsby, eds, *Handbook of Political Science*, Vol. 8, Addison-Wesley, Reading, Mass. 1975, pp. 363—415, at p. 401.
17. Haas' conclusion, however, differs from Nye and Keohane's in that he regards regional integration theory to be becoming gradually obsolete; not that it was, as Nye and Keohane imply, analytically misguided in the first place. Haas argues that the process associated with interdependence can and does go on without necessary reference to what we look for when we study integration. For more restricted purposes then, integration theory retains its relevance. See E. B. Haas, 'Turbulent Fields', pp. 208—9.
18. D. Puchala, 'European Fiscal Harmonization: Politics during the Dutch Interlude', in L. Hurtwitz, ed., *Contemporary Perspectives on European Integration: Attitudes, Non-governmental Behavior, and Collective Decision-Making*, Greenwood Press, Westport, Conn. 1980, p. 211.
19. H. R. Nau, 'Review Essay — From Integration to Interdependence: Pains, Losses and Continuing Gaps', *International Organisation*, Vol. 33 (1), 1979, pp. 119—47, at p. 144.
20. J. A. Caporaso, 'The Emerging European Community: Problems or Interest-Group Hedonism', paper delivered at the ECPR Joint Workshop Conference, Brussels, 17—21 April 1979, p. 2.
21. Haas maintains that spillover only retains its explanatory power in, for instance, the monetary sector if Economic and Monetary Union are considered necessary to further the aims of the Customs Unions. See E. B. Haas, 'Turbulent Fields', pp. 194 and 196.
22. H. Wallace, 'Institutions in a Decentralised Community', in B. Burrows, G. Denton and G. Edwards, eds, *Federal Solutions to European Issues*, Macmillan, London 1977, p. 29.

23. R. O. Keohane and J. S. Nye, op. cit., p. 386.
24. As Pinder argues, '. . . for most purposes the common European interest is served equally well by common instruments which do not suppress national instruments but work alongside them, performing a European function.' See his 'Europe as a Tenth Member of the Community', *Government and Opposition*, Vol. 10, 1975, p. 392.
25. R. O. Keohane and J. S. Nye, op. cit., 385.
26. It also gives support to Hoffman's argument: that it is the national governments, which through national interest or for more idealistic motives decide to take steps towards creating a regional government. The process is slow because of international distrust and caution, but (says Hoffman) it proceeds as the government wants it to, quite free from proddings of particular social groupings. S. Hoffman, 'Obstinate or Obsolete? The Fate of the Nation-State and the Case of Western Europe', *Daedalus*, Summer 1966, pp. 882–916.
27. R. O. Keohane and J. S. Nye, op. cit., p. 385. See also E. Kirchner and K. Schwaiger, *The Role of Interest Groups in the European Community*, Gower Press, Aldershot 1981.
28. H. Wallace, op cit., pp. 31–2.
29. Witness also the January 1981 proposal of the German foreign minister, Genscher. In a speech in Stuttgart, he recalled the old plan for a European union. Specifically, he called for the establishment of a decision centre for European Community foreign policy, co-ordination of security and arms procurement policies, a monetary union and a common energy policy. Quoted in *Frankfurter Rundschau*, 13 January 1981.
30. The complexity of the European Community as a unit for study is highlighted by Wallace when he states that the Community is best viewed as 'a multilevelled system arranged in political layers from the local to the supranational, itself contained within a wider system of inter-governmental co-operation among the industrialised democracies'. W. Wallace, 'Walking Backwards Towards Unity', in H. Wallace, W. Wallace and C. Webb, eds, *Policy-Making in the European Communities*, John Wiley and Sons, Chichester 1977, p. 316.
31. H. R. Nau, op. cit., p. 145.

BIBLIOGRAPHY

Burrows, B., Denton, G., and Edwards G., eds, *Federal Solutions to European Issues*, Macmillan, London 1977
Caporaso, J. A., *The Structure and Function of European Integration*, Goodyear, Pacific Palisades, Calif. 1974

274　*Models of Political Co-operation*

Caporaso, J. A., 'The Emerging European Community: Problems or Interest Group Hedonism,' paper delivered at the ECPR Joint Workshop Conference, Brussels, 17—21 April 1979

Deutsch, K. W. *et al, Political Community and the North Atlantic Area,* Princeton University Press, Princeton 1957

Deutsch, K. W. *et al, France, Germany and the Western Alliance: A Study of Elite Attitudes on European Integration and World Politics,* Charles Scribner's Sons, New York 1967

Deutsch, K. W., *The Analysis of International Relations,* Prentice Hall, Englewood Cliffs, NJ 1968, first edition

de Vree, J. K., *Political Integration: the Formation of Theory and Its Problems,* Mouton and Co., The Hague 1972

Etzioni, A., *Political Unification — a Comparative Study of Leaders and Forces,* Holt, Rinehart and Winston, New York 1965

Fischer, W. E., 'An Analysis of the Deutsch Sociocausal Paradigm of Political Integration', *International Organisation,* Vol. 23 (2), 1969

Friedrich, C. J., *Trends of Federalism in Theory and Practice,* Pall Mall, London 1968

Haas, E. B., *Beyond the Nation State — Functionalism and International Organisation,* Stanford University Press, Stanford 1964

Haas, E. B., *The Uniting of Europe — Political Social and Economic Forces, 1950—1957,* Stanford University Press, Stanford 1958

Haas, E. B., 'The Uniting of Europe and the Uniting of Latin America,' *Journal of Common Market Studies,* Vol. 5 (4), 1967

Haas, E. B., 'Turbulent Fields and the Theory of Regional Integration', *International Organisation,* Vol. 30, 1976

Hansen, R., 'Regional Integration: Reflections on a Decade of Theoretical Efforts', *World Politics,* January 1969

Harrison, R. J., *Europe in Question,* George Allen and Unwin, London 1974

Hay, P., *Federalism and Supranational Organisations — Patterns for New Legal Structures,* University of Illinois Press, Urbana 1966

Hodges, M., ed, *European Integration,* Penguin, London 1972

Hoffman S., 'Obstinate or Obsolete? The Fate of the Nation-State and the Case of Western Europe,' *Daedalus,* Summer 1966, (VC, No. 3)

Hughes, B. B., 'Transaction Analysis: The Impact of Operationalism', *International Organisation,* Vol. XXV, Winter 1971

Hughes, B. B. and Schwarz, J. E., 'Dimensions of Political Integration and the Experience of the European Community', *International Studies Quarterly,* Vol 16, Sept. 1972

Hurwitz, L., ed., *Contemporary Perspectives on European Integration: Attitudes, Non-governmental Behavior, and Collective Decision-Making,* Greenwood Press, Westport, Conn. 1980

Inglehart R., 'An End to European Integration?', *American Political Science Review,* Vol. 61, No. 3, 1967

Jacob, P. E. and Toscano, J. V., *The Integration of Political Communities,* Lippincott, Philadelphia 1964

Kaiser, K., 'The US and the EEC in the Atlantic System — the Problems of Theory', *Journal of Common Market Studies,* Vol. 5 (4), 1967

Keohane R. O. and Nye, J. S., 'International Interdependence and Integration', in Greenstein, F.I. and Polsby N. W. eds, *Handbook of Political Science*, Vol. 8, Addison-Wesley, Reading, Mass. 1975

Kirchner, E. and Schwaiger, K., *The Role of Interest Groups in the European Community*, Gower Press, Aldershot 1981

Lindberg, L., 'Political Integration as a Multi-dimensional Phenomenon Requiring Multi-variate Measurement', *International Organisation*, Vol. 24 (4), 1970

Lindberg, L. and Scheingold, S., *Europe's Would-Be Polity — Patterns of Change in the European Community*, Prentice Hall, Englewood Cliffs, NJ 1970

Lindberg, L. N. and Scheingold, S. A. eds., *Regional Integration, Theory and Research*, Harvard University Press, Cambridge, Mass. 1971

Mitrany, D., *A Working Peace System*, Quadrangle Books, Chicago 1966

Mitrany, D., 'The Prospect of Integration: Federal or Functional', *Journal of Common Market Studies*, Vol. IV (1), 1965–6, pp. 119 – 149

Mitrany, D., *The Functional Theory of Politics*, Martin Robertson, London 1975

Nau, H. R., 'Review Essay — From Integration to Interdependence: Pains, Losses, and Continuing Gaps', *International Organisation*, Vol. 33 (1) 1979

Nye, J., 'Comparative Regional Integration — Concept and Measurement', *International Organisation*, Vol. 22 (4), 1968

Nye, J., *Peace in Parts*, Little Brown and Co., Boston 1971

Pentland C., *International Theory and European Integration*, Faber and Faber, London 1973

Pinder, J., 'Europe as a Tenth Member of the Community', *Government and Opposition*, Vol. 10, 1975

Puchala, D., 'Of Blind Men, Elephants and International Integration', *Journal of Common Market Studies*, Vol. 10, 1971–2

Savage, I. R. and Deutsch K. W., 'A Statistical Model of the Gross Analysis of Transaction Flows', *Econometrica*, Vol. 38 (3)

Schmitter, P. C., 'Central American Integration: Spill-Over, Spill-Around or Encapsulation?', *Journal of Common Market Studies*, Vol. IX, 1970

Spinelli A., *The Eurocrats, Conflict and Crisis in the EEC*, translated by C. Grove Haines, Johns Hopkins Press, Baltimore 1966

Taylor, P. 'The Concept of Community and the European Integration Process', *Journal of Common Market Studies*, Vol. 7 (2), 1968

Tonnies, F., *Community and Association: Gemeinschaft and Gesellschaft*, translated and supplemented by C. P. Loomis, International Library of Sociology and Social Reconstruction, London 1955

Wallace, H., Wallace, W. and Webb, C., eds, *Policy-Making in the European Communities*, John Wiley and Sons, Chichester, 1977

11

The Nordic Model of Neighbourly Co-operation

Bengt Sundelius[1]

The five countries of Northern Europe, Denmark, Finland, Iceland, Norway and Sweden, are often referred to as belonging to the Nordic region. The term Scandinavia is usually used to describe Denmark, Norway, and Sweden, the countries that make up the core of the Nordic region. In many cultural, social, and political aspects, Nordic societies differ from continental European countries and have developed common characteristics not found elsewhere.

Although political scientists have explored this region far less than other parts of Europe, several studies have been made of the Nordic political systems. Often, foreign observers have been struck by the relatively successful manner in which these countries have solved their political problems and worked for social and economic reform. Concepts such as 'the politics of compromise', 'working multi-party systems', 'the politics of post-industrial change', 'co-optive politics', 'corporate-pluralism', 'the middle way', and 'stable democracy', have been used to describe the Nordic political scene. The impression prevails that in comparison to many other regions these countries are characterised by a fairly successful way of handling major domestic social problems and developments.

In this study, we shall outline the political techniques used for managing regional relations and the motives and sources of these joint problem-solving processes. We are interested in whether these countries, in their regional interactions, have been able to develop fairly successful management of joint social problems and changes. Many other studies of the Nordic area have been guided by a fascination for the rare and distinct features of these political systems. Similarly this project was initiated by a belief that the region has something new and different to offer theorists and practitioners of international co-operation and integration. Hopefully, the Nordic experiences can contribute to our increased understanding of international relations, just as these countries' domestic political activities have improved our knowledge of the process of democratic politics.

The Historical Context of Contemporary Nordic Relations

In a historical perspective, Nordic relations have been characterised as much by conflict and rivalry as by peaceful co-existence and co-operation. Efforts during the Middle Ages to form one unified Nordic state failed at the hands of Swedish nationalists. In its place, two distinct entities were gradually established. Denmark-Norway-Iceland made up one unit, which at first dominated the region, and Sweden-Finland formed another unified entity.

The traditional struggle for regional hegemony between Denmark and Sweden continued throughout the sixteenth, seventeenth, and eighteenth centuries. Numerous wars were fought, alliances were formed, and provinces were conquered and reconquered. This rivalry was further aggravated by the temporary power vacuum in Northern and Central Europe, as both Prussia and Russia were weakened by internal difficulties. Slowly these countries emerged as great powers in the region and came to dominate its political scene at the expense of both Denmark and Sweden.

These two countries had gradually consolidated themselves domestically and at the end of the eighteenth century were two fairly well integrated political units. The political administrations, legal codes, educational systems, and church organisations had all developed somewhat separately in the two kingdoms and laid the foundation for later structural differences between east and west. At the beginning of the Napoleonic Wars the Nordic region was made up of two distinct state-units, dominated respectively by the Danish and Swedish political elites.

At the end of the Napoleonic Wars, some drastic changes in the political configuration of the Nordic region had taken place. The Swedish province of Finland was seized by Russia in 1809 and turned into a semi-autonomous province until her independence in 1917. The shock in Sweden over the loss of one-third of her territory was great and resulted in a *coup d'état* and a new constitution, which remained intact until 1975. Norway was taken away from Denmark in 1814 and given to Sweden as compensation for the loss of Finland. However, Norway was never totally integrated as a part of Sweden, like Finland had been, but instead was attached in a union under the same monarch. The Norwegians had their own constitution, government, and central administration. Only in foreign policy did the Swedish government represent the Norwegians as well.

This Norwegian-Swedish union never penetrated from the political-constitutional level down to the economic-cultural-social levels. Instead, the two societies developed separately during the nineteenth century. As a result of growing cultural, social and economic differences, the political conflicts increased through the century until in 1905 the union was finally dissolved. Thus, the Norwegian union with Sweden did not have the same fundamental impact on society as the earlier association with Denmark had. Denmark was stripped of much of her possessions in 1814 and only kept Iceland. That country remained a Danish colony until it received autonomy in 1918 and finally declared itself independent in 1944, at a time when Denmark was occupied by Germany.

It seems that the period between 1800 and the end of the Second World War can be described as an era of Nordic political disintegration, as the two traditional entities in the region were split apart into five separate nation-states. This development did not take place only on the constitutional level, but with the rise of nationalism, public sentiment favoured such a division. In fact, some resentment was voiced against the former governing elites in Denmark and Sweden. For example, a part of the Finnish majority in Finland wanted to rid the country of any Swedish influence, and some Norwegians tried to re-establish their national cultural and linguistic heritage. Even today, the memories of foreign domination are on the minds of many Norwegians and Finnish-speaking Finns.

Since 1814, the Nordic region has not experienced any internal military conflict. This fact contrasts sharply with the

tradition of almost continuous wars prior to that time. At
the same time as the Nordic region after the Napoleonic
Wars was split up into many smaller entities, these countries
were then united in a common destiny as small powers, vulnerable to great power interference. Since that time one can
talk about the Nordic region as a 'area of peace', because
violent solutions have been avoided whenever serious conflict arose. For example, Norway could peacefully secede
from the union with Sweden in 1905; the Swedish-Finnish
dispute over the rights to the Aaland Islands was settled
peacefully in 1921; and the conflicting Norwegian and
Danish claims to eastern Greenland were adjudicated by the
Permanent Court of International Justice in 1933.

The original reason why violent action was avoided in
these situations was mainly the fear of great power intervention in the area. External dominance of the region was to
be avoided even if it meant making sacrifices to the neighbouring countries. Slowly, these separate decisions in favour
of compromise solutions established a tradition of regional
peaceful relations. For example, all the Scandinavian countries stayed neutral during the First World War, in spite of
strong sympathies with the different parties to the war.
Similarly, the military planning of today does not include
options for attacks by any of the other Nordic countries.
Thus, a 'pluralistic security community' has slowly developed,
where dependable expectations of peaceful settlements of
regional disputes are found.[2] This condition has clearly been
motivated by the common fear of potential great power
involvement. It is interesting that this condition was not
reached until the region was politically divided into several
states, which were reduced to small-power status.

At the same time as the Nordic region was split up into
several smaller units, the need for co-operation and joint
activity among these units increased. For a time, the memories
of the rivalries and domination inhibited such efforts. For
example, the Norwegian resentment of the union with
Sweden for some time affected relations between those
countries. Likewise, Iceland still is influenced by her recent
independence from Danish rule.

Deliberate efforts towards Nordic co-operation first took

place in the middle of the nineteenth century. During the time of liberalism and nationalism, and inspired by the movements for national unity in Germany and Italy, the period of 'Scandinavianism' occurred. An ideology of Scandinavian unity developed among the intellectual elites in Denmark and Sweden. No doubt, the recent reduction of these countries to a very marginal position in world politics influenced this desire to unite the countries into one larger, stronger Scandinavian state. Several Scandinavian conferences were held among students and other intellectuals to manifest the desire for further unity. Numerous speeches were made and pamphlets were written in favour of the movement, and the rhetoric of 'Scandinavianism' flourished.

This movement towards a Scandinavian union was also supported by the Danish and Swedish kings, who saw in it a means to unite the region under their crown. For example, the Swedish king Oscar I participated in some of the meetings and in 1856 expressed the now famous words: 'From now on, war between the Scandinavian brothers is impossible.' In particular, the Danish monarch was eager for Scandinavian support in his effort to resist the emerging Prussian empire. However, at the time of the Prussian attack on Denmark in 1864, the Swedish government declined to send military support to the Danish front. This failure to live up to the rhetoric about Scandinavian unity and brotherhood made a deep and lasting impression on the supporters of Nordic co-operation. From that time on, the efforts to create alliances or a unified Scandinavian state were abandoned in favour of more low-key, pragmatic, and functional co-operation.

During the latter part of the nineteenth century, several practical measures aimed at furthering Nordic co-operation were taken. Conferences were held on a regular basis among representatives of various scientific, legal, and political groups. Joint committees were created to harmonise national laws. In 1875, a Scandinavian currency union was established, which lasted through the First World War. Collaboration among many industrial, commercial, agricultural, and labour organisations appeared. However, it was not until the First World War that the co-operation efforts again reached the governmental level. Faced with the external threat of war, the Scandinavian governments saw the advantages of a joint position and close regional co-operation. To symbolise the new developments, the three Scandinavian heads of state met officially for the first time in December 1914. During the war, the countries tried to present a common front of neutrality towards the belligerents in spite of having different sympathies towards the participants in the war. To compensate for the loss of foreign trade, the countries engaged in extensive barter, which greatly increased regional trade. In 1918, 30 per cent of all foreign trade was with other Nordic countries. This was a significant increase from the pre-war level of 12 to 13 per cent.[3]

The regional co-operation achieved during the war was unprecedented and hopes were expressed that it could be continued after the war was over. However, the governments made no serious efforts during the 1920s to continue Nordic governmental co-operation; instead the activities relapsed into the pre-war pattern. As earlier, low-key, sectoral efforts were carried out in certain areas of low political significance. Only in the League of Nations did the Scandinavian governments co-operate extensively to increase their chances of influencing the decisions in that international organisation.[4]

Since the Second World War, Nordic relations have been characterised by a gradual but steady increase in inter-governmental co-operation. Not only have joint policy projects and intensive governmental interactions been continued from the inter-war period, but some significant institutions have been established to help channel these regional activities. This trend of increased Nordic co-operation is quite evident despite some major setbacks during the period. In fact, to many foreign observers the publicised failures seem to overshadow the many smaller, less dramatic and less well-known achievements. For example, in 1948—9 negotiations to form a Scandinavian Defence Alliance failed; continuous efforts during the 1950s to create a Nordic Economic Market led to nothing; the intensive effort in 1968—70 to establish a Nordic Economic Union (NORDEK) resulted in final collapse; and the hopes for a united front in the negotiations with the European Economic Community (EEC) in 1971—3 were not fulfilled.[5]

History seems to indicate that the Nordic countries have failed dramatically when they have tried to undertake some major, conspicuous co-operation projects. In contrast, they have been quite successful in achieving incremental and low-key steps towards closer co-operation. For example, numerous joint governmental committees and organs have been established throughout the post-war period to help co-ordinate policy in various issue-areas. As a result of these functional activities, Nordic public policy is to a great extent jointly planned, formulated and executed. A regional parliamentary body, the Nordic Council, was created in 1952 to serve as a forum for debate and initiative. Various Nordic funds have been established to finance joint cultural, industrial, and developmental projects. A Council of Ministers, with small, permanent secretariats, exists to facilitate regional co-ordination and planning.

One interesting point about all these aspects of Nordic co-operation during the post-war period is that they were created piecemeal. While the major proposals for increased co-operation failed, much of the substance of these projects has been achieved through incremental developments. The major thrusts forward in the co-operation effort have also occurred at times when the region seemed to be threatened with further disintegration due to external developments. Thus, the driving force for Nordic co-operation today is perhaps not as much a desire to unite the region as a wish to keep it intact. For example, the recent expansion of the EEC to include Denmark has been combined with a significant structural strengthening of the Nordic co-operation process.[6] Today, the regional relations are so intense and diversified that one can more properly describe them as an extension of domestic policy-making rather than as foreign relations in a traditional sense.

The Nordic Pattern of Integration

Having traced the development of a Nordic pluralistic security community and briefly touched upon the growth of regional governmental collaboration during the twentieth century, we now turn to the dynamics of contemporary inter-actions. Of interest are the processes by which a situation characterised merely by the absence of violent conflict has been transformed into a pattern of intimate collaboration. An effort will be made to sketch in a summary fashion the Nordic strategy of regional integration. The brief review is based on a more comprehensive, empirical study and only hopes to highlight the broad outlines of these processes.[7]

For the purposes of this study, integration is conceptualised as a process that reaches across the various national entities rather than links these with a higher, regional level of activity. The regional level is not seen as increasing in authority, salience, or capacity to act, to the extent that the national units lose those characteristics of statehood. The process of political integration is less one of centralisation of regional authority than of finding collective and nationally acceptable solutions to pressing national problems.

Three conceptual types of integration and seven operational dimensions of the concept may be identified. For the organising framework see Table 1 below. The three conceptual types are societal, attitudinal and political integration respectively. Societal integration is defined as the process whereby the involved societies are becoming increasingly interconnected through growing transnational ties and networks. Both regional elite interactions and various forms of aggregate transactions are studied. One potential link between societal integration and political integration is found in the attitudinal setting in the region. The responses by the public authorities to the changing degrees of societal interconnectedness are partly dependent on the attitudinal ties within the region.

Where a favourable attitudinal setting is found, a foundation for constructive responses and mutually advantageous solutions exist. In contrast, societal integration which is combined with unfavourable attitudes toward regional cooperation can easily spur hostile reactions and increase conflict among the countries. Attitudinal integration is defined as the process whereby the peoples of a region develop increasingly favourable attitudes toward their regional partners and to joint management of regional problems. Such changes are evidenced in surveys indicating a strengthening of regional identity ties and the maintenance of a supportive attitudinal setting for the co-operation processes.

Political integration is defined as the process whereby the

TABLE 1

TYPES OF INTEGRATION, THE CONCEPTUAL DEFINITIONS AND OPERATIONAL DIMENSIONS

Types of Integration	Societal Integration	Attitudinal Integration	Political Integration
Conceptual Definitions	The process whereby the regional societies are becoming increasingly interconnected through growing transnational ties and networks.	The process whereby the people of the region develop increasingly favourable attitudes towards their regional partners and to joint management of regional problems.	The process whereby the public authorities in the region increasingly manage national problems through joint processes.
Operational Dimensions	1. Increased regional transactions of goods, messages, and people. 2. Increased activity of non-governmental elites across the national boundaries in the region.	1. Strengthening of regional identity ties. 2. The maintenance of a supportive attitudinal setting for joint co-operation processes.	1. Growth of joint public institutions. 2. Increased trans-governmental interactions. 3. Increased joint public policy output.

public authorities in the region increasingly manage national problems jointly. Three aspects are involved in political integration: the growth of collective public institutions, increased transgovernmental interactions and increased joint public policy output.

We have now identified three conceptual types of integration and specified seven operational dimensions of the concept. Next, we shall outline the Nordic pattern of co-operation in terms of these types of integration. This will help identify the dynamics of the Nordic strategy as well as indicate in what areas it has proved most and least far-reaching.

The general impression of Nordic transaction-flows during the period 1952–72 is that of high regional rates combined with marked discontinuities between the region and the external areas. For all types except trade, the Nordic flows were already very intensive in 1952 and significantly more intensive than the external exchanges. Except for a marked increase in regional trade during the 1960s, the Nordic societies have not experienced any drastic increase in mutual relevance during the period studied. Instead, high rates of mutual transfers have characterised the region for a considerable time. While the volumes of Nordic flows have grown, the proportion of regional transactions to total foreign exchanges has not increased substantially. It has sometimes even declined. On the whole, it might be more appropriate to describe these transaction-flows as indicating stagnation rather than a process of rapid societal integration. The region was already in 1952 closely tied together by various flows and the changes from that time have not been significant, except for the trade data.

The growth of transnational elite activities in the Nordic region has experienced a two-stage development. First, contacts were initiated in an effort to manage common problems resulting from the high mutual relevance of the Nordic societies. The regional activities were at this time mainly responses to developments at the aggregate level of societal relations and cannot be characterised as aiming at influencing the joint governmental decision-making process. Later, the trans-Nordic contacts were channelled into more structured, formal and institutional means. An effort was made to create joint co-ordinating bodies that could ensure continuous exposure to regional considerations and serve as spokesmen for the national organisations in their dealings with the joint governmental institutions in the region. At this time, the transnational interactions intensified as contacts with the joint public organs became more important. The goal of influencing the joint governmental policy-making process also became one of the major ambitions of the trans-Nordic activities. As before, many aspects of these interest-group oriented activities are targeted at the national administrations but a second focus towards the joint institutions has also developed.

To determine the possibilities for joint management of the high level of mutual societal relevance in the region, the regional identity ties were explored. Although the data were very limited, they pointed to a continued positive evaluation of and identification with the other Nordic societies during the post-war period. In fact, some limited evidence indicated the possibility of a growing affinity among the Nordic people during the period. Thus, the high level of mutual relevance among the Nordic societies was found to be combined with substantial identity ties among the Nordic people. This combination of ties among the Nordic societies could provide a basis for constructive and mutually beneficial management of common problems. At the same time as the high rates of regional transactions make for common tasks in need of solutions, the strong identity ties can facilitate such joint solutions.

We also explored the public views of the Nordic co-operation process. Although our data were rather limited, we found a generally positive and permissive attitude towards Nordic co-operation. This process seemed to possess certain symbolic and emotional values regarding neighbourly friendliness and regional harmony and was strongly supported as an idea by the people. Specific proposals for increased co-operation were also generally supported, although a substantial number of the respondents could not offer definite opinions on these more specific questions. The general impression is that the political elites of the region have a relatively free hand in implementing the vague notion of Nordic co-operation. At the same time as no major opposition to this concept was found, we could not trace any strong support for specific, concrete measures of co-operation.

The first operational dimension of political integration explored was the growth of joint public institutions. The main observation regarding this was the great expansion of the institutional structure since the middle of the 1960s. Not only have the joint organs grown in quantitative terms since 1964, but the degree of institutionalisation in terms of size of personnel, joint secretariats, financial resources available, and activity within these organs has also expanded drastically. In particular, the changes since 1970 are important. Since that time many new important structural features have been added to the regional co-operation process. For example, a joint secretariat for the Nordic Council, a Council of Ministers with two secretariats and numerous permanent committees of high officials, a fund for industrial development, and a Nordic investment bank have been created in this relatively short period of time. Thus, this dimension of political integration has recently experienced considerable growth. This expansion of the joint public institutional structure has also induced a wave of increased trans-Nordic activity among various non-governmental groups. Apparently, there is a link between the growth of joint public institutions and the development of more structured, centralised interactions among various non-governmental elites in the region.

The growth of joint public policy was found to experience its greatest expansion before the recent structural changes in the region. Both the scope and intensity of joint policy grew significantly in the period 1954–64. Since that time, the region has mainly experienced a continued slow increase in scope, intensity and salience of joint policy. In particular, the economic sector has expanded during these last fifteen years.

One interesting observation is that the policy dimension of political integration has developed prior to and presumably independently of institutional growth in the region. Thus, the results or outputs of the joint processes operating in the area already show significant changes prior to the institutionalisation and formalisation of these joint policy-making activities. This finding leads us to question why the political elites in the countries have undertaken a major structural reorganisation of the joint activities, when obviously significant policy results were achieved prior to this change.

The answer may rest in a fear that external developments during the last ten years, such as the growth of the EEC and the enlargement of that group, would undermine the results already reached in the Nordic region. A greater structural rigidity and formalisation would, hopefully, facilitate regional co-ordination and ensure that a regional perspective was maintained on all major issues. The goal was not so much to expand the co-operative ventures but to make sure that the countries could hold on to what they had achieved when faced with a strong external challenge. To that end, both new joint structures were established and several programmes for new co-operation schemes were agreed on to help symbolise the continued importance of Nordic co-operation.

Trans-governmental interactions in the Nordic region were analysed to determine if in fact the joint policy output in the region was the result of joint processes of consultation, co-ordination and decision or if it was arrived at separately. We found an intensive network of both formal and informal interactions across the national administrations. In particular, the informal contacts seemed important to the joint policy-making process. The various joint institutions in the region were also part of this trans-governmental activity as their staffs played a crucial part as initiators and mediators of policy. In addition we examined the norms for interaction and decision among the political elites active in those trans-governmental interactions. Belief in compromise, consensual decision-making, rational choice, openness, and emphasis on politics as a means to reach practical and beneficial solutions to problems seemed to dominate the political cultures of the area. This normative structure seemed to give the Nordic co-operation process a unique style of joint policy-making. Here, informal interactions, pragmatic goals and methods, an incremental approach towards task expansion, and an emphasis on broad consensus behind decisions dominated the joint efforts.

We noted an increase in the frequency of trans-governmental interactions during the last ten years. Thus, the recent organisational strengthening of the joint co-operation process has been combined with more intensive activity within this new structure. We also found that the main actors in this regional policy-making process are the bureaucratic segments of the governments. The political leaders of each country have only limited direct involvement in the process and are heavily dependent on their staffs for guidance.

It is interesting to compare the results achieved in each of the dimensions of integration discussed in this study. The first observation is that Nordic societal integration has not been very impressive during the last twenty-five years. In many respects, the transactional dimension has stagnated or even suffered some disintegration, while the transnational elite activities have only very recently experienced a new expansion. However, the fact that the Nordic societies have not experienced a major process of integration during the last twenty-five years is mainly related to the very strong initial ties in the region.

In the three dimensions of political integration, the region has experienced a clear process of integration during the last twenty-five years. This is the case both due to lower initial levels of joint management and because of a consistent effort to further increase these joint governmental activities. The growth of joint public policy has been the most impressive dimension of political integration. Here a continuous process of joint outputs has been maintained throughout the period and has produced comparatively substantial results. The trans-governmental interactions among the public authorities in the region are also very important. In this dimension intensive political integration has been experienced.

The institutional dimension of political integration is far less impressive than the other two aspects of the process. For a long time, the Nordic region did not experience any growth in this dimension, but was characterised by stagnation. It is only during the last ten years that a considerable expansion can be noted. Since the latter part of the 1960s, a process of integration is obvious in this dimension as well. However, in comparison with other regional efforts the institutional results of this process are still modest.

Finally, we noted a continuous process of a gradually more

favourable attitudinal setting for the joint efforts. This dimension seems to have been keeping up with the changes in the other dimensions of political and societal integration during the time period. For example, we could point to the clear possibility of a strengthening of regional identity ties during the post-war period. However, we could not find any strong demands for or interest in greatly expanded governmental co-operation beyond the present levels. Thus, in these dimensions of integration it might be more appropriate to talk about a continuous acceptance of and vague support for the developments in the region rather than of a definite process of attitudinal integration.

The pattern of integration developing in the Nordic region is summarised in Table 2 below. Initial high levels of mutual societal relevance combined with modest identity ties make for transnational and trans-governmental elite activities across the countries. The trans-governmental interactions lead to joint policy results. A few joint public institutions are established to facilitate co-ordination and planning in various areas. Gradually, the growth of joint public policy increases the need for further transnational co-ordination of the major non-governmental organisations in the region. The attitudinal base for further governmental co-operation and the regional identity ties are strengthened and allow for increased co-operation. Finally, the considerable achievements made in joint policy and the intense trans-governmental interactions are co-ordinated, organised, and formalised through the creation of a new joint institutional structure in the region. In addition, the transnational activities of major groups are structurally strengthened to better fit with the new institutional features of the public policy-making process. Due to these structural changes, the policy-making process is now stabilised, institutionalised and mainly the concern of the bureaucratic elements of government. The joint co-operation effort has become clearly established and given its own organisational foundation.

Motives and Sources Facilitating Nordic Co-operation

Earlier we pointed to the prevalent desire to avoid great power interference in the region as a motivating factor behind

TABLE 2: THE DEVELOPMENT PATTERN OF NORDIC INTEGRATION

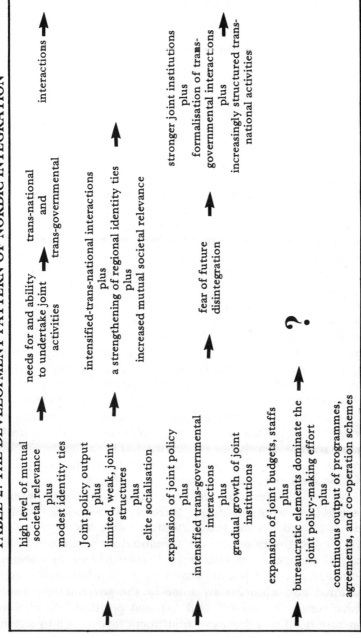

high level of mutual
societal relevance
plus
modest identity ties

↑

needs for and ability
to undertake joint
activities

trans-national
and
trans-governmental
interactions

↑

Joint policy output
plus
limited, weak, joint
structures
plus
elite socialisation

↑

intensified-trans-national interactions
plus
a strengthening of regional identity ties
plus
increased mutual societal relevance

↑

expansion of joint policy
plus
intensified trans-governmental
interactions
plus
gradual growth of joint
institutions

↑

fear of future
disintegration

↑

stronger joint institutions
plus
formalisation of trans-
governmental interactions
plus
increasingly structured transnational activities

↑

expansion of joint budgets, staffs
plus
bureaucratic elements dominate the
joint policy-making effort
plus
continuous output of programmes,
agreements, and co-operation schemes

↑   ↑   ?   ↑

the establishment of a pluralistic security community. This aspect still plays a role in the formulation of Nordic security policies. Through the dynamics of the so-called 'Nordic Balance', characterised by mutual restraint and sensitivity in security postures, the superpower presence is far less pronounced in Northern Europe than in other East-West borderline areas.[8]

It is also widely believed that the maintenance of a stable region, domestically and internationally, gives major external parties less reason to become involved in local affairs. By settling local disputes peacefully and by providing a stable and predictable economic and political setting the Nordic governments help retain their positions as autonomous nation-states. Thus, the Nordic co-operation process is not only valued for its immediate, practical results but it is also appreciated as a means towards reducing great power interests in the area.

It appears that a fundamental motive behind Nordic co-operation is of a defensive nature. The objective seems to be to help protect the nations from various forms of external domination or penetration. This dimension was mentioned earlier as a motive also behind the recent structural strengthening of the co-operation processes. It is widely accepted that each Nordic country traditionally maintains strong cultural-economic-political links with major external areas. In many ways, the countries focus their international involvements in different directions, giving room for centrifugal pressures on regional unity. Often, a favoured solution to national problems, such as security or prosperity, has been the strengthening of such outside commitments even at the expense of Nordic solidarity.

Nordic co-operation schemes have sometimes offered second-best solutions when broader international involvements proved beyond reach. In most cases, one or several of the Nordic governments have promoted such ventures in the face of major external challenges. Particularly strong attempts to maintain regional unity have been made when major international commitments by some of the governments would leave others in isolated and exposed positions. Nordic co-operation offers a defensive adjustment mechanism to serious political or economic external challenges which may undermine national autonomy and enhance foreign domination. Nordic co-operation is seen as enhancing the national postures in another respect as well. Through regional collaboration and the presentation of a united front, the governments greatly strengthen their otherwise rather limited influence on the international environment. Living by the principle of 'strength in numbers', the Nordic governments are often motivated to co-operate in order to increase their international influence. If such external efforts are to prove successful internal agreement on policy is required. Thus, the external ramifications of disunity offer strong incentives for reaching mutually acceptable solutions on many issues. It is often said that the Nordic governments find it more difficult to settle internal disputes than to find common ground in international arenas.[9]

In addition to the externally oriented motives for Nordic co-operation important local aspects are also included. It is realised that a number of domestic objectives cannot be reached without some form of joint effort. For example, the geographical proximity of the nations generates a number of common problems with transportation, migration, pollution and social and judicial services. The Nordic countries have a long and strong record on finding joint solutions to such neighbourhood issues.[10] These often low-key and informal arrangements may not be recognised as major political achievements in regional co-operation. However, the ramification for the local populations are significant as various obstacles to regional mobility interchanges and equality have been removed. They provide an important public service to the people in the countries.

Nordic co-operation is also seen as a useful mechanism to overcome the limited national resources of the countries. A number of nationally desirable objectives are only possible with the addition of externally available resources. For a number of reasons, a pooling of Nordic resources may often seem more satisfactory than collaboration with other, more distant and significantly larger partners. This motive has stimulated Nordic efforts in the educational, scientific, communications, industrial, energy, and regional development fields. In other areas, such as security and trade, the Nordic region has not offered sufficiently large collective resources to satisfy the individual national needs. In these sectors, co-operation which extends beyond the Nordic region often offers the most promising solutions.

With intensified regional interactions and heightened national sensitivities to developments in the neighbouring countries, an additional motive for co-operation has emerged. It is recognised that the Nordic economies are closely connected and that national economic policy often has implications also for the other societies. A desire to avoid policy choices with negative effects on the regional partners is evident among the governments. Through a continuous dialogue aiming at policy co-ordination, government officials hope to foster regional stability and collective prosperity. Although national priorities often make it impossible to find one common policy posture, at least several undesirable alternatives can be avoided. Continuous contacts are maintained across most areas of public policy, including judicial, financial, fiscal, industrial, energy and foreign policy.[11]

We have pointed to several external and internal motives for pursuing Nordic co-operation. It is evident from this brief review that the Nordic governments have strong incentives to participate in regional collaboration. Valuable national objectives and benefits can be achieved through such collective efforts. However, the existence of political motives for co-operation cannot alone explain the comparatively successful record of Nordic co-operation. It is also important to recognise a number of factors which facilitate the accomplishment of the desired results. The sources of Nordic co-operation can be found in the cultural heritage, social and political structures and in prevalent values and norms. Possibly, these background conditions are unique to the Nordic setting and are not easily transferred to other areas.

With the growth of nationalism in Europe a sense of a Nordic heritage developed also in this region. We previously discussed the pan-Scandinavian movement of the mid-1800s. Also more recently one can note a sense of a Nordic identity among the peoples. While this is less noted at home it becomes very evident in international dealings. The psychological distance to fellow Nordics is considerably shorter than to other foreign groups. Several opinion polls indicate the affinity of the Nordic peoples relative to other nationalities.[12]

Several factors reinforce this common feeling of belonging to a group set apart from others. The language similarities facilitate relaxed communications. The values, life-styles and interests are often very similar. One is generally relatively well acquainted with these countries and their inhabitants. During the period covered by the memories of the present generation no serious antagonising conflicts have been experienced. In addition, Nordic nationalism may serve as a substitute for traditional nationalism. While the latter notion is somewhat discredited in these very internationally oriented societies, a belief in Nordic unity, strength and even exclusiveness seems more in accord with the modern emphasis on international co-operation. In all, the Nordic region offers a focus for national identity which seems less alien and perhaps more comfortable than the larger international environment. This common perception may facilitate stable domestic support for intimate regional governmental collaboration.

In many respects, the Nordic societies and political systems have developed in parallel fashions. The common heritage of gradual, generally peaceful domestic change has not only affected the contemporary political cultures but also resulted in very similar national structures.[13] The government machineries, political parties and interest groups are organised along similar lines and serve similar functions in society. The noted parallelism facilitates close interaction among political leaders, governmental officials and interest-groups. The widely recognised similarities with the other Nordic countries also encourage using these as initial reference points and sources of inspiration for national action. The parallelism is also a primary factor behind extensive policy diffusion between the governments.

In addition, the parallel national structures may significantly facilitate the co-operation process.[14] It is easy to identify one's opposite number in the other countries. Participants in the co-operation effort generally face similar restraints and possibilities as they basically perform identical functions in society. All parties can without difficulty appreciate the details of policy-making in the other governments since these do not vary significantly from their own setting. Basic ideological beliefs and fundamental social and economic objectives are often shared across the state lines. It should be relatively easy to work together when so many of the national attributes are held in common or are very similar.

There are some notable exceptions to the dominant feature of Nordic parallelism. We previously pointed to the divergent external orientations as forces limiting regional co-operation. The economic structures of the countries also vary significantly, as do national resources, economic activity and interests. Traditionally it has been more difficult to reach agreement in the economic sector than it has been in other policy areas. Recently, the national differences in this regard have tended to be somewhat reduced as all countries have experienced similar economic trends and pressures.

Today, the sharpest economic contrasts may not be between the nations but between the southern and northern parts of the region. A pattern of stable economic activity and presumed financial dominance persists in the south while the north experiences relative stagnation and demands for government subsidies. It is not clear how the anticipated Norwegian oil exploration north of the 62nd parallel will affect this relationship between the regional periphery and centre. Possibly, the potential infusion of substantial new resources in this area may stimulate new co-operation projects among the concerned governments.

The Nordic political systems are well known for their prevalent norms of consensus-formation, compromise and fact-finding. It is widely felt that these dominant values have facilitated the development of stable, harmonious, high-performance polities. As could be expected, the norms influencing domestic developments are also crucial factors in the regional processes. The Nordic preference for consensus-formation is manifested in an emphasis on national accommodation. Decisions are not taken over the objections of any of the parties. Unanimity is the rule in the collective policy-making process. National sovereignty is recognised and respected as a vital political force. Proposals which would drastically violate the essential interests of any nation are not seriously considered. However, this emphasis on consensus-formation does not necessarily result in obstructionism leading to immobilism.

The value placed on compromise is reflected in the emphasis on accommodation to others. Mutual sensitivity to each other's needs and interests are dominant features of the co-operation process. These norms give an assurance of not being disregarded or compromised. They also involve a responsibility to respond to the demands by the other participants. Possibly, the absence of a supra-national pretence generates some confidence among the governments. They are aware that they can at any time refuse to support a policy or even withdraw from the proceedings. The existence of limited formal commitments and the strong preferences for co-operation may combine to facilitate mutually acceptable solutions.

The Nordic policy-making sequence proceeds from extensive and detailed investigations to lengthy deliberations and to final political decision. Often, this process takes several years. The value given to fact-finding prior to making a political commitment is rooted in the domestic political cultures. This bias makes for an extremely slow, often tedious and cumbersome co-operation process. However, it also gives some assurance that all ramifications of a decision are fully explored and that all legitimate interests are considered. Perhaps this drawn-out process is a prerequisite for finding common ground in the many important policy issues covered by the regional co-operation efforts. An established sense of confidence in that no vital interests are overlooked or ignored may also facilitate more far-reaching commitments than quicker decisions would allow.

Together with the other sources discussed, the dominant norms for regional interactions may be crucial factors behind the generally successful record of contemporary Nordic co-operation. The governments in this area have managed to solve numerous national problems through joint actions. They have established a solid pattern of intimate collaboration covering a wide scope of public policy. It is an open question to what extent the Nordic model for neighbourhood co-operation can be applied to other regions experiencing similar needs for collective solutions to vital concerns.

REFERENCES

1. This paper will also appear in Bengt Sundelius, ed., *The Foreign Policies of Northern Europe*, Westview Press, Boulder, Colo. 1981.
2. See Karl Deutsch, *Political Community and the North Atlantic Area*, Princeton University Press, Princeton 1957; and Raymond Lindgren, *Norway – Sweden: Union, Disunion and Scandinavian Integration*, Princeton University Press, Princeton 1959.
3. These early developments are reviewed in Frantz Wendt, *The Nordic Council and Co-operation in Scandinavia*, Monksgaard, Copenhagen 1959.
4. See Shepherd Jones, *The Scandinavian States and the League of Nations*, Princeton University Press, Princeton 1939.
5. These developments are reviewed in Claes Wiklund and Bengt Sundelius, 'Nordic Cooperation in the Seventies: Trends and Patterns', *Scandinavian Political Studies*, Vol. 2, new series, No. 2, 1979, pp. 99–120.
6. This is argued in Bengt Sundelius, 'Nordic Co-operation: A Dead Issue?', *The World Today*, Vol. 33, July 1977, pp. 275–82.
7. The study referred to is the author's 'Nordic Co-operation: A Dynamic Interaction Process', Ph.D. dissertation, University of Denver, Colo. 1976.
8. See Nils Andren, *The Future of the Nordic Balance*, Swedish Research Institute of National Defence, Stockholm 1977.
9. Nordic co-operation in international forums is reviewed in Åke Landquist, ed., *Norden på värdsarenan*, Tema, Stockholm 1968.
10. This is reviewed in Frantz Wendt, *Nordisk Rad 1952–1978*, Nordic Council, Stockholm 1979.
11. This activity is reviewed in Bengt Sundelius, *Managing Transnationalism in Northern Europe*, Westview Press, Boulder, Colo. 1978.
12. For example, see *Den nordiska allmanheten och det nordiska samarbetet*, 1973, Nu 1973:4, Nordic Council, Stockholm 1973.
13. Folmer Wisti, ed., *Nordic Democracy*, Danish Institute, Copenhagen 1981.
14. Compare Gunnar P. Nielsson, 'The Parallel National Action Process: Scandinavian Experiences', in Paul Taylor and A. J. R. Groom, eds, *International Organization: A Conceptual Approach*, Frances Pinter, London 1977, pp. 270–316.

BIBLIOGRAPHY

Anderson, Stanley V., *The Nordic Council: A Study in Scandinavian Regionalism*, University of Washington Press, Seattle 1967

Andren, Nils, 'Nordic Integration: Aspects and Problems', *Cooperation and Conflict*, Vol. II, No. 1 (1967)

Dickerman, Robert, 'Transgovernmental Challenge and Response in Scandinavia and North America', *International Organization*, Vol. 30, No. 2 (1976)

Haskel, Barbara G., 'Disparities, Strategies and Opportunity Costs: The Example of Scandinavian Economic Market Negotations', *International Studies Quarterly*, Vol. 18, No. 1 (1974)

Haskel, Barbara G., *The Scandinavian Option: Opportunities and Opportunity Costs in Postwar Scandinavian Foreign Policies*, Universitetsforlaget, Oslo 1976

Lindgren, Raymond, *Norway—Sweden: Union, Disunion and Scandinavian Integration*, Princeton University Press, Princeton 1959

Lyche, Ingeborg, *Nordic Cultural Co operation*, Universitetsforlaget, Oslo 1974

Nielsson, Gunnar P., 'The Parallel National Action Process: Scandinavian Experiences', in Paul Taylor and A. J. R. Groom, eds, *International Organization: A Conceptual Approach*, Frances Pinter Ltd, London 1977

Orvik, Nils, 'Nordic Cooperation and High Politics', *International Organization*, Vol. 28, No. 1 (1974)

Schiller, Bernt, ed., *Books, Articles, Reports Concerning Nordic Co-operation*, NU 1975:3, Nordic Council, Stockholm 1975

Solem, Erik, *The Nordic Council and Scandinavian Integration*, Praeger, New York 1977

Sundelius, Bengt, *Managing Transnationalism in Northern Europe*, Westview Press, Boulder, Colo. 1978

Sundelius, Bengt, *The Foreign Policies of Northern Europe*, Westview Press, Boulder, Colo. 1981

Sundelius, Bengt and Wiklund, Claes, 'The Nordic Community: The Ugly Duckling of Regional Cooperation', *Journal of Common Market Studies*, Vol. 18, No. 1 (1979)

Wallensteen, Peter, *et al.*, *The Nordic System: Structure and Change 1920—1970*, Department of Peace and Conflict Research Uppsala University, Uppsala 1973

Wendt, Frantz, *The Nordic Council and Cooperation in Scandinavia*, Munksgaard, Copenhagen 1959

Wendt, Frantz, *Nordisk Rad 1952—1978*, Nordic Council, Stockholm 1979

Wiklund, Claes, 'The Zig-Zag Course of the Nordek Negotiations', *Scandinavian Political Studies*, Vol. 5 (1970)

PART IV

POLITICAL CO-OPERATION:
THE ANGLO-IRISH CASE

Part IV of this volume contains one paper, that of Patrick Keatinge who, with particular reference to the communiqués of the Republic of Ireland and United Kingdom governments of 21 May 1980 and 8 December 1980 respectively, examines 'political co-operation: the Anglo-Irish case' in order, as he says, to dispel some of the confusion.

12: AN ODD COUPLE? OBSTACLES AND OPPORTUNITIES IN INTER-STATE POLITICAL CO-OPERATION BETWEEN THE REPUBLIC OF IRELAND AND THE UNITED KINGDOM
PATRICK KEATINGE

Patrick Keatinge addresses himself to three questions: (a) Does 'political co-operation' have any precise meaning in the general context of international relations? (b) To what extent can the concept help us understand the particular case of relations between the Republic of Ireland and the United Kingdom? (c) If closer co-operation is indeed the aim of both governments (as emerged in the two communiqués) in what forms might it evolve in the light of the experiences of other countries?

In reply to the first question he tells us that relations between sovereign states have traditionally been seen in terms of conflict and power, with co-operation treated as a peripheral matter. Although accepting that most of the writing in International Relations relates to multilateral relationships he suggests that the 'Complex Interdependence' model offers an appropriate framework for examining relations between Dublin and London. Thus he attempts to answer the second question under the following three headings derived from this model: (a) the patterns of interaction between the two states; (b) the political processes employed; and (c) the types of outcome which generally occur. He uses the descriptions derived, in turn, to identify the fundamental problems of asymmetry, legitimacy, and management respectively which tend to inhibit political co-operation between the Republic of Ireland and the United Kingdom.

Turning to the third question, Keatinge first makes a brief examination of three existing forms of co-operation which might 'transfer without rejection'; these are the Franco-German Friendship Treaty (1963), Benelux (1944/47/58) and Nordic Co-operation (1952/71), which he selects 'because they have been referred to by politicians or by the media over the winter of 1980–81'. In addition he recalls one hypothetical model – condominium – because it has already been raised in the context of the Northern Ireland conflict.

In each of the four cases he examines the relevance of the model in terms of the problems of asymmetry, legitimacy and management. He accepts that the four cases do not exhaust the possibilities, but hopes that these analyses will serve to promote discussion. He concludes that none of the *existing* schemes appears to encompass a relationship between sovereign states with the same mixture of territorial dispute, ethnic and sectarian divisions and transactional violence as that suffered by the Republic of Ireland and the United Kingdom in respect of Northern Ireland and that the *hypothetical* scheme invariably seems to have the adjective 'impracticable' around its neck.

Secondly, he asks, if we accept the currently prevailing assumption that political co-operation between the Republic of Ireland and the United Kingdom has not been satisfactory in the past, what then can be done to create a new framework which will prove both durable and effective? What, if any, changes can be made and what existing procedures need to be strengthened? In the context of the commitment made at the Dublin summit in December 1980 to commission joint studies relating to the 'totality of relationships within these islands' the considerations he raises relate in the first place to the possible mode of co-operation and in the second place to its likely substance.

With respect to the mode of co-operation he suggests and examines possible new structures and processes in the light of the fundamental problems already identified and of the experience elsewhere. With respect to the substance of co-operation he comments briefly on the prospects of developing further co-operation with regard to the following types of issues: economic and social policies, cultural relations, common citizenship, security against transnational terrorism, interstate security and political settlement in Northern Ireland.

12

An Odd Couple? Obstacles and Opportunities in Inter-State Political Co-operation between the Republic of Ireland and the United Kingdom

Patrick Keatinge

Holy writ, for the student of international politics, often comes in that cryptic and inscrutable form of prose known as the diplomatic communiqué. Thus it was that the term 'political co-operation' emerged to the fore in relations between the United Kingdom and the Republic of Ireland following the summit meeting in London on 21 May 1980.[1] The next summit in Dublin, on 8 December 1980, envisaged co-operation in the context of 'the further development of the unique relationship between the two countries'. Political co-operation in Anglo-Irish relations[2] is clearly something special, but the reverberations of the Dublin summit suggest that it is a phrase which is open to a wide variety of interpretations.

The purpose of this paper is to attempt to dispel some of the confusion surrounding the application of this concept to the Anglo-Irish case, while recognising that where confusion is wilful and information is negligible that may not be possible. To this end three questions are raised: (a) Does 'political co-operation' have any precise meaning in the general context of international relations? (b) To what extent can the concept help us understand the particular case of relations between the Republic of Ireland and the United Kingdom? (c) If closer political co-operation is indeed the aim of both governments, in what forms might it evolve in the light of the experiences of other countries?

Inter-State Political Co-operation:
Towards a Definition of the Concept

The common-sense usage of the term political co-operation implies merely that two or more states work together in pursuit of some common interest. This manifestly happens most of the time, in war as well as peace, between many states, and it may be incorporated in many sorts of relationship. At one extreme the context of political co-operation may be seen as that of the 'power' or 'realist' model of inter-state relations. In this traditional and still popular view the anarchical international system, embodying enormous disparities in the distribution of material and human resources among legally 'equal' states, implies endemic conflict and the use of force as the ultimate instrument of policy. Political co-operation here will be limited, intermittent and precarious. It will be manifested in the 'grand designs' of major states, and will be more or less imposed on smaller, client states, through the central diplomatic and military agencies of the great powers.

At the other extreme the context of inter-state political co-operation is a situation where there is intensive and durable co-operation on a wide range of issues. Here the legally independent sovereign states agree, however reluctantly, to engage in a process of 'joint decision-making' which may even bring them together with aspirations to form a new integrated political entity. Hence the emergence of a body of writing rather loosely termed 'integration theory'. This focused on the pioneering evolution of the European Community, and is examined in more detail elsewhere.[3] The label 'integration' deserves comment. Some of the original formulations posited a new integrated political entity arising from the co-operation of existing participants, often in more or less clearly held visions of a federal Europe. With the persistent refusal of reality to match these expectations, however, more attention was paid to integration as a political process which might lead somewhere.

As integration theory wilted somewhat during the Seventies the problems arising out of inter-state co-operation came into greater relief. A variety of quite disparate factors emerged: the decline of the *Pax Americana,* confusion in the management of the international economy, instability in many third world countries, and the apparent proliferation and increased importance of non-state entities such as multinational corporations and terrorist groups – the so-called *transnational* actors. All this did not necessarily imply a diminution in inter-state co-operation. Nevertheless, it did seem to impose serious limitations on the ability of national governments not merely to control their external relations as traditionally conceived, but their internal direction of economic and social policy as well. In response to these developments, a body of literature – less clearly defined even than integration theory and often less optimistic – examined the effects of 'interdependence'. In their concern with the interplay between economic mechanisms and political processes, and their emphasis on the role of transnational actors, these writers have usually applied their ideas to global issues and, like integration theorists, they have tended to envisage political responses as being multilateral in form.

In short, the academic literature on inter-state political co-operation has not, with one or two exceptions, made much of co-operation in the often claustrophobic and inherently unstable *bilateral* context. Even less has the particular case of bilateral co-operation which is the concern of this paper been a focus of attention. There is a tantalising suggestion of what could have been explored in an early work by one of the leading integration theorists, Karl Deutsch.[4] Over twenty years ago Deutsch argued that Ireland and the United Kingdom (together with the United States and Canada) formed 'a group of four countries among whom the largest number of conditions favouring integration seemed fulfilled already, so that one might think of them as a potential North Atlantic nucleus'.[5] That this lead was never pursued can be largely explained by the fact that the academic study of international relations hardly existed in Ireland, and, while the Irish Free State had always been paid some attention by students of the Commonwealth, British experts on international relations in general not unnaturally felt that they had far larger fish to fry.

There are, therefore, no obvious leads in trying to pick up the conceptual threads which Deutsch left loose in the late

Fifties. The first choice that must be made is to decide whether Anglo-Irish relations approximate more closely to the 'power' or 'interdependence' models of international relations. It is not a simple choice, but given the former model's emphasis on conflict, where 'at least one of the parties to the conflict has both the will and the capacity to employ force',[6] it is not appropriate for our purposes, for on balance that condition has not been met in Anglo-Irish relations, particularly since 1945.

The 'power' model is eschewed, then, in favour of a model of 'complex interdependence' which has been developed by Keohane and Nye.[7] Of particular interest is the authors' application of the model to bilateral relations between the United States and Canada. There is an obvious asymmetry in power between the two, but, largely because of the nature of their interactions, they use political processes and reach levels of agreement which do not reflect this asymmetry in any clear or consistent manner.

The parallel with Anglo-Irish relations is, as we shall see, by no means perfect, but at the very least this model provides a plausible descriptive framework. Thus the second part of the paper will examine the relationship between the Republic of Ireland and the United Kingdom under three main headings derived from Keohane and Nye: first, the patterns of inter-actions between the two states; second, the political processes employed; third, the types of outcome which generally occur. On the basis of this description an attempt is made to identify the fundamental problems which tend to inhibit political co-operation.

The Republic of Ireland and the United Kingdom: A Case of Very Complicated Interdependence
Patterns of Interaction

It is now part of the conventional wisdom, in Dublin at least, that 'the uniqueness of the relationship between our two countries derives from the extraordinary close economic, social and cultural links between our two islands that are the product of our joint history.'[8] Perhaps too much is made of 'uniqueness' in this respect, for what we have here is in effect the 'multiple channels of contact' which is the first set of conditions for the existence of Keohane and Nye's model of 'complex interdependence'. It is worth looking briefly at the major elements of these channels of contact and the most noticeable trends in their evolution over the last twenty years or so.

Bilateral trade is summarised in Table 1. From Dublin's point of view there has been a noticeable reduction in the significance of the United Kingdom as an export market, explained in large part by the opportunities for export diversification following membership of the European Community in 1973. Yet the UK is still by far the most important single export market, and its significance as a source of about 50 per cent of the Republic's imports has barely changed at all since the Sixties. From London's point of view, the Republic as an economic partner is by no means so omnipresent; in 1978–9 she took 5.7 per cent of the UK's total exports and accounted for 3.7 per cent of the UK's total imports. Yet although these figures indicate a different order of significance it is worth noting that since the early Seventies the Republic has been ranked higher as a source of imports into the UK and particularly as an export market for the UK than it was previously. Thus its position, for example, in 1979 as the UK's fifth most important export market cannot be dismissed as negligible.

The Republic's trade dependence on the United Kingdom is not the only economic link of substance. Historical patterns of capital flows – in both directions – are generally considered to be significant, though financial and commercial networks were so intertwined that it has not proved possible to quantify this phenomenon with a degree of certainty. However, direct foreign investment in the Republic during the Seventies has been monitored more closely. A detailed study of the situation in 1974, for example, showed that in that year the aggregate employment created by UK investment was just under 20 per cent of the total employment created by foreign investment, and that the UK share was far behind that deriving from North America (38 per cent) and other European Community countries (33 per cent) – see Table 2. This decline in the significance of British investment in the Republic is borne out even more sharply in figures relating to fixed asset investment in new projects during the late Seventies. Here the predominance of the United States becomes obvious, while even Germany outranked the UK as an investor in 1978 and 1979 (see Table 3). However, this must be seen in the light of long-established British investments of all types in the Republic.

TABLE 1

UNITED KINGDOM AND THE REPUBLIC OF IRELAND

BILATERAL TRADE

Exports

	The view from Dublin		The view from London	
	Exports from Irl to UK as percentage of total Irish exports (NI figures)	Importance of UK market to Irl	Exports from UK to Irl as percentage of total UK exports	Importance of Irish market to UK
1959–60	73.8 (13.8)	1	3.2	10
1972–3	57.8 (9.9)	1	4.9	4
1978–9	46.8 (8.0)	1	5.7	6

Imports

	The view from Dublin		The view from London	
	Imports into Irl from UK as percentage of total Irish imports (NI figures)	Importance of UK as source of Irish imports	Imports into UK from Irl as percentage of total UK imports	Importance of Irl as source of UK imports
1959–60	50.5 (3.8)	1	2.7	11
1972–3	50.8 (3.8)	1	3.6	7
1978–9	49.8 (4.4)	1	3.7	8

Sources: D. McAleese, 'The Foreign Sector' in N. Gibson and J. Spenser, eds, *Economic Activity in Ireland: A Study of Two Open Economies*, Gill and Macmillan, Dublin 1977. Annual Statement of the Trade of the United Kingdom, HMSO, London.

TABLE 2

REPUBLIC OF IRELAND

Foreign Investment in New Industry: 1974

Source of foreign investment	Aggregate employment created	Aggregate employment by source of foreign investment as percentage of total
1. North America (USA and Canada)	13,849	38.43
2. EEC other than UK	11,797	32.73
3. UK	7,119	19.75
4. EFTA	2,378	6.60
5. Joint ventures	898	2.49
Total	36,041	100.00

Source: D. McAleese, *A Profile of Grant-Aided Industry in Ireland*, IDA, Dublin 1977, p. 21.

TABLE 3

Shares of fixed asset investment by overseas companies in new manufacturing enterprises in Republic of Ireland, 1976–9 (percentages)

	1976	1977	1978	1979
United Kingdom	11	7	2	2
United States of America	69	34	59	81
Federal Republic of Germany	7	2	16	5

Source: IDA Annual Reports, 1976–9.

The multiple channels of contact include the movement of people as well as the exchange of goods and finance – indeed it was this feature which seemed to make most impression on Deutsch in his early work on political communities.[9] The prevailing trend historically has been the constant and considerable emigration from the Republic, one result of which was the creation of large Irish communities in many of the major British urban centres, corresponding perhaps to the earlier establishment of the 'British-Irish' in the north east of Ireland.[10] Again, the Seventies saw a change in this pattern, with a substantial (13,600 per annum) rate of net immigration, probably accounted for by former emigrants returning to a more prosperous Republic. Some of this new type of migration was 'cross-border' rather than 'overseas' in character; whether either type of migration will persist in the Eighties, with the combination of a rapidly growing population and economic recession, is open to question.[11]

Patterns of more short-term mobility (business or personal visits, tourism) are more difficult to monitor, though some assessments have been made. For example, Birch maintained that in 1975, allowing for the difference in size of population, the intensity of travel between the Irish Republic and the island of Britain was of much the same order as that between Northern Ireland and Britain; in other words inter-state mobility is not in this case significantly different from the periphery-centre mobility within a large state.[12] Tourists from the United Kingdom (including Northern Ireland), while contributing a much reduced share of the Republic's revenue from tourism compared with the situation prevailing twenty years ago, still represent about 50 per cent of the tourist market (see Table 4).

Even such a rapid sketch of the multiple channels of contact indicates some obvious fundamental conclusion. First, the relationship between the two sovereign states is markedly asymmetrical; the United Kingdom looms very much larger in the public domain of the Republic than does the Republic in that of the United Kingdom. Second, there is, however, evidence that during the last twenty years the Republic's dependence on the United Kingdom has declined in some important respects. Nevertheless, even assuming the con-

TABLE 4

Percentage of Republic of Ireland's Tourist Revenue by Market Area

Market	1960	1978
United Kingdom	79	52
(NI)	(21)	(13)
North America	16	26
Continental Europe	3	19
Other areas	2	4

Source: 'Tourism Policy', NESC 1981.

tinuation of this decline, a third point is clear. The various interactions we have examined cover a wide range of activities, are often intensive and have proved to be durable; they do, therefore, fulfil the conditions of complex interdependence. Of their nature they will give rise to persistent problems of policy and administration for the respective governments. A case in point is the dilemma of the Dublin government with regard to exchange rate policy following the Republic's decision to join the European Monetary System (EMS), the United Kingdom's decision to remain outside and the marked divergence in Punt/Sterling rates, especially since the summer of 1980.[13] The consequences of the end of a *de facto* common currency are not yet clear, and are not yet reflected in the available economic indicators referred to above. In the long term there may be a significant impact on trade and capital flows; in the short term the major effect is added inflation in the Republic and an added sense of 'foreignness' which did not previously exist. Policy responses cannot be seen in a traditional 'national' framework; on the one hand, the politically sensitive area of contacts with Northern Ireland is affected, on the other a diplomatic objective — persuading the United Kingdom to join the EMS — is indicated. In the short term interdependence can be very complex indeed.

Complexity also arises because of the *transnational setting* in which the intergovernmental relationship exists. Given the framework of the mixed economy, non-governmental structures and processes are bound to be influential, and they do not necessarily recognise the territorial boundaries of the sovereign states. Financial interactions have already been referred to. Dublin's experience of implementing exchange rate controls is as yet very limited; up to 1979 when currency parity ended non-governmental financial institutions and networks operated with the minimum of reference to territorial distinctions. The increasing role of foreign firms, especially in export-oriented manufactured products, was one of the most remarkable developments in the Irish economy during the last two decades, while trade activities have both 'all-Ireland' structures (the Irish Congress of Trade Unions) and 'Britain-Ireland' structures (Irish branches of large British unions). Hence it is obvious that management of labour policies cannot be confined simply to a closed national perspective. Irish governments must struggle to match expectations of wage levels and social welfare benefits derived from British experience. Sporting and cultural organisations, and above all the churches, straddle the Anglo-Irish land border.

These transnational structures are the tip of an iceberg of broad cultural affinity and interpenetration. This is seen most sharply in the multiple loyalties or multinational identities of the Irish-in-Britain or the British-in-Ireland, but also has broader effects. The employment of a common language within and between two states is not unique, but it does provide a minimal means of communication (though not necessarily of empathy) which is by no means the norm in interstate relations. Here again, though, asymmetry rears its head. While allowing for quite a distinctive contribution by the smaller society (from Anglo-Irish literature to the 'Irish Joke'), the predominance of the English language can still touch some raw nerves and can be divisive as well as integrative in the all-Irish context. But language is not only a vehicle of political symbolism; it can also be seen as a means of transmitting a broad range of values and information. Cultural penetration in the Republic can be seen in the acceptance of the British media, especially in the main urban concentration in the Dublin region. The circulation of British daily newspapers has made some inroads since the late Sixties, though without making a major impact.[14] Much more striking than this, though, is the reach of United Kingdom television

channels. Of the 80 per cent of all adults who watch television 29 per cent watched UK channels. This national figure
is distorted, however, by the fact that the south-west of the
Republic does not receive these transmissions; in Dublin the
audience for UK channels was 59 per cent of the total
audience (see Table 5). There is some more limited movement in the other direction, in the access of Northern Ireland
viewers to the Republic's two television channels, and of
some British radio audiences to the Republic's radio services.

It must be emphasised that this type of cultural penetration is not unique in international relations — Canada and the
United States, Austria and Germany are other comparable
examples — but it is anomalous in the context of the realist's
view of the sovereign state. So too is the extent to which, in
relations between the Republic of Ireland and the United
Kingdom, there are noticeable gaps in the barriers which
sovereign governments usually throw up in order to control
transnational flows, whether they be economic, social or
cultural. Two such gaps deserve comment. First, there is
no passport control between the two states (the free travel
area concept); second, there is the right of Irish citizens
resident in the United Kingdom to vote in British general
elections, a right which not before time is apparently to be

TABLE 5

Percentage Television Viewing by Adults (15+ years), 1979–80

Viewing Yesterday	Total	Region				Community	
		Dublin	Rest of Leinster	Munster	Connacht Ulster (part)	Urban	Rural
TV at all	80	79	80	81	82	80	80
RTE	71	62	73	80	70	69	74
UK networks	29	59	33	2	22	40	14

Source: B. Chubb, *The Government and Politics of Ireland*, 2nd ed., Oxford
University Press, London, forthcoming; based on figures made available
by Irish Marketing Surveys Ltd.

reciprocated by the Irish government.[15] These actual or potential elements of common citizenship derive from a tradition of uneasiness, in both Dublin and London, about some of the practical consequences of dissolving the union of 1801. Historically, this can be seen on the Irish side during the treaty negotiations in 1921 and the Nationality and Citizenship Act of 1935; the British government for its part stood over the provisions of its 1948 Nationality Act when Ireland decided finally to leave the Commonwealth later that year. To have imposed the normal differentiation between the two states implied largely unpredictable costs for both parties, and from the British point of view might have disrupted the evolving and complicated transition from Empire to Commonwealth.

Whatever the historical antecedents of these 'anomalies', some of them possess a staying power which in large part may be attributed to bureaucratic convenience, if not inertia. From time to time during the past decade the establishment of passport control has been suggested as a means of reducing a transnational flow which was not widely envisaged in 1948 — the urban terrorist and his military supplies — only to be turned down by the British government on the grounds that it was impractical.[16] This is not to say that the particular anomalies found in the regulation of interactions between the Republic of Ireland and the United Kingdom will continue to survive come what may; indeed, one important anomaly — the financial freedom deriving from currency parity — all but disappeared in 1979. It does indicate, however, that for the most part the interstate relationship contains the sort of paradox and qualification associated with the model of complex interdependence.

The jarring note in these patterns of interaction is of course the position of Northern Ireland, or rather the positions adopted by each state towards the *Northern Ireland issue*. At first sight this question seems to place Anglo-Irish relations not in a framework of complex interdependence so much as in the more conventional one of a gladiatorial contest between sovereign states, where considerations of power and coercion hold sway. There is after all a dispute as to which state ought to be the sovereign power in Northern Ireland; the United

Kingdom is 'in possession' and the Republic of Ireland has staked its claim in the most formal manner possible.[17] At this primary 'constitutional' level the ultimate stated goals of both governments seem to be mutually incompatible, given the configuration of constitutional politics in Northern Ireland. There is, however, another level of interaction on this issue, and this does not necessarily lead to conflict between the sovereign governments. The secondary level of interaction involves attempts to respond to short-term developments and to establish the basis for partial or comprehensive settlements within Northern Ireland itself. It involves, too, as a constant theme the response to organised military action from a transnational source – principally the Provisional IRA.

For the unionist population in Northern Ireland one issue above all others in this latter context arouses bitterness and the attitudes and language of acute conflict. The existence of a state border is one of the principal resources of the transnational terrorist who can play on the widely held tradition of denying extradition for political offences. The Dublin government's position on this issue has been interpreted as evidence of indifference, bad faith and hostility. On occasion such interpretations have been reflected in British policy, but one of the striking features of Anglo-Irish relations – as relations between sovereign governments – is the secondary place which the problem of the fugitive offender has held over the last twelve years as a whole. Rather the emphasis on the 'security' issue has been on military considerations, and while this is characteristic of the power model of interstate relations, the objectives of both governments are not fundamentally or necessarily incompatible at this level. 'The enemy' for both is non-governmental, whatever form it takes.

This uncertain mixture of incompatibility at one level and possible co-operation at another has combined with the internal dynamics of the Northern Ireland conflict to produce at least four distinct patterns of diplomatic interaction on the 'Northern issue' between Dublin and London, since the present replay of the 'troubles' began in 1968.[18] The first pattern, in which intergovernmental positions were only first articulated in August 1969, lasted until August 1971.

At the primary level the United Kingdom position (Northern Ireland-is-a-domestic-issue) was pronounced formally in the Downing Street Declaration and at the UN Security Council, though there is evidence that British leaders were aware that that might not be the end of the matter. The Irish government attempted to intervene in the role of protector of the Minority community, but tended to soft-pedal the constitutional claim. At the secondary level of interaction we see a tentative, *ad hoc* search for a *modus vivendi,* in which two essentially unprepared, even bewildered, national administrations tried to recover their balance. The fragility of this *modus vivendi* was most clearly seen in the difficulty of establishing ground rules for dealing with the transnational security problems; British naval boardings and the cratering of border roads were early portents of the propensity of this type of interaction to cause trouble between the governments.

Indeed, it was the increasing transnational security problem – the start of the Provisional IRA campaign in the early spring of 1971 and the British response to it through internment – that introduced a second pattern of interactions from August 1971 to March 1972. Primary positions were articulated bluntly (the Lynch-Heath exchange of telegrams after internment being typical), while diplomatic behaviour depended on day-to-day developments on security issues, the period following Bloody Sunday marking the depths of diplomatic confrontation. Overall, this pattern of interaction – the diplomacy of protest – corresponded quite closely to the conventional image of interstate conflict.

The third pattern of interstate interaction over Northern Ireland was in marked contrast to the second. The replacement of the provincial government at Stormont by direct rule from London in itself underlined the role of the sovereign governments, and the Dublin government was increasingly brought into a consultative role in an active search for political settlement. The possibility of movement at the primary level of interaction allowed both governments to gloss over some quite serious problems arising at the secondary level. The transnational security challenge remained acute for most of the period, at one stage tempting the British government to deal directly with the Provisional IRA with the incidental effect of undermining the authority of the sovereign government in Dublin. But such problems did not prevent the highest level of inter-governmental accord being reached in the Sunningdale agreements in December 1973.

The collapse of that formula in 1974 was ample illustration of a failure by both governments to follow through their agreed objective, and the succeeding pattern of interaction can be described as one of sustained inter-governmental passivity or 'drift'. The primary level of interaction was put on the long finger by both sides: policy in London was increasingly influenced by intractable economic issues and parliamentary and electoral considerations, while Dublin's attempt to revive the 'interim' objective of power-sharing within Northern Ireland met with little response. More and more Anglo-Irish relations were seen in terms of secondary issues; thus, early in 1978, for example, inter-governmental contacts at the highest level were characterised by a series of accusations and counter-accusations which obscured both the very real level of co-operation on security and the equally real problems still posed by transnational terrorism. On a more positive note, though, there was the development of a sharper focus on 'cross-border' economic co-operation.

A further impetus to change in the pattern of interaction came with a new government in the United Kingdom in May 1979 and the Haughey succession in the Republic in December that year. The Thatcher/Haughey summits in 1980 were presented as an end to the sterility of inter-governmental relations following the collapse of Sunningdale, and to the extent that that promise is realised we may already be in a fifth pattern of interactions. Some clearer guidelines on that point may be gained by taking a closer look at the political processes employed over the whole range of issues between the Republic and the United Kingdom.

Political Processes

Let us look first of all at the manner in which *governmental goals* are articulated and the *inter-governmental agenda* is formed. There is a danger in this respect of giving excessive weight to the 'fever chart' interpretation of Anglo-Irish relations, as presented by political leaders on occasions and by media commentators more often than not. The 'fever chart' reflects the immediate and dramatic event, conflicts of personality, and explanations of behaviour in terms of parochial, party or sectional interests. Of course such factors do influence government policy, but they rarely reflect either the whole range of issues at stake or the continuity of contact and purpose at the bureaucratic level. It cannot be emphasised too often that for the whole of the period since 1969, while the fever chart rose and fell on Northern Ireland, both sovereign governments were either involved in negotiating membership of the European Community or, from the beginning of 1973, actually participating in the policy-making of the Community. This too has its fever chart, or even a series of fever charts related to specific policy areas, and it is difficult to find a clear and persistent alignment or cleavage between the Republic of Ireland and the United Kingdom over the whole range of problems which they both encountered.

Even within the narrower bilateral confines of the Northern Ireland issue the goals of both governments were frequently unclear. It is possible to acquire the impression, for example, that for London, especially in the early Seventies, interpreting Mr Lynch was, rightly or wrongly, a task suitable for hardened Kremlinologists. In the same period it is not difficult to find manifest confusion among British political leaders, both in government and opposition, with regard to their views of Irish unity and the extent to which they should incorporate it in their strategy. This is not surprising; in both countries the incoherence or ambiguity of stated policy reflected the strong negative effects arising out of the interplay of party politics and intraparty politics (in the Republic) or of electoral considerations (in the United Kingdom). In both cases governments sought to reduce the uncertainties of a volatile and emotive issue through broadly bi-partisan approaches which had the effect of reducing the articulation of objectives to the lowest common ambiguity.

Thus while a settlement of the Northern Ireland issue was usually presented as being 'at the top' of the inter-governmental agenda (almost always by Dublin), it is not self-evident that it was always alone at the top. Nor did the agendas of

Anglo-Irish relations during the Seventies always reflect the security interests of the more powerful state, negotiating from a position of military strength and coherence of purpose. Sometimes this could be seen, but as often as not the Dublin-London agenda was determined by Danes or Frenchmen operating out of Brussels, or by transnational terrorists or political clerics operating out of West Belfast or Ballymena. Hence, perhaps a certain bewilderment in 1981 at the unusual sight of the two heads of governments trying to re-establish their role in defining the content and form of the bilateral relationship.

Turning to the types of *governmental agency* involved, multifaceted political processes associated with complex interdependence can again be seen in relations between the Republic and the United Kingdom. However, it must be admitted that these have since the early Seventies co-existed with an increasing role for the traditional agencies of power-oriented inter-state relations, the Foreign and, to a lesser extent, Defence ministries. The Republic's Department of Foreign Affairs had no officials specifically and exclusively assigned to Anglo-Irish relations before the Northern Ireland conflict re-emerged in the late Sixties; now there are two sections assigned to this task, within an Anglo-Irish and Information Division.[19] From 1980 a more overt role has been played by senior officials in a much expanded Department of the Taoiseach, which had in any case been increasingly involved from the early Seventies. In London in the late Sixties relations with Dublin were channelled through the Commonwealth Office, an historical anomaly which was only ended by the merger of that ministry with the Foreign Office in October 1968. One consequence of this was that at this critical juncture in Anglo-Irish relations the Foreign Office found that 'it knew very little about' the Republic.[20] In contrast, some senior officials at the Treasury and other economic departments did have quite a close working relationship with their Dublin counterparts, particularly through the negotiation and operation of the Anglo-Irish Free Trade Agreement which came into effect in 1966. The near hiatus in the diplomatic relationship was not the only administrative anomaly in Whitehall — when the need arose in 1969 to 'establish relations' with their own provincial government in Belfast the British government relied on seconded Foreign Office officials. At the ministerial level of contact, however, this pattern is not always so clear-cut; the Republic's Minister for Foreign Affairs may have quite frequent meetings with the Secretary of State for Northern Ireland as well as with the British Foreign Secretary or their respective Junior Ministers. Indeed the complexity of Whitehall's bureaucratic networks dealing with Ireland, both North and South, may well be an influence on British policy which deserves further investigation. After more than a decade during which it has changed quite considerably, remarkably little is known about it.

The development of these policy-making structures does not, therefore, unambiguously support the view that Anglo-Irish relations are a highly politicised confrontation in which the symbols of sovereign authority are manipulated and exchanged through traditional diplomatic channels. This view may indeed have some relevance, but is far from representing the whole truth. In the first place it takes no account of the increasing involvement, during exactly the same period, of the bulk of the 'economic' departments in both Dublin and London on the extensive range of matters relating to membership of the European Community. Secondly, it is arguable that it is an over-simplified presentation of the bureaucratic *dramatis personae* even within the context of the bilateral issue of Northern Ireland. Particularly this is true of the networks established in recent years to deal with Anglo-Irish economic co-operation. A Steering Group of senior officials, with a North/South sub-group, was established in November 1977. It identified four policy areas of common interest (transport, energy, customs, economic planning) in addition to North/South issues. In the latter context alone a report in June 1980 listed four quite comprehensive 'cross-border' projects and 'contacts and developments' covering thirty-six specific policy areas.[21] These networks involve not merely a wide range of government departments in both states, but also include semi-state agencies (e.g. trade or tourist promotion), private sector organisations and local authorities. The mode of contact appears to be informal and the work as yet at a planning stage. Nevertheless, it seems that personal contacts are close: this sort of bureaucratic pluralism or 'transgovernmentalism is an important yardstick for measuring the future development of political co-operation. Two types of *policy instrument* employed during the past twelve years merit comment. First is the increasingly frequent resort to direct heads of government discussions (summit meetings), associated with frequent ministerial-level contacts. On the one hand, this does demonstrate the degree of politicisation of Anglo-Irish relations, and a few of these summits have had the hallmark of the imperious summons by the stronger party in order to administer some form of public chastisement to the weaker.[22] But two qualifications must be made to such an interpretation. This bilateral summitry has coincided with even more frequent, regular and, since 1975, institutionalised multilateral summitry in the context of what we now know as the European Council, and here the flea may meet the elephant in less claustrophobic circumstances. European multilateral summitry leads in turn to more bilateral summit meetings with 'third parties' which may provide opportunities for promoting the small state's position. A good example was the Haughey/Schmidt meeting of 31 March 1981, when Chancellor Schmidt supported the treatment of Northern Ireland as an 'international question'. A second qualification stems from the agreement in May 1980 to establish a routine procedure of regular bilateral summits, and one moreover in which there is reciprocity in location. This will not in itself guarantee agreement on co-operation, but it may make it rather more difficult for the larger state to hurl thunderbolts at the smaller.

And, as the fever charts show, relations between the Republic of Ireland and the United Kingdom have seen the employment of 'thunderbolts' as an instrument of policy. Diplomatic confrontations — the exchange of insults and generalised threats — have not been one-sided. In 1972 the Republic's Foreign Minister referred to Britain's 'lunatic policies'; in 1978 the British Minister with responsibility for Northern Ireland described the Republic as 'a haven for terrorists'. This is not the place to explore the veracity of such statements; they are reproduced as illustrations of the extent to which governments can go in trying to establish a favourable image for their own positions. This image-building — 'propaganda' when the other party is doing it — is not limited to occasional ministerial pronouncements, but is a continuous process involving contacts with third-party governments and the media. We can only speculate as to what proportion of the running costs of Anglo-Irish relations is absorbed by these efforts to keep the fever chart up-to-date. We can only speculate, too, about the significance of a rather different and less dramatic form of policy instrument — the maintenance of routine face-to-face contact between officials. There is some evidence to suggest, however, that on the whole this form of communication has been sustained on a fairly even keel through good times and bad. Probably the most serious test came after the Bloody Sunday shootings in January 1972. The Irish government was at a loss to interpret British intentions, and made a serious diplomatic protest in the form of the withdrawal for consultations of the Irish ambassador in London. This act probably served its purpose as a diplomatic signal, and the potential weakening of communications at official level appears to have been avoided. The then British ambassador in Dublin has recorded the survival of his working relationship with the Dublin government (at a time when his embassy was burned by a mob), though it is not clear that his own superiors (both official and political) understood the messages he was conveying.[23] Yet within a few months of this crisis Anglo-Irish relations had entered one of its most co-operative periods and the British ambassador had retired to live in the Republic. Other serious crises, such as the assassinations of the British ambassador, Christopher Ewart-Biggs, in 1976, and of Earl Mountbatten in 1979, and the consequent shadows over Dublin as a posting for British diplomats, did not appear to have detrimental effects in the long term. It is plausible to assume some degree of empathy at the official level, which provides the basis for persistence of 'quiet diplomacy'.

The final set of policy processes we must consider covers the role of *international organisations* and *issue linkage*. A persistent theme in many of the points already examined has been the effects of Irish and British membership of the European Community and their participation in one of the world's most complex systems of multilateral political co-operation. It can be argued that this factor has some positive effect for the smaller state in the bilateral relationship, and these may now be summarised briefly.

First, there have been substantive economic effects, tending to reduce, though not eliminate, Irish economic dependence on the United Kingdom. A less tangible consequence arising from this has been the development, among some key political leaders and senior officials at least, of a quite confident attitude towards the United Kingdom; this can be seen in the willingness to 'go it alone' in the European Community in the face of possible British withdrawal in the mid-seventies and British non-participation in the EMS in 1979.

A second type of effect relates to the joint policy-making process at the European level. This is characterised by the formation of different inter-governmental coalitions on this or that policy, and ultimately the possibility of a veto being imposed by any member-state. In short, the inherent instability of bilateral power relationships is no longer the central fact of diplomatic life. Moreover the Irish government is presented with opportunities to be 'helpful' on certain issues, or on occasions such as the Irish occupancy of the Presidency of the Council of Ministers, when a mediatory role can be played. This opportunity to break through the wall of great power indifference may also be reinforced by the way the multilateral political process provides a regular timetable of summit contact. Not only can these be used for exchanges on bilateral issues,[24] but in a more general way they may allow for the creation of personal relations between political leaders. Mrs Thatcher, for example, absorbed a different view of Mr Haughey at Brussels than that which she found in the political columns of the media.

Finally, there has occurred the opportunity for Irish governments to attempt to influence joint positions on issues of global significance in the foreign policy consultation procedure (European Political Co-operation, where the term 'political co-operation' is used formally but narrowly). The fact that to date the outcome of this process has generally been in the form of minimalist positions on selected issues suggests that by and large a small state can have it both ways.

At the same time there is access to a lot of information and a little influence and prestige, without the costs of rigid compliance with the policies of one or more great powers. The Republic's position as 'odd man out' with regard to NATO membership has not yet proved to be a public issue at the European level, whatever significance defence co-operation may in the future prove to have either bilaterally or multilaterally.

To what extent has joint membership of this international organisation permitted either Dublin or London to indulge in *issue-linkage*, or bargaining on the basis of what are often intrinsically unrelated issues? In a power-oriented relationship we would expect the larger state to call the shots in this respect. But life in the European Community is not quite so simple. There is some evidence of British Ministers trying on occasions to behave in this way. For example, Garret Fitz-Gerald claimed that when he was Minister for Foreign Affairs the then Foreign Secretary, Anthony Crosland, attempted to influence the Republic's EEC fisheries policy by threatening Anglo-Irish relations in general.[25] Crosland's ploy did not work and FitzGerald's tale is one of very few to have emerged over more than a decade when the opportunity for great power manipulation of issue-linkage in the European Community existed. On the other hand such opportunities may equally arise for the smaller state, and Irish pressure to have cross-border projects introduced through the European Community could be seen as an example.

At this stage, though, a note of caution must be sounded. Membership of the international organisations has *moderated* the bilateral relationship but there are definite limits to the extent to which it has facilitated the adoption of new policies. It must be remembered that the European Community is in itself a source of conflicts between its members. On the Common Agricultural Policy, in particular, the London and Dublin governments are opposed, while more generally the United Kingdom's lack of enthusiasm for the development of European integration has often been at odds with Dublin's professed attachment to a *communitaire* approach.

Also, the attempts to apply the logic of functional (i.e. economic and social) integration in an all-Ireland context during the last twelve years, in which European Community principles, mechanisms, and finances are increasingly brought into play, have not yet shown signs of yielding significant *political* results in the bilateral relationship. There is after all a strong unionist tradition in Northern Ireland of representing functional co-operation as the thin end of the wedge of Republican irredentism, and, quite apart from the European Community's own stumblings on the ever steeper slopes of integration, expectations that it would have a determinable effect on the Northern Ireland conflict show few signs of realisation.

Outcomes

The outcomes to be expected of a relationship of political co-operation do not, where complex interdependence exists, necessarily reflect the full asymmetry between the states involved. It must be stressed, however, that neither do they imply the attainment of some form of seamless harmony; we are dealing, after all, with the government of men, not of angels. Disputes on specific issues will persistently arise and some may prove persistently intractable, but what will be equally persistent will be the attempts of the governments concerned to find an accommodation of their conflicts well short of the recourse to military threat. Moreover, efforts will be made to present areas of conflict in the relationship as being only a part of a more comprehensive range of common interests. In a more general sense the outcome of a relationship of political co-operation finds expression in a particular type of *'international regime'*, or 'networks of rules, norms, and procedures that regularise behaviour and control its effects'.[26] Such a regime, it must be emphasised, does not necessarily take the shape of a formal inter-governmental organisation but may simply be an unwritten code of conventional behaviour, understood by official and political leaders in both countries and taken for granted by their publics. Indeed, one of the critical questions about political co-operation facing any government is the extent to which the international regime requires formal organisation, and if it does what form it should take. So far as relations between Ireland and the United Kingdom are concerned this question is of the utmost topicality.

Before 1969 such arrangements evolved from a tradition on the Irish side of a national independence struggle and on the British of imperial domination, through the often ambiguous, shifting stages of Commonwealth membership, to a regime of 'friendly relations' in the Fifties and Sixties. This was notable for a relatively low intensity of inter-governmental contact and the survival of many anomalous practices from previous bilateral or multilateral regimes. Both sides saw a common interest in not disrupting transnational flows by imposing a rigid pattern of 'normal' inter-state relations.

Since 1969, however, it has not proved so easy to find a mutually acceptable bilateral framework. Briefly the main attempts may be summarised as follows:

(a)   August 1969—August 1971. Tentative and fragile bilateral *modus vivendi,* moderated by joint participation in EEC negotiations.

(b)   August 1971—March 1972. Diplomatic confrontation, moderated by successful culmination of EEC negotiations.

(c)   March 1972—May 1974. Increasing, but largely *ad hoc,* creative political co-operation, enhanced by accession to EEC.

(d)   May 1974—September 1977. *Ad hoc* bilateral *modus vivendi,* moderated by joint participation in the EEC.

The autumn of 1977 is speculatively presented as a turning-point in the search for a satisfactory bilateral regime. While the fever chart over the winter of 1977—8 showed a classic display of continuing recrimination at a political level, it was at this time that the inter-governmental steering-group was established to co-ordinate Anglo-Irish economic relations, including cross-border economic co-operation. This very tentative move towards establishing a systematic and institutionalised governmental regime was reinforced in 1980 with the convention of the regular summit meeting, the second of which has committed both governments to a comprehensive review of 'the totality of relationships within these islands'.[27] Whatever that famous phrase may or may not include, and whatever the political motives behind it, it cannot avoid the question of the bilateral inter-state regime.

It is against this background, then, that we must try to identify the fundamental problems of political co-operation between the Republic of Ireland and the United Kingdom.

Fundamental Problems

It is generally accepted that any inter-state system with less than five members has an inherent tendency to break down, a tendency which becomes all the more marked if there are only two.[28] In practice Anglo-Irish relations do not exist in a purely bilateral world, and we have already referred to the moderating effects of multilateral structures. Nevertheless, this underlying propensity to disequilibrium is reflected in three inter-related but rather different problems, the most obvious being that of *asymmetry*. Although felt most keenly on the Irish side — for that is after all the essence of the problem — the natural imbalance between the states is a fact of life which would pose persistent strain even without a territorial dispute (see Table 6). Nor is it simply a matter of the greater substantive dependence of the one side on the other, important though that may be; its effects are more pervasive. A former British ambassador to Dublin, Sir John Peck, has written of what he calls 'the Isle of Wight syndrome', an attitude which in its extreme form induces a tendency 'to forget entirely that Ireland is independent'.[29] Indeed,

TABLE 6

THE REPUBLIC OF IRELAND AND THE UNITED KINGDOM

Bilateral Asymmetry: the bedrock

	Area (1,000 Sq.Km.)	Population (thousands)
Republic of Ireland	70.3	3,221
United Kingdom	244.0	55,902
Size of Republic as percentage of size of the United Kingdom	29%	6%

Source: 1981 Administration Yearbook and Diary, IPA, Dublin 1980.

there is something to be said for the view that, in spite of continuing economic contacts, the British political establishment tended to forget about both parts of Ireland between 1949, when the Republic left the Commonwealth, and the outbreak of disorder in Northern Ireland in 1968. Even with the often painful reminders of the existence of the island in subsequent years, the Isle of Wight syndrome has not died easily, for many other pressing interests compete for the limited attention of the British political leadership. Those officials and political leaders in the United Kingdom who do take the relationship with the Republic seriously have generally had a more arduous task in bringing their views to bear on the more complex policy-making process in London, than do their counterparts in Dublin. From the Irish point of view there has often been a natural anxiety about gaining access to the top level of British policy decision-making and, even where this is achieved formally, of being really consulted.

A second pervasive problem of Anglo-Irish relations is that of *legitimacy*. On both sides there are vocal minorities which simply do not accept that contacts between Dublin and London have any legitimate basis. The extreme nationalist tradition in Ireland, both North and South, has never accepted the twenty-six county government as a legitimate sovereign authority, empowered to engage in external relations. For the unionist tradition in the United Kingdom (and not only in Northern Ireland), the territorial claim in Article 2 of the Republic's constitution, rightly or wrongly associated with transnational terrorism, puts the Dublin government out of court.

But it may also be the case that more general but more widely held attitudes inhibit a general acceptance of the validity and utility of Anglo-Irish diplomacy. On the Irish side asymmetry can contribute to an inferiority complex, in which it is argued that the Republic will inevitably be bested in any close association with the much larger power; hence the best strategy to pursue is one of 'avoidance' or even isolation. This defensiveness may not perhaps be typically found amongst those officials who are actually engaged in Anglo-Irish relations, but the further we move away from this small circle the more likely it is to emerge. It can be traced back from the ethos of the Irish Sovereignty Movement, through de Valera's emphasis on self-sufficiency, to the traditional Sinn Féin image of the 'isolated republic'. On the British side the Isle of Wight syndrome, already referred to, may have variants in the view that small states in general (a) don't matter, (b) are a persistent nuisance, or (c) at best will have to wait their turn for occasional handouts. Whether the attitude in either country be one of suspicion, contempt or indifference, if it is persistently manifested in party politics or in the media, the legitimacy of interstate co-operation will suffer.

The third problem is one of *management* — the way in which governments of industrialised societies attempt to control, to regulate and direct both the inter-governmental and transnational interactions which often threaten to disrupt their policy and ultimately their legitimacy. In recent years there has been a widely held view that these societies are in some sense 'ungovernable', or at least that their governments suffer from 'overload'. This suggests that the role of the government as 'manager' of public affairs is to be questioned on the grounds of efficiency; are its activities co-ordinated, internally consistent and making the best possible use of scarce resources? Manifest inefficiency is one important factor, after all, leading to doubts about a government's legitimacy.

The Republic and the United Kingdom (Isle of Wight syndrome notwithstanding) do have patterns of interaction which raise problems of management, and even a superficial evaluation of both governments' performance raises questions. For more than a decade they have both been engaged in costly military and legal measures to face the transnational security challenge — and at best containment has been achieved. Both governments face increasingly serious economic difficulties, and while the appropriate responses may well be found beyond the level of bilateral co-operation, can we be sure that the most is being made of bilateral policy in this context?

In brief, there is little basis for complacency in this allegedly unique diplomatic relationship. It is, therefore, worth looking at the experience of other countries in trying to establish and sustain modes of political co-operation, in order to see whether any lessons can be learned in order to 'lift the situation to a new plane'.[30]

Political Co-operation: Some Suitable Cases for Emulation?

The characterisation of relations between the Republic of Ireland and the United Kingdom as 'unique' – the word has been scattered over recent British and Irish policy statements like confetti at a wedding – often seems more appropriate as an incantation to dull the critical senses rather than as a guideline to policy. Every bilateral relationship is unique in some way. Yet in so far as this relationship is unique, in its precise combination of co-operation and antagonism, learning by analogy from the experience of others must be exercised with great caution. The emphasis in the following attempt to learn from others is on trying in the first place to identify forms of political co-operation which might transfer without rejection by our extremely sensitive bodies, but unfortunately there can be no guarantee the transfer will be successful until the experiment is made. The academic observer can only suggest possibilities; it is for the politician to make them work.

The method employed here is to make a brief examination of three existing forms of political co-operation, selected in the first place because they have been referred to by politicians or by the media over the winter of 1980-81. In addition, one hypothetical model will be recalled, largely because it has already been raised in the context of the Northern Ireland conflict. The four cases do not exhaust the possibilities, but serve merely to initiate further discussion. In each case the relevance of the model will be examined in terms of the problems of asymmetry, legitimacy and management. Then in a final section an attempt is made to extract those elements which seem most pertinent in the Anglo-Irish context, and thus to assemble some of the material for an eventual synthesis.

The Franco-German Friendship Treaty (1963)
In the early sixties President de Gaulle, having failed to

mould EEC political co-operation in his own inter-governmental rather than supranational image (via the Fouchet
plan), resorted to a bilateral variant of the scheme. The
other partner in this arrangement was arguably not so much
Germany as the then German Chancellor, Konrad Adenauer.[31]

The Treaty provided for: (a) detailed procedures of regular
consultation between the administrations; (b) specific measures of military co-operation, which in retrospect seem
innocuous enough, the more so since both states were already
in NATO, but which at the time proved to be politically contentious; (c) measures of cultural co-operation, in order to
transform attitudes in the long term through youth and
educational exchange, with a particular emphasis on lowering
the barrier of language; (d) a general commitment to harmonising economic policy, which added little or nothing to
the existing multilateral (EEC/ECSC) commitments of both
states.

Through this model, unlike some of the following ones, is
bilateral (and in that respect close to the Anglo-Irish context)
it is not a case of marked asymmetry. France and Germany
are, and were then, two major European powers and the
political 'love affair' between their two leaders was very
much based on shared and somewhat grandiose visions of
global strategies. From the point of view of asymmetry,
therefore, comparisons are fruitless.

There are lessons to be learned, however, with regard to
legitimacy, for an important function of this Treaty was
to set the final seal on the process of Franco-German reconciliation after a history of the most appalling conflict. Yet
the Treaty in itself was not the primary instrument of that
reconciliation, which was the result of a very complicated
combination of forces (arguably including the very depths
to which Franco-German enmity had descended). Moreover, the circumstances surrounding the Treaty are an object
lesson in the fragility of this sort of process; two signatures
on a piece of paper are not enough. Indeed, a week before
signing de Gaulle transgressed the spirit of the accord by not
consulting Adenauer on his rejection of British membership
of the EEC. After signing Adenauer soon retired and his
successors would have virtually nothing to do with the

Treaty. Moreover, in the process of ratification the legitimising role of the Treaty was devalued to some degree in both parliaments, which permitted party considerations to intrude.

This latter difficulty may have been partly a consequence of the emphasis on the executive branch of government, particularly marked in the Fifth French Republic, and in general manifested in a traditional approach to the 'proper' conduct of foreign relations. The procedure of political co-operation in the Franco-German Friendship Treaty is almost exclusively at the executive level. But if the representative (i.e. parliamentary) level of government is to be kept at arm's length, the legitimacy of that type of political co-operation is bound to be overdependent on the attitude of this or that head of government – and heads of government do change, even in the Fifth French Republic.

With regard to managing Franco-German political co-operation, the Treaty was a supplement to already existing multilateral networks in both the EEC and, for a time, in NATO. Its major contribution to management processes seems to have been twofold. The provision of a routine or timetable for regular bilateral intergovernmental contacts may seem mundane enough nowadays, but it is interesting to see this sort of procedure re-emerge in the multilateral context in the European Political Co-operation and European Council processes. A second contribution that has been generally accepted as successful was the programme for youth and cultural exchanges. On the whole, though, the considerable degree of substantive political co-operation at the highest levels which now prevails is dependent on the respective leaders' shared views of their countries as leading Western European powers, rather than on the mechanisms of the Friendship Treaty.

Benelux (1944/47/1958)

This form of political co-operation between Belgium, the Netherlands and Luxembourg has evolved from a Customs Convention in 1944 to an economic union in 1958.[32] The emphasis is on joint decision-making on a wide range of economic issues, and in this, as in its quite elaborate institutional structure, Benelux is closely associated with the evolution of the European Community approach to integration.

The position of Luxembourg, so very much smaller than the other two members, is a curious one. Do we leave her to one side, as a country whose main purpose in international life is to provide a splendid outlet for the energies of Gaston Thorn? It is not often that an Irishman has the opportunity to wield the Isle of Wight syndrome, but if parallels are to be considered the spotlight might more aptly be played on Belgium and the Netherlands and on the cultural and linguistic division which does not correspond nearly to the state boundaries. On the other hand, if Luxembourg is considered, does the strongly asymmetrical relationship between Belgium and Luxembourg, manifested in an economic union (BLEU) since 1922, provide us with a parallel to the United Kingdom and the Republic? Or is Luxembourg to the other two what an *independent* Northern Ireland might be to Dublin and London, with a splendid outlet for the energies of Dr Paisley? Such flights of fancy may not afford us much guidance on the problems of asymmetry.

So far as legitimacy is concerned, the progressive nature of treaty-making is of interest. This was not a once-and-for-all gesture, but the step-by-step development of a network of contacts which are not exclusively executive in character. There is a Consultative Inter-parliamentary Council and an Economic and Social Advisory Council; thus elected representatives and sectional interests are directly involved in the political process. On paper this contributes to the legitimacy of the whole process, though at the same time it is probably fair to say that there are no acute problems of legitimacy at the inter-state level, whatever about the position within one member state, Belgium. In the public mind the creation of the 'full' Benelux political system in 1958 was in any case largely overshadowed by the establishment of the EEC.

As a system of managing interstate co-operation Benelux has been subsumed to some extent within the broader multi-lateral arrangements of the European Community; in so far as the latter tends to proceed at two or even more speeds (where it proceeds at all) Benelux can be seen as a viable fall-back for its members. Indeed, it is as a coalition of often like-minded member-states within the Community that the political significance of Benelux seems to lie. Though sectional economic interests are by no means identical, it has proved possible to formulate common positions on political strategies. However, this unity of purpose should not be exaggerated and when it does not exist the organisation simply marks time. This was the case in the early Sixties, for example, indicating 'the extent to which political agreement and will to act among the three members is a prerequisite for almost any kind of action'.[33]

Nordic co-operation (1952/1971)

Nordic co-operation can, like Benelux, be seen as a progression of treaties and institutionalisation, from the establishment of the inter-parliamentary Nordic Council in 1952 to the intergovernmental Council of Ministers in 1971, and encompassing a wide range of bodies, mainly executive or administrative in character, with detailed specific functions. The institutional framework was developed some time after the establishment and growth of many transnational networks.[34]

It is of course a multilateral grouping of five states (Norway, Sweden, Denmark, Finland and Iceland), in which only one — Iceland — is markedly smaller than the others. It is not, therefore, a model of political co-operation with very obvious relevance to the problem of bilateral asymmetry. It does, though, raise some interesting points about the legitimacy of inter-state co-operation. First, there is the fact that its original formal manifestation was parliamentary in form; in this case the strictly inter-governmental institutionalisation followed, with a felt need for high level co-ordination, with the Council of Ministers. This suggests a low level of politicisation of inter-state co-operation, that is to say that legitimacy was not a serious problem. Cultural affinities and common political values, with a strong emphasis on social democracy, may go far to explain this.

Yet the legitimacy of the process was a potential problem in that these governments did not and still do not have a bland view that there was nothing to prevent their coming together in this way. Two sorts of issues could be divisive. One is the question of national sovereignty. After all, two members, Norway and Sweden, dissolved their political union in 1905, not so very long before the Anglo-Irish union dissolved in 1921. As it happened, this was not done at the insistence of a small minority on shooting its way out, and that may well have helped people accept the modest measure of re-integration that Nordic co-operation implies. This historical background does mean, though, that the participants in the process do not see it in terms of an eventual new form of political union: 'there is no clear target to work toward and no uniform image of what the future will bring'.[35]

A second potentially divisive issue is that of defence, but only potentially because the member states have evolved a tacit agreement to maintain the broad status quo, the so-called 'Nordic balance'. Norway and Denmark are both members of NATO (with varying reservations about the deployment of nuclear weapons), Sweden is a traditional and relatively uninhibited neutral, Finland is a 'front-line' and correspondingly inhibited neutral, while Iceland uneasily possesses an important NATO base but reserves her military prowess for the successful prosecution of cod wars. This diversity of military behaviour is a necessary condition of Nordic co-operation, and like the issue of national sovereignty, usually remains outside the legitimate scope of the process.

There remains, nevertheless, a great deal of activity within the process. This is not the place to survey it in detail,[36] but rather to suggest that a detailed sector-by-sector investigation both of the form and content of Nordic co-operation might prove fruitful, the more so since this may offer a rather different alternative to the conventional wisdom as formed by the Brussels system. So, too, an examination of the inter-parliamentary network might be of interest. In particular, the case of Denmark illustrates some of the problems of belonging to more than one network of broad political co-operation. There is considerable institutional complexity and to some degree a competing pull between the two regional groupings.

Condominium

None of the existing schemes of co-operation examined above appears to encompass a relationship between sovereign states with the same mixture of territorial dispute, ethnic and sectarian divisions and trans-national violence as that suffered

by the Republic of Ireland and the United Kingdom in respect
of Northern Ireland. One model of political co-operation
which, it has been suggested, might fit these circumstances
is that of condominium or joint control of a single territory
by two sovereign states. While it is not strictly speaking
hypothetical (witness the recently defunct Franco-British
condominium in the New Hebrides), no attempt will be
made here to draw lessons from experience, but simply to
re-introduce a proposal made early in 1973 by Sir Charles
Carter, and to examine it briefly in the light of the relationship between the sovereign states.[37]

The first point about 'Carter's condominium' is that the
problem of asymmetry is tackled head-on, in the sense that
the instrument of joint control (the Council for Northern
Ireland) consists of an equal number of individuals nominated
by the sovereign governments in Dublin and London (though
the nominees do not necessarily come from these governments
or indeed their jurisdictions). The powers reserved to the
Council could, given the assent of a majority of each of its
two classes of members, be transferred to the parliament of
one of the two sovereign states for specified periods. Here the
legal principle of sovereign equality is maintained despite the
natural asymmetry of power.

Legitimacy — in the inter-state context — will clearly be
reinforced from the Irish Republic's point of view by the
composition of the Council for Northern Ireland, and by
the fact that the condominium is created by a formal treaty
between the sovereign powers. Moreover, it is envisaged that
Northern Ireland would have elected representatives in both
London and Dublin. Legitimacy *within* Northern Ireland is
to be derived from a provincial Assembly elected by proportional representation with the functions of a powerful
local authority; the Assembly's decisions can be challenged
by the joint Council. Behind these institutional arrangements
is the argument that both communities within Northern
Ireland and both the sovereign states surrender something,
if not all of their original positions. Unlike the SDLP's con-
temporaneous proposal for a similar scheme, this form of
condominium was not envisaged as a staging post on the way
to a United Ireland.

The Carter proposals did not develop in detail the problems arising from the management of inter-state co-operation, though it is interesting that such sensitive functions as 'police and internal security' appear among the suggested powers reserved to the Council. As it happened, the proposal was virtually ruled out by the ground rules for constitutional reform which had been established following the imposition of direct rule, and the concept of condominium invariably seems to have the adjective 'impracticable' around its neck. In the present context it is worth making two points. The initial allocation of powers between the joint Council for Northern Ireland and the Dublin and London governments would require a comprehensive review of all matters of inter-state co-operation. Moreover, it is arguable that it would be necessary to aim for quite a high level of uniformity on policy between the sovereign governments in order to maintain the arrangement in the long term. External security or defence, for example, would surely have to be explicitly co-ordinated.

More Models . . .

The four models introduced above may well represent a small selection of real or imagined examples of inter-state co-operation. Two others come to mind immediately, for they too have been raised in the Anglo-Irish context. The possibility of the Republic of Ireland rejoining the Commonwealth is one such suggestion, which met with short shrift from the Taoiseach following the London summit in May 1980.[38] There may be a sharp problem of legitimacy on the Republic's side, and such a diversity of interests and diffusion of behaviour in the Commonwealth itself as to make this model inappropriate; nevertheless, it might merit more attention than an abrupt negative. Then there is the proposal for a formal but loosely structured entity encompassing the two (not quite British) Isles, or as its author, Mr Geoffrey Taylor of *The Guardian,* tactfully calls them, the Islands of the North Atlantic (IONA). This may beg a good many questions, but we are perhaps at the stage where the sovereign governments are making a serious attempt to find some of the answers.

Dublin and London: Political Co-operation 'On a New Plane'?

If we accept the currently prevailing assumption that political co-operation between the Republic of Ireland and the United Kingdom has not been satisfactory in the past, what then can be done to create a new framework which will prove both durable and effective? What, if any, changes can be made and what existing procedures need to be strengthened? It would be presumptuous to produce a neatly blue-printed prescription at a time when the combined resources of two sovereign governments are being applied to this very task, but at least some general considerations may be raised. These relate in the first place to the possible mode of co-operation, and secondly to its likely substance.

Before proceeding, however, the co-operation between the sovereign governments must be placed in the context of the commitment made at the Dublin summit in December 1980 to commission joint studies relating to 'the totality of relationships within these islands'. Quite what the phrase 'totality of relationships' means proved to be a matter of controversy following the summit. Taking the broadest interpretation it can be seen to represent a variety of different types of political relationships (see Figure 1); of these the inter-state relationship, between the sovereign governments in Dublin and London, is but one.[39] The ways in which the other types of relationship might relate to the Dublin/London axis are not at all clear at this stage of public debate. The comments which follow, therefore, are tentative in the extreme, and necessarily disjointed.

The Mode of Co-operation

In cases of asymmetrical inter-state relations which are characterised by a high degree of complex interdependence — the United States and Canada being the obvious example — the mode of co-operation may not include formal bilateral organisations. It proceeds according to the conventions of 'quiet diplomacy', among a myriad of contacts between officials from many government agencies. There is indeed something of this mode of co-operation in the Anglo-Irish context, but the effects of the three fundamental problems identified above suggest that it may not be enough.

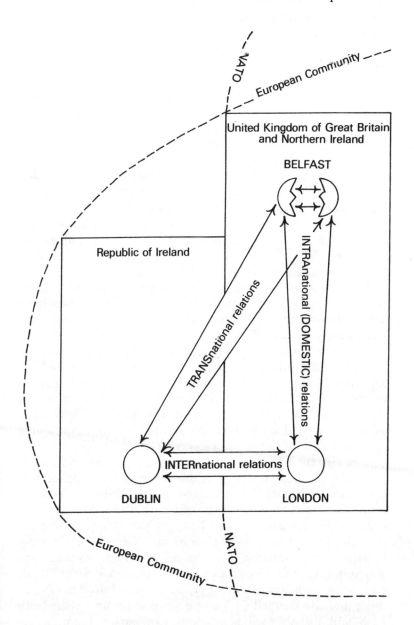

FIGURE 1: THE TOTALITY OF RELATIONSHIPS

Of these problems, asymmetry is in a material sense the most intractable, being a product of the distribution of natural resources and size of the population, and change in these areas is both slow and unpredictable. Yet the experience of the last ten years has shown that change can occur (through membership of the European Community) and the potential significance of a further development of multilateral political co-operation should not be neglected. The effects of psychological asymmetry — the Isle of Wight syndrome and its converse — can also be reduced, though hardly eliminated, by adopting more self-consciously formal modes of diplomatic contact at the bilateral level, thus ensuring access for the weaker partner. Here lies the case for institutionalised rather than *ad hoc* summitry, and a corollary of this may be a rather more formal mode of inter-governmentalism all down the line, for nothing backfires quite like a badly-prepared summit meeting. The 1980 summits may yet prove to be, at least procedurally, a new departure in this respect, while it is significant that the subsequent joint studies have led to the direct involvement of some very senior and centrally-placed British officials.

But if asymmetry is in the long term a problem we have to live with, the effects of legitimacy — or rather the lack of legitimacy — are immediate and corrosive. They will not be written off by signing a treaty containing general aspirations and statements of goodwill, though in the long term they might be eroded by a series of periodic treaties containing agreements of increasing substance. But a treaty, like a constitution, is an instrument of legitimacy which cannot be rewritten at short intervals without losing credibility. How then can legitimacy be sustained in the short or medium term? Summit meetings may serve this purpose to some degree, but the case for involving parliamentary representatives in this respect is a strong one. There already exist informal links between the Houses of the Oireachtas and Westminster, including groups of interested parliamentarians who both exchange and host visits, and the European Parliament and the Council of Europe serve as forums where both Irish and British parliamentarians can pursue their professional activities together.

So far, so good, but it can reasonably be argued that this type of interaction neither brings a sharp, systematic focus on the bilateral relationship nor is it visible enough to make much impact on the general public. Here lies the case for a joint assembly, possibly on the lines of the Nordic Council. Composition of such a body could take several forms, either reflecting asymmetry in varying degrees or giving equal representation to each parliament. It is in this type of arrangement that an opportunity would arise, through design or convention, to include significant participation by Northern Ireland politicians. For example, in an assembly of, say, fifty members membership could be in the ratio of thirty London-nominated members to twenty Dublin-nominated members, thereby reflecting some degree of asymmetry; of the thirty nominees, ten would be Northern Irish, five from each tradition, thus providing overall for a 25/25 stalemate on deeply divisive issues. Such an Anglo-Irish Assembly would play a mainly consultative role, perhaps meeting alternately in Dublin and London for an annual plenary session, at which it would review the work of previous summits and other ministerial meetings, and be able to advance its own suggestions for following summits. This implies the existence of a small secretariat with sufficient resources to formulate proposals independently of either national administration, though it would of course have to maintain close contact with both. Continuity would be maintained both by the secretariat and an executive committee elected by the members of the Assembly. Alternatively, if such a structure seemed to be over-ambitious and politically vulnerable, a less visible means of involving parliamentarians would be to have private meetings of functional committees drawn from both parliaments. These would have more restricted terms of reference, but might establish precedents for more comprehensive arrangements.

The problem of management really deserves investigation on a sector-by-sector basis. There will remain, though, the questions of overall co-ordination and ultimately of political accountability. The former seems to imply a regularisation of summit and ministerial contacts, perhaps on the lines of the Franco-German model, and the latter would involve the preparation of detailed reports to the joint Assembly as well as to the national parliaments. There is a possible danger, however, arising from such requirements, for if informal modes of inter-governmental contact, which to date seem to have prevailed to quite a large extent between Dublin and London, are pushed into a rigid, formal bureaucratic framework they could become less rather than more efficient. It may be a question, then, of discovering a fine balance between the need for a more formal bilateral regime, because of asymmetry and legitimacy, and the need to retain managerial flexibility within and between the two administrations. Finally, any change in administrative structures and procedures would have to be closely related to the multilateral policy-making systems in which both administrations are involved, and in particular that of the European Community.[40]

The Substance of Co-operation

Institutional structures and the regularisation of procedures do not in themselves indicate the substantive issues on which the two governments are most likely to co-operate; rather, these issues stem from the interplay of forces within the societies concerned, and the consequent patterns of inter-action between them. Following the December 1980 summit meeting widely divergent views about the content of Anglo-Irish co-operation emerged. Some quickly acquired an almost legendary quality, and nearly all were obscured by innuendo, rhetoric and expectations of historic progress or disaster, depending on the observer's political origins. A combination of diplomatic confidentiality and pre-electoral manoeuvring in both parts of Ireland proved to be a recipe for confusion. Prudence suggests, therefore, that each major type of issue should be examined separately before any general conclusions are drawn.

(1) Economic Co-operation. There is a clear 'track record' in this field of activity, and an embryonic bilateral procedure in the Steering Group established in 1977. The December 1980 summit communiqué specified four sectors — energy, transport, communications, and the development of particular cross-border areas (in geographical terms centred on the Foyle, the Erne and the Cooley Peninsula). Energy, for

example, involves the possibility of large-scale projects, such as an electricity link between the Republic and Britain and a natural gas link between the Republic and Northern Ireland. In addition, the promotion of tourism is a common North/ South interest, while the case for common promotion of industrial development could also be made. In the broader Anglo-Irish context the divergence of currencies suggests the need for a comprehensive examination of financial structures and procedures.

In many of these matters European Community guidelines will tend to establish the scope of joint action and may provide resources for the implementation of agreed policies. National, bilateral and multilateral policy-making will have to be reconciled with some care, and it is clear that the great part of Anglo-Irish co-operation, in terms of the continuous application of administrative resources, will be in the context of economic policy.

(2) Social Policy. The harmonisation of the objectives and mechanisms of social policy is a process which has been engaged in for some time at the European level, and bilateral consultation may be seen as an inherent part of this process.

But the real problem in establishing effective bilateral reciprocity in social policies stems from the overall economic asymmetry between the two sovereign states. The Republic cannot yet match the level of resources allocated by the United Kingdom, whatever convergence might be effected in the long term. This disparity in itself suggests that there will continue to be problems in harmonising social policy and hence a need for routine consultations between governmental agencies in both states, involving, perhaps, the development of transnational links between the relevant interest groups.

(3) Cultural Relations. The existence of a common language, as well as the relatively low level of state funding of cultural activities in the Republic, may account for the peripheral place which cultural relations have suffered in official Anglo-Irish relations — the need has not been felt keenly enough. But this may no longer be so, and some prospects of systematic co-operation may emerge. An awareness of different levels of knowledge and understanding of

'the other side' can be seen in the response to the television histories of aspects of the 'Anglo-Irish problem' broadcast by the major British networks in the winter of 1980/81. This indicates possibilities of co-operation in the educational field; one example among many might be the reconsideration of an interdisciplinary focus on 'Anglo-Irish Studies' at the university level.[41]

(4) Common Citizenship. Many important elements of common citizenship already exist, and, as we have seen, reciprocity in voting rights for United Kingdom nationals resident in the Republic is not a controversial issue in the Republic. In the short term the political effects of such a change would hardly be dramatic, but the psychological effects on the individual voter might have some significance. Under present nationality legislation a Northern unionist resident in the Republic can vote — as an Irish citizen — but may see the act as a betrayal of his British nationality; with full reciprocity no such inhibition arises.

Of course political participation is not the only element of a citizen's rights, but the further development of the concept leads into more controversial areas of Anglo-Irish relations and will probably depend on the state of play under the headings which follow.

(5) Security against transnational terrorism. The label 'security' in the Anglo-Irish context has only recently acquired the conventional inter-state connotation of 'defence'; generally it covers above all else the bilateral responses to transnational terrorism. It may be further broken down into two types of co-operation, military and policing activity on the one hand, and agreement on the legal ground rules under which that activity takes place on the other.

Co-operation on the former aspect of cross-border security has been developing quite intensively for nearly twelve years now. It is of necessity largely surrounded by secrecy and a matter within the competence of a small sector of the executive branch of the two governments and their respective security forces.

However, legitimate public concern arises out of the consequences of this activity, particularly as they impinge on the provision of security itself and on legal principles and practices within both societies. Here there would seem to be an opportunity for a significant inter-parliamentary review — possibly within the institutional structures suggested above — of all the issues and policies within this field. In the first instance this would have to be based on the provision of options by an expert body, the obvious precedent being the Law Enforcement Commission established following the Sunningdale Agreement in 1973.[42] It should be remembered that this body was given an impossible timetable (by the standards of legal deliberation), so that it declared itself simply unable to develop the concept, raised at Sunningdale, of a 'common law-enforcement area'. Since that period bilateral policy has taken the form of extra-territorial jurisdiction and attempts continue at the European level to find workable arrangements to bring transnational terrorists to justice. The political impact of all this, however, has been very slight, and the demand for the extradition of political offenders remains the *minimum* expectation of Northern unionists from any form of political co-operation. Hence the legal aspects of security and indeed the whole field of civil rights require review. Ultimately this could lead to a juridical system involving European as well as British and Irish judges.[43] In the interim, the search for a workable system would remain one of the major yardsticks of the legitimacy of co-operation as a whole.

(6) Inter-state security (defence policy). The coincidence of the marked deterioration in global East-West relations over the winter of 1979/80 and Mr Haughey's accession to power, in conjunction with Mrs Thatcher's reputed interest in military matters, have resulted in co-operation on defence being the subject of much public conjecture in the Republic. It might be more accurate to speak of 'neutrality' rather than 'defence' in this regard, and it may well be that any significant change in the situation will founder on the rock of neutrality, which is after all a traditional test of the legitimacy of Anglo-Irish relations.[44] And whatever the speculation, it seems that Ireland is not the finger in the dyke of western defence.

The stated positions at present are thus: the Irish government will only review the existing position in the event of an all-Ireland political settlement or a 'full political union' in the European Community.[45] The British government, it seems, envisages any defence co-operation in a multilateral rather than a bilateral framework.[46] These (arguably long-term) perspectives would not necessarily preclude a very general commitment, in the context of a friendship treaty, that neither state would allow its territory to be used as a base for attack on the other. Such statements have been made repeatedly by Irish governments since the foundation of the state, and can hardly be represented as an alliance commitment.

(7) Political settlement in Northern Ireland. Again, the Dublin summit of December 1980 has aroused widely divergent expectations. Mr Haughey's emphasis on inter-state co-operation 'on a new plane' has been presented in the context of an agreed solution to the conflict in Northern Ireland and this, from the perspective of Dublin (and Ballymena), has been interpreted by some to mean fundamental constitutional change in the direction of a federal Ireland. Mrs Thatcher from the first claimed that constitutional change did not arise, though for more than three months the Irish government did not go out of its way to make it clear that where 'constitutional' referred to the constitutional status of Northern Ireland this did not indeed arise in the post-summit joint studies. When this was conceded, in the short term at least, the 'totality of relationships' faded along the London/Belfast axis, with an apparent divergence of views about the time-scale of any 'constitutional' evolution, however defined.[47]

The Dublin-Belfast axis is only a little more firmly sketched in, with some broad statements of intent. Mr Haughey's reminder that at the May 1980 summit he had accepted that change in the constitutional status of Northern Ireland would only come about with the consent of a majority in Northern Ireland implies the possibility of a long-term process.[48] Add to this some general appeals to unionists to enter into 'a constructive partnership' and promises of 'guarantees of civil and religious liberty,[49] and Dublin's northern policy appears to rest on the assumption that in the interim circumstances will change sufficiently for Irish unity to be a realistic goal. Inter-state co-operation between Dublin and London is thus seen both as a change in the circumstances in itself and as a framework for further change.

Against the background of the experiences of inter-state co-operation elsewhere, this studied vagueness is hardly surprising. When an issue is acutely divisive it is usually avoided or excluded from the process in the interest of sustaining the level of co-operation that already exists. The eventual inclusion of such issues is not necessarily ruled out, but is likely to be a matter of glacial progress. Anglo-Irish co-operation 'on a new plane' may well be a necessary precondition to a process of political settlement in Northern Ireland, but it is hardly a sufficient measure in itself. Moreover, if the possibility of constitutional change is admitted, what necessity is there in the logic of the process for it to be change in the direction of a united Ireland rather than a united British Isles? Ultimately the game will be resolved in the playing and not only in the definition of the rules.

Four months after the December 1980 summit, in an atmosphere of electoral hysteria in both parts of Ireland, there is a risk that Anglo-Irish political co-operation as a whole could fall foul of inflated expectations, for or against its presumed consequences. Such an outcome would be regrettable; there is a manifest need for co-operation on many matters and a strong case both for regularising procedures and ensuring that co-operation is regarded as a legitimate process in both countries.

REFERENCES

1. 'The Taoiseach and the Prime Minister agreed that they wished to develop new and closer political co-operation between their two governments.'
2. This ambiguous but widely-used phrase refers here to the relations between the two sovereign states, as presently constituted, i.e. the United Kingdom of Great Britain and Northern Ireland and the Republic of Ireland. The term 'Republic of Ireland' is used throughout this paper to refer to the sovereign state, Ireland, in order to avoid confusion with the geographical entity, Ireland.
3. See Emil Kirchner's paper, 'The Theory of Political Integration', above.

4. K. W. Deutsch *et al.*, *Political Community and the North Atlantic Area*, Greenwood Press, New York 1957.

5. ibid., p. 199.

6. D. Vital, *The Survival of Small States: Studies in Small Power/ Great Power Conflict*, Oxford University Press, London 1971, p. 118.

7. R. O. Keohane and J. S. Nye, *Power and Interdependence: World Politics in Transition*, Little, Brown and Company, Boston 1977.

8. Garret FitzGerald in the Dail, 11 December 1980 (Dail Debates, 325, 981–2).

9. Deutsch *et al.*, op. cit., p. 151.

10. Chubb estimated in 1970 that nearly three-quarters of a million British residents had been born in the Republic of Ireland. See B. Chubb, *The Government and Politics of Ireland*, Oxford University Press, London, p. 46.

11. J. Sheehan and R. W. Hutchinson, *Demographic and Labour Force Structure in the Republic of Ireland and Northern Ireland*, Co-operation North, Dublin and Belfast 1980, pp. 8–11.

12. A. H. Birch, *Political Integration and Disintegration in the British Isles*, Allen and Unwin, London 1977, p. 40.

13. C. McCarthy, 'The Exchange Rate of the Irish Pound: Performance and Policy', *Irish Banking Review*, December 1980.

14. B. Farrell, 'The Mass Media and the 1977 Campaign', *Ireland at the Polls: The Dail Elections of 1977*, American Enterprise Institute for Public Policy Research, Washington D.C. 1978, p. 99.

15. See Charles Haughey's expressed intent in the Dail, 11 December 1980 (Dail Debates, 325, 970).

16. Unfortunately we do not know how many travellers now carry passports anyway as the most prudent means of identification in security checks.

17. Bunreacht na hÉireann (Constitution of Ireland), Articles 2 and 3.

18. The *international* aspects of the Northern Ireland conflict have not received much attention from political scientists. I was most fortunate to have access to early drafts of a Ph.D. thesis now being prepared by Michael McKinley at the Australian National University in Canberra.

19. In 1977 this included eight officials of diplomatic rank. See P. Keatinge, *A Place Among the Nations: Issues in Irish Foreign Policy*, Institute of Public Administration, Dublin 1970, pp. 212, 269.

20. J. Peck, *Dublin from Downing Street*, Gill and Macmillan, Dublin 1978, p. 17.

21. See Reports on Economic Co-operation, June 1978 and Report to Ministers on North/South Economic Co-operation, June 1980.

22. Chastisement may be administered by the host country's media rather than its government, but during the Lynch-Heath summit in September 1971 it issued from both sources.

23. See Peck, op. cit., for the most detailed account yet available of official diplomatic contacts.

24. A good example is the Lynch-Callaghan meeting in Copenhagen in April 1978.
25. See Dail Debates, 303, 1439, 15 February 1978.
26. Keohane and Nye, op. cit., p. 19.
27. Communiqué of British and Republic of Ireland governments, 8 December 1980.
28. For a clear statement of this proposition, see P. A. Reynolds, *An Introduction to International Relations*, 2nd ed., Longmans, London 1980, pp. 205–6.
29. Peck, op. cit., p. 18.
30. Charles Haughey at the Fianna Fail Ard Fheis, 16 February 1980. This phrase was used in the context of an inter-governmental approach to the problem of Northern Ireland.
31. See L. P. de Menil, *Who speaks for Europe? The Vision of Charles de Gaulle*, Weidenfeld and Nicolson, London 1977, ch. 5.
32. See G. L. Weil, *The Benelux Nations: The Politics of Small Country Democracies*, Holt, Rinehart and Winston, New York 1970, ch. 10.
33. ibid., p. 229.
34. See Bengt Sundelius' paper, 'The Nordic Model of Neighbourly Co-operation', above.
35. Bengt Sundelius, 'Coping with Transnationalism in Northern Europe', *West European Politics*, Vol. 3, No. 2, May 1980, p. 227.
36. See Sundelius, 'The Nordic Model'.
37. See C. F. Carter, 'Permutations of Government', *Administration*, Vol. 20, No. 4, Winter 1972.
38. This position was enunciated in response to a question at the press conference after the summit.
39. The narrowest interpretation of 'the totality of relationships' is that it is confined to the inter-state relationship itself; this, to Garret FitzGerald on 11 March 1981, seemed to be 'the grammatical sense of the communiqué'. See Dail Debates, 327, 1429.
40. From a Dublin perspective, administrative changes would make the existing set of administrative ground rules, the Devlin Report of 1969, even more out of date than it became following entry to the European Community.
41. A proposal mooted in the early years of the British-Irish Association.
42. See K. Kyle, 'Sunningdale and after: Britain, Ireland and Ulster', *The World Today*, November 1975, pp. 445–7.
43. See the proposals in D. Barrington, 'After Sunningdale?', *Administration*, Vol. 24, No. 2, Summer 1976, especially pp. 257–60.
44. See the often fraught debate in the Dail on 11 March 1981, Dail Debates, 327, 1391–1490. This was the fullest debate on neutrality for many years, and was directly attributable to speculation following the Anglo-Irish summit of December 1980.
45. Dail Debates, 327, 1394 and 1396.
46. See Mrs Thatcher's comments, reported in the *Irish Times*, 7 March 1981.
47. See the controversy following the comments of Brian Lenihan,

Minister for Foreign Affairs, reported in the *Irish Times*, 19 March 1981.
48. *Irish Times*, 26 March 1981.
49. Charles Haughey's speech at the Fianna Fail Ard Fheis, *Irish Times*, 13 April 1981.

BIBLIOGRAPHY

Barrington, D., 'After Sunningdale?', *Administration*, Vol. 24, no. 2, Summer 1976
Birch, A. H., *Political Integration and Disintegration in the British Isles*, Allen and Unwin, London 1977
Carter, C. F., 'Permutations of Government', *Administration*, Vol. 20, No. 4, Winter 1972
Chubb, B., *The Government and Politics of Ireland*, Oxford University Press, London 1970
de Menil, L. P., *Who speaks for Europe? The Vision of Charles de Gaulle*, Weidenfeld and Nicolson, London 1977
Deutsch, K. W. *et al.*, *Political Community and the North Atlantic Area*, Greenwood Press, New York 1957
Hancock, W. K., *Survey of British Commonwealth Affairs Vol. I. Problems of Nationality 1918–1936*, Oxford University Press, London 1937
Harkness, D. W., *The Restless Dominion*, Macmillan, London 1969
Harkness, D. W., 'Mr de Valera's Dominion: Irish Relations with Britain and the Commonwealth, 1932–1938', *Journal of Commonwealth Political Studies*, Vol. VIII, No. 3, 1970
Hull, R. H., *The Irish Triangle*, Princeton University Press, Princeton 1976
Keatinge, P., *A Place Among the Nations: Issues in Irish Foreign Policy*, Institute of Public Administration, Dublin 1978
Keohane, R. O. and Nye, J. S., *Power and Interdependence: World Politics in Transition*, Little, Brown and Company, Boston 1977
Kyle, K., 'Sunningdale and after: Britain, Ireland, and Ulster', *The World Today*, November 1975
Lynch, J. M., 'The Anglo-Irish problem', *Foreign Affairs*, Vol. 50, No. 4, July 1972
McAleese, D. F., 'Political Independence and Economic Performance — Ireland outside the United Kingdom' in E. T. Nevin, ed., *The Economics of Devolution*, University of Aston Press, Birmingham 1978
McCarthy, C., 'The Exchange Rate of the Irish Pound: Performance and Policy', *The Irish Banking Review*, December 1980
Mansergh, N., *Survey on British Commonwealth Affairs: Problems of External Policy 1931–1939*, Oxford University Press, London 1952

Mansergh, N., *Survey of British Commonwealth Affairs: Problems of Wartime Co-operation and Post-war Change 1939–1952*, Oxford University Press, London 1958

Peck, J., *Dublin from Downing Street*, Gill and Macmillan, Dublin 1978

Reynolds, P. A., *An Introduction to International Relations*, 2nd ed., Longmans, London 1980

Sundelius, B., 'Coping with Transnationalism in Northern Europe', *West European Politics*, Vol. 3, No. 2, May 1980

Vital, D., *The Survival of Small States; Studies in Small Power/Great Power Conflict*, Oxford University Press, London 1971

Weil, G. L., *The Benelux Nations: The Politics of Small Country Democracies*, Holt, Rinehart and Winston, New York 1970

The publication of the hardback and paperback editions of this volume has been made possible by a grant from the European Commission. The publication of the paperback edition of this volume has been made possible by a grant from the Ireland Fund. The Organising Committee which commissioned the contributions to this volume are deeply indebted to both for their financial assistance.

THE IRELAND FUND

CULTURE · PEACE · CHARITY